Austin Gough is Professor of History at the
University of Adelaide.

PARIS AND ROME

PARIS AND ROME

THE GALLICAN CHURCH AND
THE ULTRAMONTANE CAMPAIGN
1848–1853

AUSTIN GOUGH

CLARENDON PRESS · OXFORD
1986

Oxford University Press, Walton Street, Oxford OX2 6DP
Oxford New York Toronto
Delhi Bombay Calcutta Madras Karachi
Petaling Jaya Singapore Hong Kong Tokyo
Nairobi Dar es Salaam Cape Town
Melbourne Auckland
and associated companies in
Beirut Berlin Ibadan Nicosia

Oxford is a trade mark of Oxford University Press

Published in the United States
by Oxford University Press, New York

British Library Cataloguing in Publication Data
Gough, Austin
Paris and Rome: the Gallican church and the
ultramontane campaign 1848-1853.
1. Catholic Church—France—History
2. France—Church history
I. Title
282'.44'0934 BX1530
ISBN 0-19-821977-6

Library of Congress Cataloging in Publication Data
Gough, Austin.
Paris and Rome.
Bibliography: p.
Includes index.
1. Catholic Church—France—History—19th century.
2. Gallicanism. 3. Ultramontanism—France.
4. France—Church history—19th century. I. Title.
BX1530.G58 1986 282'.44 85-31437
ISBN 0-19-821977-6

Set by Hope Services, Abingdon, Oxon.
Printed in Great Britain
at the Alden Press, Oxford

Preface

WHEN preparations began for the First Vatican Council the Roman Curia was under no illusions about the persistence and strength of gallicanism in the French Church. Ultramontane controversialists had announced the death of gallicanism on several occasions since the end of the Old Regime—it had been dealt a mortal blow by the Napoleonic Concordat in 1802, it was untenable at any time since the fall of the Bourbons in 1830, the life had been crushed out of it in the fifties, it was completely outmoded by 1869, an empty husk, an anachronism—but Rome was not carried away by rhetoric. After many decades of close observation of French affairs and with personal knowledge of the men who had risen to episcopal rank under the Second Empire, it was easy enough for the Curia to predict that a substantial body of French bishops would appear at the Council ready to support a broadly gallican position. At least twenty-five of them would align themselves with the outright opposition to papal infallibility, and a larger number, perhaps as many as two-fifths or a half of the French episcopate and including some of the most formidable figures in the Church, were certain to oppose the schemata on papal jurisdiction which they recognized as a more serious and concrete problem than infallibility, and to raise fundamental arguments about the structure of the Church and the status of bishops. It was clear in advance, for example, that the French would argue against any dogmatic definition of the right of the papacy to exercise 'ordinary' or 'episcopal' jurisdiction throughout the Catholic world, which they interpreted to mean in practice that their dioceses would increasingly be governed by the Roman Curia.

Their special bitterness with regard to the whole question of Roman jurisdiction arose from a unique experience two decades earlier, an episode still fresh in the minds of the French Minority bishops at the Council. An important battle had been lost, and they hoped not to lose another. At the end of the 1840s, when some of them had already been bishops and others had been

young vicars-general or seminary directors, Sulpician gallicanism
had been the customary doctrine of the French Church and the
basis of ecclesiastical management in France, tacitly accepted
and condoned by Rome. In gallican theory, arrived at after
centuries of argument over authority and jurisdiction, the
Church was a constitutional monarchy in which each bishop,
holding an office of fully scriptural origin, enjoyed a certain
degree of independence as an administrator and a judge of
doctrine; and, culturally, it was a plural society in which the
Holy See was able to tolerate a wide variety of national styles and
customs. That was, so to speak, before the deluge. In a rapid and
energetic ultramontane campaign between 1848 and 1853 the
French dioceses had been compelled to give up their local
liturgies and adopt the *rit romain*, the Roman Index had swept
through French ecclesiastical libraries with devastating effect,
and the Roman Curia, suddenly stirred into life, had begun
handing down judgements, opinions, and rescripts, interfering,
encouraging appeals, and generally undermining episcopal
authority. An ultramontane opposition, with Roman support,
had appeared at every level of Catholic affairs; and the campaign
had culminated in the encyclical *Inter multiplices* of March 1853
condemning Sulpicianism and the entire concept of 'the liberties
of the Gallican Church'.

For the gallicans these five years were decisive. They remembered every step in the process, and found it hard to believe that
they had been watching the unfolding of a beneficent design of
the Holy Spirit. The circumstances of the ultramontane victory
created a profound mood of cynicism towards the theory of
Roman supremacy and even towards the papacy itself; old
friendships dissolved and new alliances formed; by 1854 the
nucleus of the French Minority party at the Vatican Council of
1870 was already in existence, with its main arguments clearly
defined. The purpose of this book is to explore the ultramontane–
gallican conflict of 1848–53—in essence, a conflict between the
belief that the challenges of post-Revolutionary society could be
met only by a centralized Church, uniform in doctrine, style, and
discipline, controlled by an infallible Pope and a vigilant Roman
administration, and the contrary belief that the Church would
lose all influence in modern society unless it had deep roots in
national character and local institutions, and a looser, federal,

collegial structure. As a historical episode it is not at all well known, although in recent years theologians have been investigating the long-abandoned goldmine of gallicanism, picking their way carefully past the notices warning of the danger of falling into bottomless pits of error; some of them have suggested tentatively what the Sulpician seminaries used to teach with the utmost confidence, that Catholics might be allowed to believe in the indefectibility of the papacy without having to accept the infallibility of the Pope.

The slightly lopsided plan of the book, with five introductory or explanatory chapters and then eight chapters of detailed narrative history, reflects the peculiar shape of the conflict itself, in which a number of potential sources of disagreement which had existed for a long time beneath the surface suddenly came into the open in a series of confrontations, manifestos, accusations, and personal victories and defeats. I have begun by discussing the state of seminary education and the careers of priests, to indicate some of the reasons why the lower clergy were so receptive to the ultramontane case against gallicanism in the 1830s and 1840s, and then gone on in chapters II to IV to describe gallicanism and ultramontanism as cultural entities, as theories of Christian society and as strategies for dealing with the intellectual challenges of the mid-nineteenth century. A fifth chapter is devoted to the career of Louis Veuillot before and after his conversion to Catholicism, and to the immense influence *veuillotisme* came to exercise in the Church. It is remarkable how much of what was to be known as 'clericalism' derives from the work of a self-taught layman, but churchmen who had been happy to accept Joseph de Maistre as a theologian and to put his books on seminary library shelves alongside the Fathers of the Church saw nothing incongruous in allowing themselves to be led by Veuillot. From the 1840s until after the Vatican Council his role in the ultramontane movement was paramount; some of the arguments and incidents of 1848 to 1885 are best seen through Veuillot's eyes, and I have presented them in this way.

I have taken the risk of writing straightforward narrative history for the eight main chapters of the book because I want to convey the powerful cumulative effect this episode had on the minds of the French gallicans. As in other historical areas where there are distinct analogies with the subject of this book, for example the dilemmas and moral agonies of West European communists in dealing with Moscow in the mid-twentieth century, or the relations between the Allied generals after the invasion of Europe in 1944, only an old-fashioned step-by-step narrative can do justice to the heady moments of fellowship, the grappling of giant crustacean personalities, the cool betrayals of faithful acolytes and admirers, the stunning reversals of long-familiar policy, the appeals and petitions received only with calculated silence, the *démarches* which produced the opposite effect from the one intended. My aim has been to understand the complex and painful memories the leading participants shared after 1853, and to suggest how this collective experience influenced their later attitudes.

Some of the sub-themes which I have touched on only briefly, and perhaps unsatisfactorily, deserve books to themselves. One example is the part played by French nationalism in resisting the concept of a supranational Catholic polity. It was always at the back of the minds of French churchmen, especially in Parisian circles, that with a convincing display of firmness France could recover the intellectual place in the Church it had held centuries earlier when the Sorbonne and the archdiocese of Paris had formed the northern pole of Christendom, not in any way inferior to Rome in theological substance; but even the most *exalté* papalists could not help noticing that the Roman hierarchy were, after all, Italians: 'I have seen a great many priests return after a long stay down there beyond the mountains', says the seminary director in Ferdinand Fabre's novel *L'Abbé Tigrane*, 'and I have never known one who has not picked up a strong taint of Machiavellianism. Machiavelli is Italy in a nutshell.' The relation of the social origins of churchmen to their ultramontane or gallican beliefs is another question of endless complexity. I have not tried to build large conclusions on what is frequently impressionistic evidence, full of subtleties and contradictions. On close examination the factors which made one man a gallican and another an ultramontane often turn out to have less to do with class or educational background than with the personal relations between an uncle and a nephew, or between two brilliant student rivals in the graduating class of a seminary; and some of the personal dramas arose from the need of middle-aged celibate clerics for sons, and the need of young priests to find fathers and mentors to replace the real parents they had hardly seen since entering the

petit-séminaire. Only detailed individual biography can solve some
of the puzzles. It is clear, all the same, that at times we are
looking at a very widespread phenomenon in modern history,
one which has become a dynamic political force in the twentieth
century: the yearning on the part of social groups deprived of
power, or conscious of having lost an influence they used to
enjoy, for an infallible leader whose unshakeable will has the
status of a historical force and is capable of reversing the direction of
history in their favour. Confronted by the unprecedented problems
of the Church in nineteenth-century Europe, by indifference
amongst the masses and a fundamental critique of religion always
gaining ground amongst the educated classes, gallicans and
ultramontanes reacted in opposite ways. The gallican and liberal
churchmen, most of whom had middle-class backgrounds and
some education outside the seminary system before entering the
priesthood, felt at least moderately confident about meeting the
challenge from the educated public; they were prepared to plunge
into the secular milieu, to write for newspapers and accept
lectureships in the universities, and to argue with the intellectual
opponents of Catholicism as nearly as they could on equal terms.
The leading ultramontanes, who came predominantly from the
minor nobility or from rural or working-class backgrounds, were
more inclined to hold themselves aloof from the whole mechanism
of the secular world and to put their trust in the idea that they
were bound to prevail in the end because of the semi-divine
powers of their leader. 'At Rome', the bishop of Beauvais wrote
in 1851, 'there is a mouth from which issue the oracles of truth,
which with one word resolves uncertainties, dissipates doubts,
traces the route to be followed. In this voice we hear the voice of
God.'

But it would be wrong to rely on a complete antithesis based
on social origins; and we have to be cautious also about other
generalizations, such as the observation often made that the
ultramontanes did at least understand the masses. There is no
doubt that some aspects of the ultramontane style of piety were
welcomed, especially in rural areas, because they satisfied a popular
taste for enthusiastic and sometimes exotic devotions, while the
gallican tradition had been cool towards miracles and towards
what the older generation of clergy saw as excessive devotion to
the Virgin Mary; but here again there are nuances which I have

mentioned in the later chapters of the book. Congregations were reluctant to adopt the Roman liturgy if it meant abandoning a familiar diocesan liturgy and losing the feast-days of popular local saints, and they greatly disliked having to listen to Gregorian chant, or to learn it themselves; and there was considerable scepticism about the Pope, made embarrassingly obvious at the time of the Roman Question in 1860 when rural parishioners could not be persuaded to contribute to a fund for the defence of the Papal States, and shouted down priests in the middle of sermons about the temporal power—as one congregation told an official of the *Ministère des Cultes, 'le curé nous ennuie avec son pape'*. Further investigation here would lead into the broad and better-known field of popular *mentalités*; and this book is essentially a history of a conflict of ideas amongst a clerical élite, in which the great moments of passion took place in bishops' studies and seminary libraries—a conflict, however, which was to have a profound effect on the development of Catholicism.

Acknowledgements

I T is a pleasure to express my gratitude for the help and encouragement I have received while writing this book: from the Warden and Fellows of St Antony's College, Oxford, and, at different times, from Wilfrid Knapp, James Joll, Theodore Zeldin, Donald Charlton, Stuart Woolf, Bruce Mansfield, Alan McBriar, and fra William McLoughlin OSM; from the late Cardinal Marty, Archbishop of Paris, who gave permission for the use of the Sibour papers; and from Dr Luigi Cajani for invaluable help with the Roman archives. I have to thank my excellent and understanding colleagues in the Adelaide history department, and especially Robert Dare who brought a fresh viewpoint to bear on a partly completed version of the manuscript, with salutary results.

A.G.

December 1985

Contents

Abbreviations

ABBREVIATIONS FOR MANUSCRIPT SOURCES

A. Arch. Paris   Archives of the Archdiocese of Paris: period of Archbishop D.-A. Sibour 1848–57: Series 1. D. vi. (4)

AN   Archives Nationales, Paris. The main collections cited are:

AN F. 19   Archives of the Ministère des Cultes: especially the following:

834, 840–61, 1424–34: séminaristes: bourses, etc.
1924 Nonciature de Paris
1931 *Correspondance de Rome* (journal)
1933 Divisions de l'Église
1934 Encyclique de 1864
1947 Congrégations romaines: Index
2450 Auditeur de Rote: Protonotaires apostoliques
2479–596 Évêques: dossiers personnels (also 6176–9: Chapitre de Saint-Denis)
2609, 2459, 6522–33 Candidatures, nominations épiscopales
2790–813 Vicaires Généraux
3955–4089 Séminaires: bibliothèques, etc.
4064 Petits-séminaires
4090 Facultés de théologie
4092–3 École des Carmes
5434–5 Liturgie
5591 Conciles provinciaux

Donnet/AN   Papers of Cardinal F.–F. Donnet, Archbishop of Bordeaux (160 AP)

Dupanloup/AN   Papers of Mgr Félix Dupanloup, Bishop of Orleans (AB XIX. 520–6).

S. Sulp/AN   Papers of the Seminary of Saint-Sulpice, Archdiocese of Paris (AB XIX. 510–19).

ASV Francia   Archivio Segreto Vaticano, Rome: Fondo Segreteria di Stato: rubrica 248, Affari religiosi di Francia (1848–56).

ASV Parigi	Archivio Segreto Vaticano, Rome: Fondo Segreteria di Stato: Nunziatura di Parigi (i.e. papers of the Paris Nunciature, removed to Rome after the Separation of Church and State in France).
BN	Bibliothèque Nationale, Paris: Départment des Manuscrits. (Numbers cited in notes refer to the Series *Nouvelles acquisitions françaises*.) The main collections cited are:
Circourt/BN	Papers of the comte Adolphe de Circourt (N.a.f. 20501).
Dupanloup/BN	Papers of Mgr Dupanloup (N.a.f. 24672–715).
S.Sulp/BN	Papers of the Seminary of Saint-Sulpice (N.a.f. 24716–25).
V/BN	Papers of Louis Veuillot and of *L'Univers* (N.a.f. 24220–39 and 24617–35).
Kergorlay/Arsenal	Papers of the comte Louis-Gabriel-César de Kergorlay, Bibliothèque de l'Arsenal (Paris) (Nos. 14091–115).

ABBREVIATIONS FOR PRINTED SOURCES

Bettoni	*Le relazioni diplomatiche fra lo Stato pontificio e la Francia, III Serie: 1848–1860, vol. iii (1850–3)*, ed. M. Bettoni (Rome 1976).
Corboli Bussi	*Rapporto di Mgr G. Corboli Bussi sopra alcuni affari religiosi di Francia . . . nell'anno 1849* (Rome 1851) (Biblioteca Apostolica Vaticana, R. G. Storia II. 1399).
DHGE	*Dictionnaire d'histoire et de géographie ecclésiastique*, directed by Baudrillart, Aubert and Van Cauwemberg (Paris 1909– in progress).
DTC	*Dictionnaire de théologie catholique*, directed by Vacant and Mangenot (Paris 1903–50).
Épiscopat	*L'Épiscopat français depuis le Concordat jusqu'à la Séparation (1802–1905)*, ed. Mgr L. Baunard (Paris 1907).
Garibaldi/Mathieu	*Correspondance inédite entre Mgr Antonio Garibaldi, internonce à Paris, et Mgr Césaire Mathieu, archevêque de Besançon*, ed. P. Poupard (Paris 1961).
Guéranger/Bouvier	Ambroise Ledru, *Dom Guéranger, abbé de Solesmes, et Mgr Bouvier, évêque du Mans* (Paris 1911).

Maurain: Saint-Siège	*Le Saint-Siège et la France de décembre 1851 à avril 1853: documents inédits,* ed. J. Maurain (Paris 1930).
Louis Veuillot	*Louis Veuillot,* 4 vols. (Paris 1902–13): vols. i–iii by Eugène Veuillot, vol. iv by François Veuillot.

I

The education of the parish clergy: a pass degree and an honours degree

The parish clergy and their problems

DURING the first half of the nineteenth century every serious enquiry into the affairs of the Church of France sooner or later had to acknowledge that the clergy were very badly educated. There was an obvious and embarrassing gap between the standards expected in the secular schools and universities and the kind of education available to priests in the seminaries. Even those Catholics who believed most strongly that the clergy should play an active role in public life had to admit that they were ill-fitted for it, and would find it nearly impossible to keep abreast of modern developments in science, economics, or politics. Saint-Simon, who had once hoped that much could be accomplished by well-educated parish priests—the new scientific age, he thought, should reach the general public through the pulpit—said that the state of seminary education in the post-Revolutionary period was so bad as to be a sin on the part of the Pope and the cardinals.[1] The most pointed reproach levelled at French priests, however, was that they were not very good at the academic subjects in their own professional sphere, ecclesiastical history, canon law, and biblical criticism. The Church was extremely defensive on this point. When the duc de Broglie criticized the inadequate training of priests in a parliamentary report of 1844 he was answered by an indignant open letter from the abbé Dupanloup, director of the *petit-séminaire* of Saint-Nicolas-du-Chardonnet in Paris.[2] Dupanloup argued defiantly that no other profession had to undergo such a rigorous intellectual preparation, and he went on to paint a glowing

[1] Henri de Saint-Simon, *Le Nouveau Christianisme* (1825). First dialogue. (Unless otherwise indicated, all printed works cited in footnotes were published in Paris.)

[2] Abbé Félix Dupanloup, *Lettre à M. le duc de Broglie, rapporteur du projet de loi relatif à l'instruction secondaire* (1844).

picture of eighty diocesan seminaries, each one with its learned professors of law, dogma, philosophy, and theology and its qualified teachers of secular subjects; hundreds of ecclesiastical high schools, the *petits-séminaires*, which passed on to the seminaries a stream of properly educated young men with vocations; and below this again a presbytery school system in which boys were placed by their parents in the household of a parish priest to learn Latin and be taught to serve mass and sing in the choir. Privately, Dupanloup knew quite well that he was describing an ideal, not the reality. It would have been remarkable, in fact, if the Church had been able to re-create a convincing seminary education in the forty years since the Concordat.

In practice much of the effort devoted to clerical training was nullified by the awkward facts of clerical recruitment. In the early part of the century there was a severe shortage of priests, and more than half of those who were available for parish work in the Restoration period were over fifty years of age. Recruitment to the clergy rose and fell according to the prevailing political climate; ordinations rose at times of official favour to the Church, like the reign of Charles X, and fell off sharply after displays of public anticlericalism like those following the Revolution of 1830, when a career in the priesthood seemed precarious or even dangerous. The seminaries could not keep pace with the erosion of numbers, and it was not until the 1850s that ordinations began to prevail over deaths and retirements; even in the Second Empire there was a good deal of *binage* and a newly ordained priest might find that he had to look after two or three parishes. The problem of recruitment was made more acute by the reluctance of the middle and upper classes to consider the priesthood as a career, even in periods of benign official patronage of religion. The pattern of recruitment established in the seventeenth and eighteenth centuries, when the Church had been able to offer great opportunities to educated young men, had been broken by the Revolution. In spite of repeated appeals by bishops throughout the century there were hardly any vocations amongst the sons of the wealthy Catholic landowners, industrialists, and high civil servants. They were educated at Jesuit colleges and occasionally joined the Society of Jesus or one of the other religious orders, but the Jesuits themselves were inclined to smile at the idea of a vocation to the parish clergy.[3] Middle-class boys were not placed in presbytery schools; if they attended a *petit-séminaire* they treated it simply as a Catholic school, and did not mix with the predominantly lower-class boys who were going on to join the priesthood. 'The *petits-séminaires*', wrote one bishop, 'normally send on to the seminary only the tail of the graduating class, while the head goes off to seek its fortune elsewhere.'[4] Recruitment was mainly from the poorer and less well-educated classes; in 1845 the Allignol brothers estimated that seven-eighths of the parish clergy came from *les classes laborieuses*, and recent studies of individual dioceses confirm this general picture.[5] At least 60 per cent of all seminarians in the early nineteenth century came from peasant backgrounds; in some dioceses the proportion was much higher. The rest were mainly from lower-middle-class and artisan families, and less than 10 per cent were middle-class boys, the sons of notaries, doctors, civil servants, or businessmen, who already had the benefit of reasonably good education before entering the clergy. About half of the 8000 seminarians in France were receiving financial assistance in the form of government bursaries:[6] in some seminaries all the students were on bursaries. They came generally from families who could not afford to pay fees, but not from the very poorest class. In an unofficial way the seminaries discouraged vocations from absolute paupers: it was known from

---

[3] René-François Guettée said that a Jesuit professor tried to dissuade him from joining the diocesan clergy by describing to him with much satirical detail 'the typical *curé*, the typical vicar-general and the typical bishop': *Souvenirs d'un prêtre romain devenu prêtre orthodoxe* (1889), 25.

[4] Quoted by the abbé Bougaud, *Le Grand Péril de l'Église de France* (1878), 135; and see Bougaud's chapter 5, 'De l'obstination des classes riches à s'éloigner du sacerdoce'; also a pamphlet by 'Un vicaire de campagne', *Pourquoi les hautes classes n'entrent pas dans le sacerdoce* (1852); J. Brugerette, *Le Prêtre français et la société contemporaine*, 3 vols. (1933–8), vol. i; on the persistence of certain problems of recruitment over a century and a half, F. Boulard, *Essor ou déclin du clergé français* (1950).

[5] AN F. 19. 834, 840–61 (candidatures for bursaries); F. 19. 1424–34. Amongst the most important studies of dioceses are G. Cholvy, 'Les vocations sacerdotales et religieux dans le diocèse de Montpellier 1801–1856', *Annales du Midi*, lxxi (1959), 222–9; C. Marcilhacy, *Le Diocèse d'Orléans sous l'épiscopat de Mgr Dupanloup* and *Le Diocèse d'Orléans au milieu du XIXᵉ siècle* (1964); P. Huot-Pleuroux, *Le Recrutement sacerdotal dans le diocèse de Besançon 1801–1960* (1966); M. Lagrée, *Mentalités, religion et histoire . . . Le diocèse de Rennes 1815–1848* (1977).

[6] AN F. 19. 834; F. 19. 1430–4.

experience that indigent parents would fasten on the son who
was a priest, and try to move the whole family in to live at the
presbytery, with dire results. Seminary directors knew that many
vocations were suspect. The decision to enter the priesthood was
often influenced by the approach of the annual conscription
ballot, or arose from the endless struggle of rural families to
evade the laws of inheritance; rather than see a property split
into infinitesmal parts under the *loi du partage forcé* a family would
persuade one or two sons to go into the clergy, usually the ones
thought to be hopeless farmers. In large rural families the
parents and older children worked in the fields and the younger
children were allowed to run wild; if a boy became uncontrollable
the family would sometimes place him in the *curé*'s household 'to
straighten him out', and from that point he might go on until he
was ordained.[7] In 1865 the bishop of Coutances warned his
seminary instructors to be discriminating in their choice of
peasant recruits: 'Keep away from the sanctuary those who want
to enter it out of calculation . . . from the hope of being able,
without effort, to eat the bread that they could not expect from
their own families. Take poor boys, certainly, but not those poor
who have nothing in their hearts but vicious jealousies and low
servile feelings.'[8]

The kind of education a young man received in his way
through the *école presbytérale*, the *petit-séminaire* and the *grand-
séminaire* depended to a large extent on his own intelligence and
determination; at times the teaching seemed designed to put
obstacles in his way. At the first stage, the personality and tastes
of the priest-tutor in whose household a boy first learned Latin
and Christian doctrine could have a decisive influence on his
whole career. Some priests had great respect for scholarship but
too many were embittered survivors of the Revolution who
passed on to their pupils a distrust of the secular learning which
they thought had been the ruin of a whole generation of clergy in

[7] The impression that seminary directors gained about their pupils is borne out by
the sociological studies made for the *Société d'économie sociale*: on peasant children see,
for example, M. Callay, 'Paysan du Laonnais' (1861), *Les Ouvriers des deux mondes:
Études*, 1st series, iv.

[8] Bougaud, *Le Grand Péril*, 114 n. The point about grasping indigent families is
noted by the abbé Aguettand, *Le Curé instruit par l'expérience, ou vingt ans de ministère dans
une paroisse de campagne* (1856), chap. 7; and cf. the Trouche family in Zola's *La Conquête
de Plassans*.

the eighteenth century. The boys in the *école presbytérale* were constantly reminded of their separateness from the world. In the Orleans diocese the official instructions for priests who had boys under their care emphasized that 'they must inspire their young pupils with the great verities of faith which will be the solid basis for their careers: the fear of God, the horror of sin, the brevity of man's life, the nullity of earthly things, the reality of eternal punishment'.[9] In most *petits-séminaires* this isolation was intensified; the boys destined for the priesthood worked and played separately, and were taught a reduced curriculum without mathematics, science, or history; even on holidays with their families they were supposed to be under the supervision of the local *curé*.

It was at the level of the *grand-séminaire*, however, that clerical education was most deficient. Given the urgent need to staff the parishes with zealous and practical young men, and the low educational qualifications of the great majority of recruits, the seminaries resigned themselves to offering a plain course with the minimum of intellectual demands. They were constrained also by the poverty of their own resources. In the ten-year hiatus at the beginning of the century there had been no seminaries at all; many able men had died, religious orders and learned societies had been disbanded. Where was the Church to find competent seminary instructors? At about the time when Stendhal has Julien Sorel studying at the seminary of Besançon, the Archbishop of Besançon was complaining about the ignorance of most of the teachers in that establishment, and the lack of books for those who did want to improve themselves.[10] Ecclesiastical libraries had been largely dispersed in the Revolution; but in any case there were far too many seminaries. The concordatory arrangement by which each diocese was to train its own priests had been a mistake in strategy; the Church and the Government obviously would have done better to have amalgamated the eighty seminaries in groups of five or ten, combined their libraries and staffs, and created a proper clerical university in each province. In the post-Revolutionary period it was impossible to find eighty

[9] Abbé Gaduel, *De la vocation ecclésiastique*, cited by Marcilhacy, *Le Diocèse d'Orléans au milieu du XIXᵉ siècle*, 226. Gaduel was regarded as a liberal in theology.
[10] Letters of Cardinal Mathieu to the abbé Boiteux 1834–6, in S. Sulp/AN AB XIX 517; and AN F. 19. 2504 (Mathieu).

good teachers of biblical studies, eighty canonists, and eighty
theologians, especially men prepared to lecture for 600 francs a
year, and seminary directors complained that when they did
manage to secure a learned professor it was only a matter of time
before the ministère des Cultes offered him a bishopric, at twenty
times the salary. The more capable teachers were in great
demand also for administrative chores in their dioceses: a man
who was simultaneously Professor of Theology, Vicar-General,
Archpriest of the Cathedral and Director of Ecclesiastical Music
would have to cut down his seminary lectures to perhaps one a
fortnight. The 'chairs' of philosophy and theology were often
occupied by third-year students who knew little more than their
pupils, and at their worst were 'simply peasants in soutanes'.[11]

The four-year course[12] was divided into two years of 'philosophy'
and two of 'theology', but the main emphasis in practice was on
the need for a basic re-Christianization of France and the
restoration of religious observance. The subjects given most
attention were sacred eloquence, the correct form of mass and
other ceremonies, and personal piety; there was little time for the
patient study of academic subjects. The priesthood was learned
as a trade. Fifteen times a day the bell called seminarians to
spiritual exercises which developed self-discipline but were a
positive handicap to study. The principal textbooks of philosophy
and theology, Bailly's *Theologia dogmatica,* Bouvier's *Institutiones*
theologicae and *Institutiones philosophicae* and the *Philosophie de Lyon*
by the Oratorian Vallat were not negligible works—Bailly and
Bouvier contained passages of very distinguished abstract
argument and substantial treatments of the gallican question[13]—
but they had been written to refute the errors of earlier centuries.

[11] Guettée, *Souvenirs,* 15. These egotistical but illuminating memoirs give a
sardonic account of the seminary at Blois which is confirmed by all the other available
evidence. Very interesting material on the libraries and the teaching in seminaries is
scattered through a long series of files in the Ministère des Cultes series, AN F. 19.
3955, 3968, 3973–4, 4065, 4071, 4086–9. For a comparative study of Italian
seminaries, G. Brocanelli, 'Seminari e clero nelle Marche nella seconda metà
dell'Ottocento', *Rivista di storia della Chiesa in Italia,* xxxi (1977), 68–100, 391–424.

[12] Some seminaries introduced a five-year course in the 1840s, with very reluctant
approval from the bishops who knew that it would slow down the rate of ordinations;
the longer course became general later in the century.

[13] Louis Bailly, *Theologia dogmatica et moralis ad usum seminariorum,* 8 vols., first
published in 1789, and eighteen subsequent editions; J.-B. Bouvier, *Institutiones*
theologicae, 6 vols. (Le Mans 1817), and *Institutiones philosophicae,* 3 vols. (Le Mans
1825).

Locke and Descartes were dealt with by extracting lists of 'erroneous propositions' and showing how each one could be confounded from papal encyclicals. The better part of a year was spent studying the doctrine of grace, as if a priest's main adversaries were to be the Jansenists. The teaching of academic subjects took the form of rapidly dictated commentaries 'in Latin which would have made Cicero laugh',[14] followed by sessions of rote learning. Seminary directors argued that if the teaching were to be in French the students would come to regard Latin as simply another subject in the curriculum and would lose the ability to read papal encyclicals, canon law, and indeed the great bulk of ecclesiastical literature; in any case many seminarians in the provinces during the first half of the century spoke patois and found French almost as difficult as Latin.[15] Only a handful of the better seminaries had any written examinations: examining was oral, and earnest enthusiasm counted for more than knowledge. Ecclesiastical history, which might have helped priests to understand their theology better, was taught by reading it aloud at mealtimes; all that the average priest knew about the early Councils or the medieval papacy amounted to a few sentences half heard through the clatter of plates. Montalembert said that in the 1830s only five out of the eighty seminaries taught history seriously; many of them did not have a single history textbook.[16] Napoleon had wanted priests to have a good knowledge of their own times and 'a decent degree of plain worldliness', but in practice seminarians heard nothing about politics or current affairs, and hardly ever saw a newspaper. At Angers in 1815 they never heard about the Hundred Days. At Chartres they became aware of the Revolution in 1830 when the prayer said after mass

[14] Guettée, *Souvenirs*, 19.

[15] Dupanloup, *Seconde lettre à M. le duc de Broglie* (1844).

[16] Quoted by Mgr Baudrillart, 'Le renouvellement intellectuel du Clergé', *Le Correspondant* (15 Jan. 1908). An attempt by the director of the Dijon seminary to conduct examinations and to fail the weaker students had to be abandoned because of the acute shortage of priests: G. Chevallier, *Mgr Rivet* (Dijon 1902), 43–6. On the deficiencies of seminary education in the nineteenth century, abbé Duine, 'Souvenirs et observations', unpublished manuscript, BN N.a.f. 12997–13000; abbé G. Moreau, *L'Église de France et les réformes nécessaires* (1880); F. Garilhe, *Le Clergé séculier français au XIXᵉ siècle* (n.d.); abbé E. Baudaire, 'La Formation intellectuelle du clergé', *Annales de philosophie chrétienne*, 3rd Series, v (1904–5), 153–69, 267–307; abbé J. Guibert, 'Nos grands séminaires', *Revue pratique d'apologétique*, xi (1910) 561–87. There are some excellent literary sources, notably Ferdinand Fabre's novel about a seminary director, *L'abbé Tigrane* (1873), and his memoir, *Ma Vocation* (1889).

for the reigning monarch, the *Domine salvum*, startled them by naming a different king. At one seminary in February 1848 they guessed from the sudden silence and reserve of their teachers that 'something extraordinary had happened', and then all their incoming mail was cut off and visits from relatives forbidden; eventually, in the middle of March, the director announced the news from Paris and indicated that the clergy should prepare themselves for martyrdom.[17]

Equipped, then, with not much more than an outline of the main philosophical 'errors' and a knowledge of the liturgical calendar, the young priest was sent out to face the secular world. The bishops, in desperation, encouraged the ecclesiastical publishers to issue sets of ready-written sermons and homilies for every occasion: the abbé Laveau's four-volume collection *Le Curé de campagne*, the sermons of Fr. Brydaine SJ in seven volumes, sermons and addresses by Canon Martel and the abbé Jouve, an eleven-volume *Somme du prédicateur* and a *Dictionnaire des exemples à l'usage des prédicateurs*. Armed with one of these a priest could gain an undeserved reputation as an orator. His congregation would marvel at his high-flown eloquence and have no idea that the same sermon was being given on that Sunday all over the country; but too often the books gathered dust on the presbytery shelves because the priest could not pronounce the long words in sermons composed by professors of sacred eloquence. Even when well delivered the standard sermons were 'old-fashioned, authoritarian and pedantic' when they dealt with aspects of the modern world such as education or the relations between capital and labour.[18] Many of them had been first published under the *ancien régime*; they evoked cynical smiles from middle-class parishioners and sometimes open hostility from peasants. Throughout their training priests had been given a very exalted picture of the role the clergy should play in modern society, but it required only a few weeks' exposure to the village voltaireans, the sub-prefect, the mayor, the doctor, the notary, and the schoolmaster, for a

[17] Fabre, *Ma Vocation*, chap. 9; and this was at Montpellier, one of the most progressive of the provincial seminaries.

[18] A contemporary priest's opinion, in Canon Le Sueur, *Le Clergé picard et le Concordat 1801–1904*, 2 vols. (Abbeville 1929–30), ii, 56. The better sermons, for example those by Père Brydaine SJ, were too densely theological for the average congregation, and the less sophisticated collections like *Le Curé de campagne* rose to great heights of innocent absurdity.

young *desservant* to be made painfully aware that he was perhaps the worst-educated man in the parish, and likely to be the least influential.[19]

His segregation from the world since the age of ten or twelve years had left him completely out of touch with the current of everyday life. Once again, attempts were made to solve this problem by publishing books designed to improve a priest's power of conversation and argument. The abbé Migne's printery in Paris issued a *Dictionnaire des anecdotes chrétiennes* and over fifty other dictionaries of sacred subjects for presbytery libraries: compilations of 'political and social errors', 'marvels of Christian art', 'religious statistics', a *Dictionnaire de l'athéisme réfuté par les athées* and a *Dictionnaire des objections populaires contre le dogme . . . contenant pour chaque difficulté une réponse claire et précise.* The most widely read instructional manuals were the handbooks of parish management written by experienced priests: *Le Guide des curés* and *Le Bon Curé au XIX*e *siècle* by the abbé Dieulin, *Du ton et des manières d'un ecclésiastique dans le monde, par un homme du monde,* and a great many didactic memoirs like the abbé Epineau's *Mémoires d'un vicaire de campagne* which ran to several editions.[20] These books are full of excellent and timeless advice—the abbé Aguettand's *Le Curé instruit par l'expérience* is particularly good and would have been equally useful to country schoolmasters or policemen—but when they turn to discuss the correct demeanour and style of a priest the shadow of the seminary falls across the pages. In relations with the laity they advise an obsessive degree of caution. The young priest must not align himself in any way with factions in the parish: 'do not agree too completely with this man or that; say "possibly", or "it may be so . . ." '. He must not look a man, or, most particularly, a woman, straight in the eye, but fix his gaze on a point four or five paces ahead, or to the side. 'Every profession has its characteristic defects', wrote an exasperated layman:

---

[19] Under the Concordat there were approximately 3400 *curés*, or priests in charge of major parishes, enjoying security of tenure; 7500 *vicaires* assisting *curés* in the larger parishes; and 30,000 *desservants* in charge of minor parishes (*succursales*).

[20] Some other examples are the abbé Réaume's *Le Guide du jeune prêtre,* (several editions between 1844 and 1959); *La Voix du bon pasteur* by the abbé Parel (1842); abbé H. Barbier, *Les Mystères du presbytère et de la vie religieuse, par le Solitaire* (1844); abbé Augustin Devoille, *Mémoires d'un curé de campagne* (1854).

the deviousness of priests is like that of peasants . . . The peasant feels himself at a disadvantage in business affairs, and has to devise a method of dealing with them, by ruse and subtlety. Every time I find a priest taking refuge in these shuffling evasions, unwilling, for example, to say 'yes' or 'no' to the simplest and least compromising question, I say to myself: here is the same instinct as that of the peasant *vis-à-vis* the bourgeois.[21]

No amount of good advice could hide the basic fact that the parish clergy were in an intensely uncomfortable situation, expected to deal on equal terms with the leaders of local society without having the bourgeois advantages of education and money. The salary of a *desservant* was 800 francs a year; a skilled worker in the mid-nineteenth century could earn 2000 francs, and the income of an established notary would usually be at least 4000 francs. How well or how badly a priest survived depended on the infinite nuances in the broad pattern of religious geography.[22] In devout regions where religious practice was high a priest could earn a supplementary income or *casuel* amounting to 100 or 200 francs a year from fees for weddings, funerals, and special masses. If he had a group of boys under his care the fees paid by their parents in cash or kind would allow the household to live in moderate comfort; a flourishing presbytery school could be a great consolation and helped to dispel the loneliness and depression of a celibate priesthood. In some parts of the country the ancient tithes were still collected until well into the nineteenth century, a more reliable resource for priests than the fluctuating *casuel*.[23] As the map prepared by Boulard and Le Bras shows, however, religious practice was generally low and large areas of central France were virtually dechristianized.[24] Many villages did not see a priest for thirty or forty years after the Revolution, and had no wish to restore the clergy as arbiters of morality or guides in politics. A young *desservant* in the middle of

---

[21] Undated note by Louis-Gabriel-César de Kergorlay, Kergorlay/Arsenal 14094: 407.

[22] The present study does not deal directly with the question of religious practice, on which there is a vast literature: see F. Boulard, 'Aspects de la pratique religieuse en France de 1802 à 1939', *Revue d'histoire de l'Église de France*, li (1973), 269–311.

[23] M. Lagrée, *Le Diocèse de Rennes*, 272–5.

[24] The map is appended to Canon Boulard's *Premiers itinéraires en sociologie religieuse* (1955/1966); see also the surveys of dioceses summarized in J. Maurain, *La Politique ecclésiastique du Second Empire* (1930), chap. 12.

the century could find a crumbling church, a tiny congregation of elderly women, and local society dominated by middle-class people who read the Parisian newspapers which now arrived each day by the railway, and who treated him with ironical reserve; the municipal council and the *conseil de fabrique* which supervised parish expenditure were often run by outright anticlericals.[25] The peasants were maddening in their casual immorality, secretiveness, and meanness, and in times of trouble they were inclined to rely on dubious local cults and 'wise women' rather than on the powers of orthodox Catholicism. In dioceses like Gap, Angoulême, Moulins, and Tulle the average *casuel* was less than 20 francs a year. One young priest told the vicar-general of Orleans that at mass he had thirty women and two or three men, and at vespers nobody. On Sunday nights 'I retreat to my presbytery and try to shut out the sound of singing from the men who are brutalizing themselves at the cabaret, and the violins at the dance which is leading the women and girls to perdition.'[26] Parish work in the industrial cities was even more difficult and unproductive. It is not surprising that the occupant of a presbytery sometimes felt that he was manning an isolated outpost in hostile territory. His only guide was a shelf of books urging him to apply himself to a series of more or less impossible tasks. In the midst of his parish duties he was to spend five hours each day in meditation and penance. He had to listen patiently in the confessional to young women telling him about their sins in graphic detail, while at the same time performing herculean mental exercises to preserve his own chastity.[27] He was to 'adopt a Christian *politique*' without committing himself to any party or any opinion, to display learning without having any, to 'be the friend and mentor of the people of the countryside' who showed no interest in either his friendship or his authority; and to watch his table manners. Printed at the back of the handbooks of parish management there was a bewildering and threatening array of legislation arising from the Concordat, ordinances, decrees, and penalties covering every aspect of clerical life from his relations

[25] See the essays by R. Magraw and A. Gough in T. Zeldin (ed.), *Conflicts in French Society* (London 1970).

[26] Bougaud, *Le Grand Péril*, 29.

[27] On the confessional as a source of strained relations between priests and parishioners, Theodore Zeldin's brilliant essay, 'The conflict of moralities', in *Conflicts in French Society*.

with the *conseil de fabrique* to the exact shape of his hat. On Sundays he had to read government notices from the pulpit, and in election campaigns he was expected to make some favourable reference to the government's official candidate; if he took this, mistakenly, to mean that he might venture a few political comments of his own, his sermon was reported by the *police des cultes* and he received a stern warning to 'remember the purely spiritual nature of your mission'. He belonged, in effect, to the most over-supervised and underpaid branch of the French civil service. By the age of forty, says the hero of Fernand Lafargue's novel *Les Ouailles du curé Fargéas*, a parish priest is like a stunted oak-tree, battered by storms from every quarter of the horizon.[28]

Where was the priest to turn for support and encouragement? Not to the aristocracy, who might have been 'clerical' in politics but treated the humble parish clergy with aloof condescension. And not, unfortunately, to the bishops. Since the Concordat a state of tension had existed between the hierarchy and the lower clergy which compelled them to behave as adversaries. The bishops of the nineteenth century were not only more diligent and businesslike than the languid absentee prelates of the *ancien régime*; they were also far more powerful. Before 1789 a bishop's authority had been subject to the checks and balances provided by parliaments, cathedral chapters, and the diocesan consultative committees called *officialités*. Under the Concordat the bishops inherited virtually all the powers of these bodies over ecclesiastical affairs; they were even invited to write their own diocesan regulations, within the terms of the Organic Articles of 1802. The gulf between hierarchy and lower clergy was very wide. For a parish priest to be raised to the episcopate—a very unusual occurrence—was like being promoted from private to general in one step: a bishop's salary was 12,000 francs a year, or 20,000 if he occupied an archbishopric, plus a further 10,000 if he was made a cardinal;[29] he was in absolute charge of five or six hundred priests, a seminary, and dozens of schools and colleges.

[28] Some of the lesser known books of the major French novelists deal with the dramas and frustrations of clerical life: e.g. Balzac's *Le Curé de Tours* and *Le Curé de village*, George Sand's *Mlle La Quintinie*, and Prosper Mérimée's *L'Abbé Aubain*.

[29] Retired bishops were appointed as Canons of Saint-Denis on a pension of 6000 francs a year; a parish priest after a lifetime of service received a pension of 500 francs which could be revoked by the diocesan bishop for various offences, including engaging in controversy.

He dealt with prefects, cabinet ministers, and academicians; he travelled to Rome, to Germany, to England. In particular, the management of clerical patronage under the new system emphasized the power of the concordatory bishops and the helplessness of the diocesan clergy, and the resentment created by the question of tenure (*inamovibilité*) was to be one of the principal factors which turned priests' minds towards ultramontanism. Under the *ancien régime* the bishop had been only one of the authorities who could nominate to benefices; apart from the monarchy itself, cathedral chapters, universities, several mitred abbots, and hundreds of influential laymen exercised the right to nominate. The clergy appointed in this way looked to their patrons rather than to their bishop for further advancement, and a bishop had to treat his priests with a certain amount of caution. Under the Concordat the bishops gathered all this patronage into their own hands. Only the *curés* of 3400 major parishes throughout the country were granted security of tenure; nominations to these enviable posts were to be made in consultation between the bishop and the ministère des Cultes. The 37,500 *vicaires* and *desservants* were appointed by the bishop of the diocese and could be moved or even revoked altogether by him, without consultation or any form of due process. The bishop exercised complete control over a priest's career from the seminary to the retirement home. He could move a man without warning from a congenial parish to a remote and unfriendly one; almost every priest had experienced the shock of receiving a letter instructing him to leave his parish immediately, after fifteen or twenty years. Ferdinand Fabre describes the case of a priest who had spent every penny of his own private inheritance in building a church and a hospital for his village, and was then transferred at one day's notice, without explanation; if priests are timid, evasive, mumbling creatures, Fabre says, it is out of fear of their bishops.[30]

In the middle of the July Monarchy, when the concordatory system seemed most securely established, the dissatisfaction of the lower clergy came to the surface in a movement of protest which was a prelude to the larger struggle of gallicans and ultramontanes. In 1839 two very refractory priests of the diocese

---

[30] Ferdinand Fabre, *Les Courbezon: scènes de la vie cléricale* (1862).

of Viviers, the Allignol brothers, who after several arguments with the bishop had retired to their family home rather than accept postings to remote mountain parishes, published a compendium of grievances. They were supported by a campaign of petitions from priests, all to similar effect:[31] clerical salaries ought to be doubled; something should be done to improve the status of priests in society, beginning with better education—'the century has left the priests behind'; and, above all, the parish clergy should be protected from the arbitrary proceedings of bishops who moved or revoked them without regard for their rights in canon law. What had happened, the Allignols asked, to the old *officialités*, which were supposed to consist of two vicars-general and two 'consultors' from the lower clergy, and might have compelled the bishops to conduct proper hearings before a priest was moved, or a fair trial if he was accused of some misdemeanour? Too many of the bishops evidently took the line that 'canon law in this diocese, *c'est moi*'.

Several bishops joined the controversy, with the general support of their colleagues and of the ministère des Cultes.[32] There were sound reasons for the system as it stood. France since the Revolution was a *pays de mission*, and proven talent had to be deployed wherever it could do the most good; a bishop could not allow a good preacher or a saintly confessor to vegetate amongst people already converted, but had to throw him into the front line of parish work in areas of indifference. To be moved could sometimes be a compliment. Some of the more drastic actions, such as that of the new bishop of Valence who was criticized for having moved 150 priests during his first months in the diocese, were actually attempts to revive zeal in regions where Catholicism was moribund. There were certain administrative subtleties: when a new *curé* was appointed to one of the bigger urban parishes the three or four assistant priests there might have to be

[31] Allignol frères, *De l'état actuel du clergé de France* (1839). Petitions in AN F. 19. 1948; and see J.-B. Duroselle, 'L'abbé Clavel et les revendications du bas-clergé sous Louis-Philippe', *Études d'histoire moderne et contemporaine*, i (1947).
[32] The biographies of July Monarchy bishops all describe the debate over *inamovibilité* and the *officialités*; one of the most interesting is the life of the Allignols' diocesan bishop, J. Paguelle de Follenay, *Vie du cardinal Guibert*, 2 vols. (1896), vol. ii, chap. 2. For juridical comment, Émile Ollivier, *L'Église et l'État au Concile du Vatican*, 2 vols. (1877), vol. ii, chap. 3; abbé Fabre, *Du rétablissement des tribunaux ecclésiastiques* (1857).

moved so that the *curé* would not have to contend with the
jealousies and entrenched interests of men whose loyalties were
with his predecessor. With regard to the revocation of priests
because of complaints or local scandals, the bishops could hardly
dispute the technical point that their way of proceeding *ex
informata conscientia* instead of summoning the *officialité* was
irregular, but they argued that it was more sensible to act neatly
and without publicity. In the opinion of a senior official of the
ministère des Cultes, 'a simple administrative action by the
bishop, without ruining the man's career altogether, can remove
him from harmful influences and give him a chance to render
useful services in some other parish'. A trial before representatives
of the clergy, although canonically correct, might lead to a
complete disaster even if the priest were to be found innocent.[33]

The Allignol brothers went to Rome in the hope of support,
and received a benevolent but very guarded welcome. The
Sacred Congregations were pleased at the tendency of the
European lower clergy to think of Rome as a court of appeal, but
there were disquieting elements in the clerical agitation of the
1840s. To add weight to their case for tenure the Allignols had
cited the 'Richerist' argument of 1789: if bishops are the heirs of
the apostles, priests are equally of scriptural origin, being the
heirs of Christ's disciples; the government of a diocese properly
lies in the 'the community of its priests'—and there was even a
hint that the lower clergy should elect the bishops. To revive the
officialités would have stimulated this effervescence and might
have had unwelcome results. Rome, anyway, was reluctant to
extend security of tenure more widely because this would have
increased the number of clerical appointments which under the
Concordat had to be approved by the ministère des Cultes.
Above all, the papacy did not wish to create any embarrassment
for the government of the July Monarchy with which its relations
at that time were good but very delicate. No formal brief or
encyclical was issued on the subject. The Secretary of State,
Cardinal Lambruschini, was authorized to write to the Allignols'
bishop, Mgr Guibert of Viviers, assuring him that the priests'
movement had not been endorsed at Rome. Lambruschini
himself was heard to say privately that he wished security of

[33] Note by A. Tardif, 1 Oct. 1855, AN F. 19. 6118.

tenure could be abolished in Italy.[34] The debate on clerical tenure helped the French bishops to define their own principles, but it convinced a very large number of parish priests that concordatory gallicanism in practice was a system under which they were bullied by their superiors. Although Rome had been hesitant and unsatisfactory on this occasion, the impression remained, fostered by the ultramontane literature being widely circulated at the time, that there was no relief to be expected from bishops or governments, and that the papacy would be the ultimate refuge of a hard-pressed clergy.[35]

The honours degree

The Church in France could hardly have survived without a minority of more gifted or simply better-educated priests who had higher expectations. The bleak picture of intellectual nullity in the seminaries has to be qualified by recognizing the existence of something in the nature of an honours degree, a more adequate education designed primarily for those young men of middle-class origin who had been recruited in the *petits-séminaires* in spite of the many disincentives, or who had come directly to the seminaries after receiving their secondary education in state colleges. This clerical élite, however, who were to be the future bishops, seminary directors, vicars-general, editors of Catholic journals, and *curés* of city parishes, cannot be equated simply with the 5 to 10 per cent of middle-class recruits. The son of a peasant or a tradesman could find himself in the honours stream, so to speak, if he was lucky enough to have been placed in the care of one of those exceptional parish priests with a taste for scholarship. The ecclesiastical historian René-François Guettée was given his first education by a *curé* who was a keen amateur scientist and entymologist. He taught Guettée that a priest could be an intellectual; when the boy passed on to the *petit-séminaire* he found it a distinct let-down, and wrote that the headmaster 'understood nothing of the social and scientific mission that a priest should fulfil'.[36] Another historian, Louis Baunard, who

---

[34] *Corboli Bussi*, Articoli i, ii, iv; Follenay, *Guibert*, vol. ii, 79 and 96; A. Mater, *L'Église catholique* (1906), 195–204.

[35] Anon., *Lettre à M. l'abbé Dupanloup sur cette question: pourquoi le clergé n'est plus et ne peut plus être gallican* (1845); N.-M. La Senne, *La Condition civile et politique des prêtres* (1847).

[36] Guettée, *Souvenirs*, 9.

later became rector of the Catholic University of Lille, began his career in the household of the abbé Méthivier of Neuville, a distinguished classicist and a member of the Asiatic Society.[37] François Mathieu, later archbishop of Toulouse, was a farmer's son who was placed *chez le curé*; when this excellent priest was moved to another parish he took the boy with him, taught him Latin and guided his reading in the classics; Mathieu was ready for tertiary education at fourteen.[38] Some priests supported their brightest pupils through the seminary if their parents were reluctant to pay the fees. At the level of the *petit-séminaire* great efforts were made to encourage vocations amongst the middle-class students who would not otherwise have considered a career in the clergy. The flattering attention given to an intelligent boy often combined with family circumstances to produce a decision. Henri Didon entered the *petit-séminaire* of Grenoble in 1848 at the age of nine, and won six prizes in the first year. He graduated with brilliant results and could have had a place at the École Normale, but his father died, and his mother did not feel able to support him as a student in Paris. Didon entered the seminary and later became a Dominican.[39] Ferdinand Fabre was at a *petit-séminaire* when his father went bankrupt; an aunt lent the family money, and expressed a wish to have a nephew in the clergy. Ferdinand was urged to 'pray for the vocation'.[40] In reading the biographies of churchmen, however, one cannot help being struck by how often the decision was made by the boy himself, drawn to the clerical life by his admiration for a particular teacher or confessor. Many careers began under the influence of the abbé Dupanloup at Saint-Nicolas-du-Chardonnet. Dupanloup himself had been the protégé of a noble family. He had a wide literary culture, great eloquence, and very distinguished manners, and earned a considerable reputation during the July Monarchy as a confessor to the aristocracy. Through his personal friendships with diplomats, deputies, and journalists he had become convinced that the Church in Europe was doomed in the nineteenth century unless it could recover its appeal to the educated classes. Saint-Nicolas, a school which already had a good academic reputation, offered Dupanloup a chance to

[37] L. Mahieu, *Vie de Mgr Baunard* (1924).
[38] E. Renard, *Le Cardinal Mathieu* (1925).
[39] S. Reynaud, *Le Père Didon* (1904).   [40] Fabre, *Ma Vocation*, chap. 1.

experiment with an improved pattern of clerical education. He encouraged the directors of Catholic schools in the provinces to send him their best pupils; one of his recruits was Ernest Renan, who had won all nine of the first prizes at his school in Brittany. Under Dupanloup's supervision they read Cicero, Plutarch, and Racine, the usual fare of a good nineteenth-century college, and went on to Victor Hugo, Larmartine, and Michelet. Renan said that it was the most cultivated and worldly school in the capital. In order to broaden the outlook of his gifted seminarists he enrolled an equal number of academically able boys from the upper classes; to these, with astute psychology, he spoke of the priesthood as a heroic career to which only the strongest and most intelligent should aspire. 'Supernatural motives alone, of course, should determine vocations', he wrote; 'none the less it is true that the children of the upper classes entering the clergy bring with them certain human advantages which, in a century like this one, can be a powerful means of influence for good'.[41] Dupanloup established a similar school at Orleans when he became bishop in 1850; Saint-Nicolas and Orleans were responsible for a number of notable vocations, although Dupanloup was always disappointed that there were not more.[42]

At the tertiary level even the least enlightened seminaries took proper care of the better-educated students who were marked out for careers in the hierarchy, and they were allowed all kinds of privileges. They could walk unaccompanied around the town, have their own books, and correspond with people other than their own families. Guettée, at Blois, was allowed to study for weeks at a time in the municipal library and given full use of the bishop's own books; when he produced the first volume of his *Histoire de l'Église* as a student the diocese paid to have it published. Maurice d'Hulst, an aristocratic recruit who came to the seminary from the fashionable Collège Stanislas, continued to have lessons from private tutors.[43] Alexandre Jandel was permitted to live in lodgings because his family said that the

---

[41] Mgr Dupanloup, Pastoral of 26 May 1855, quoted in Bougaud, *Le Grand Péril*, 90 n.

[42] Dupanloup/AN AB XIX 510 (Petit-séminaire de Saint-Nicolas); P. Schoenher, *Histoire du petit-séminaire de Saint-Nicolas-du-Chardonnet 1612–1908*, 2 vols. (Lille 1909), vol. ii; Mgr Lagrange, *Vie di Mgr Dupanloup*, 3 vols. (1883–4), vol. i, chaps. 8–9.

[43] A. Baudrillart, *Vie de Mgr d'Hulst*, 2 vols. (1912).

seminary of Nancy was cold and damp.[44] Everything possible was done to guide these superior students past the danger points, the moments of doubt, crises of celibacy, and attacks of homesickness when they might have been tempted to give up their studies. Seminary directors noted that homesickness was a major cause of erosion amongst the middle-class students, who could at any moment return to a more comfortable life and better prospects, by contrast to the harsh derision that a peasant boy could expect if he left the seminary.

At the heart of the gallican system, and indeed essential to the survival of gallicanism, stood a small group of seminaries which could claim some intellectual distinction and had something to offer to the more intelligent student. Montpellier, for example, conducted by the Lazarist Order and under the patronage of a learned bishop, had some of the leading intellectuals in the clergy on its teaching staff. The seminaries in the archiepiscopal sees kept up a generally high standard, at least in the teaching of religious subjects; but the one most nearly approaching the status of a university was the great Parisian seminary of Saint-Sulpice. The Sulpician Order controlled twenty of the diocesan seminaries. They had been lucky in having been able to preserve a library in Paris and a nucleus of teachers who had taken university degrees before 1789. The Sulpicians understood the need for a learned clergy but they were conscious of being spread too thinly to be able to maintain high standards everywhere. Some of their best scholars were taken away by Cardinal Fesch to train the clergy of Lyons, and the Sulpician seminaries at Bordeaux and Orleans also had good staff and libraries. The order's main concern, however, was to restore Saint-Sulpice in Paris to its pre-Revolutionary status when it had attracted the best students from provincial dioceses and had given its élite seminarians the opportunity to attend lectures at the Sorbonne. After some years of difficulty under the Empire, when the talented and energetic director André Emery guided the order through several conflicts with Napoleon and the ministère des Cultes, the seminary revived with great success. Once again the dioceses were invited to send in their best pupils; at the end of the Restoration only about 20 per cent of the students were Parisians

---

[44] H. Cormier, *Vie du révérendissime père A.-V. Jandel* (1890).

by origin. Saint-Sulpice took a high proportion of those well-educated recruits who entered the priesthood directly from a good secular schooling, and it also encouraged vocations amongst older men who had already begun careers as lawyers or civil servants. Students spent the first part of their training at the Sulpician house at Issy on the outskirts of Paris, in surroundings much more pleasant than the grim fortress-like seminaries of the provinces. Although the Sulpician curriculum was still, like all seminary education, essentially backward looking, the scholarly abbé Gosselin at Issy urged his pupils to take philosophy seriously and to read widely in Pascal, Malebranche, Leibniz, and even Victor Cousin. There was no barrier to spending one's leisure time studying mathematics or botany, which many seminary directors thought unsuitable for priests. In the evenings the students walked in the great park of Issy with their clever and charming instructors, and it was not difficult to obtain passes to scour the bookshops or visit friends in Paris. After two years of this benevolent régime they came into Saint-Sulpice for two further years of theology, ecclesiastical history, and biblical studies. Here the discipline was tighter. Passes were given more reluctantly, and the seminarians had to ask friends outside to buy books for them. As the time approached for ordination a greater emphasis was placed on personal dedication and the study of Catholic doctrine; but there were compensations. Standard texts like Bailly's *Theologia dogmatica* came to life through more intensive study and more intelligent commentaries, and the abbé Baudry introduced students of his classes on dogma to wide-ranging speculation on the work of modern thinkers. Students who could demonstrate special ability were encouraged to take Hebrew and Middle Eastern studies with two first-rate scholars, Garnier and Le Hir, and were released to attend lectures at the Sorbonne and the Collège de France.[45] The Sulpicians were prepared to accept the criticism that their protégés might become

[45] Garnier had been offered a chair at the Sorbonne. On Sulpician education, Ernest Renan's *Souvenirs d'enfance et de Jeunesse* (1883); J. Pommier, *La Jeunesse cléricale d'Ernest Renan* (1933); L. Bertrand, *Bibliothèque sulpicienne*, 3 vols. (1900), vol. ii; P. Boisard, *Issy, le séminaire: esquisse historique* (1942); J. Leflon, *Eugène de Mazenod*, 3 vols. (New York 1961), vol. i. Sainte-Beuve is describing Saint-Sulpice, from excellent sources, in the seminary chapter of his novel *Volupté*. An idea of the spiritual and devotional side of Sulpician teaching may be gained from the description of Baudry's lectures in X. de Montclos, *Lavigerie, le Saint-Siège et l'Église* (1965), 64–71.

intoxicated by these intellectual adventures; there was a certain amount of suppressed glee in the other seminaries when Ernest Renan abandoned Christianity after taking the Sulpician course in biblical literature.

In every seminary there was an annual *concours* for the men who were about to be ordained. The most academically able students were called up to read papers in Latin on the sacraments or the Epistles of Saint Paul, and the top student of the ordination class was invited to debate some theological topic publicly with the seminary director or the bishop of the diocese. Then, while the rank and file packed their bags and prepared to go out to remote and dismal parishes, the better-educated ordinands discussed their future with the director. This one would be attached to the cathedral as an administrator; that one would be secretary to his uncle the bishop of X . . .; others had already been asked for to fill chairs in seminaries; one lucky candidate might be offered a city chaplaincy to allow him to be near a university library. Most would be vicars-general before they were thirty-five. There was one thing, however, that they all had in common: a training in gallicanism. The majority of priests, for whom the gallican system would mean only a lifetime of hard work in a country parish, could be excused for not enquiring too deeply into the theory behind it; but for the better students of the Sulpicians and Lazarists and the more serious 'honours students' in the other seminaries, whose careers would be devoted to managing the gallican apparatus, each step in their studies of ecclesiastical history, philosophy, or patristic literature had had the effect of reminding them that the Church of France was a national Church with certain traditional procedures, and that it took a particular and characteristic view of its own relations with the State and with the Roman papacy.

II

Gallicanism under the Concordat

I T was part of the strategy of the ultramontane movement in the 1830s and 1840s to state firmly that gallicanism was dead, and that its defenders were no more than ghosts of the Old Regime. The abbé Desgenettes told Cardinal Lambruschini in 1840 that 'since the Concordat gallicanism exists in France only as a political instrument of the civil power; in religious matters it is extinct and can never return to life'.[1] Desgenettes was trying to conjure away the awkward reality that under the concordatory arrangements of the nineteenth century gallicanism was in some important respects as well entrenched as it had been before 1789. He was right to distinguish *gallicanisme ecclésiastique* from *gallicanisme parlementaire*, but the sharp antithesis he made between these two aspects of the doctrine is misleading.

Gallicanisme parlementaire

The real significance of the Concordat of 1801—in itself a mixture of high statesmanship and cynical pragmatism—lay in the way it was interpreted and administered; and until well after the middle of the century the official management of ecclesiastical affairs was in the hands of very determined gallicans who had no doubt that the ministère des Cultes had inherited the full powers of the old monarchy in matters of religion, and that their function was to control the Catholic Church. The ministry had been set up as an integral part of the Napoleonic structure and embodied the voltairean assumptions of that period. Portalis, the first ministre des Cultes, wrote that State religions,

> even false ones, have the advantage of putting obstacles in the way of arbitrary doctrines . . . The Government is reassured by the existence of a known and unchanging dogma. Superstition is, so to speak,

---

[1] Desgenettes to Lambruschini, 7 June 1840, in J.-P. Martin, *La Nonciature de Paris et les affaires ecclésiastiques de France sous le règne de Louis-Philippe* (1949), 281–2.

regularized, circumscribed and enclosed within limits that it cannot, or dare not, exceed.[2]

In dealing with the Church Portalis and his successors at the ministry were able to go far beyond this reductionist formula, and to deploy an effective weaponry of argument drawn from centuries of gallican jurisprudence. With very few exceptions the ministres des Cultes (the portfolio was usually combined with Public Instruction) were outstandingly able men who had studied ecclesiastical affairs and were able to debate religion and Church history at an academic level. Villemain, who was at the ministry from 1839 to 1844, at the height of the Catholic campaign against the secular *Université*, was a professor of literature at the Sorbonne and perpetual secretary of the Académie française. Fortoul (1852–6) had taken a doctorate in art history and held university chairs at Toulouse and Aix before his election to parliament in 1848; he had inherited the papers of the abbé Sieyès, and was planning a book on the Church in the Revolutionary period at the time of his death in 1856. Rouland (1856–63) had been *procureur général* of Paris; he was a powerful irritant to the hierarchy, who found him altogether too well informed on religious matters for a layman. The vicomte de Falloux, whose brief tenure in 1848 left a distinct mark on both education and episcopal appointments, was, exceptionally, an ultramontane, but he had been very active as a religious controversialist and was not at all overawed by theologians. The senior civil servants in the ministère des Cultes, Contencin, Jourdain, Nigon de Berty, Tardif, and Hamille, held their posts for long periods and made intensive studies of the very subjects which the clergy usually neglected, canon law and ecclesiology. They acquired extensive experience in monitoring the relations between French dioceses and the Roman bureaucracy, assessing the political nuances in sermons and pastorals, and dealing with more mundane questions of clerical appointments and diocesan finance. Adolphe Tardif, personal assistant to several Ministers, was a formidable savant who published a book on the *Privilèges accordés à la couronne de France par le Saint-Siège* (1855); Tardif and his colleagues were always ready to lecture a vicar-general on the Pragmatic Sanction of 1438 or to advise a bishop on the

---

[2] J. E. M. Portalis, *Discours, rapports et travaux inédits sur le Concordat de 1801* (1845), 10.

canonical rules for nominating a coadjutor.[3] In view of the general support for the concordatory system in press and parliament, the ministère des Cultes was not disturbed by ultramontane rhetoric about the death of gallicanism. At any time between 1830 and 1870 there was a large body of informed lay opinion in parliament and in society which accepted the main outlines of gallican theory as it was defined by the influential jurist A.-M. Dupin in his *Manuel du droit public ecclésiastique français, contenant les libertés de l'Église gallicane*; the *Manuel*, first published in 1824 and reprinted almost biennially until the 1860s, was the principal textbook on Church–State relations for law students and was used as a handbook in the ministère des Cultes, and Dupin himself, as President of the Chamber of Deputies and later a senator of the Second Empire, was extremely influential in debates on ecclesiastical questions.[4]

The gallican position expressed by Portalis, Dupin, and the ministry was that the period from the Civil Constitution of the Clergy to the Concordat represented a hiatus but not a fundamental break in the continuity of ecclesiastical tradition. In formulating policy for the nineteenth century the gallicans went back unhesitatingly to the classic authorities of earlier centuries: the decrees of the Sixth Council of Paris as cited in Gratian's *Decretum* of 1140; Pierre Pithou's *Les Libertés de l'Église gallicane*, written for Henry IV in 1549, and cited constantly by jurists and *parlementaires* under the Old Regime; the Four Articles of 1682; the *Dissertation sur l'autorité du Roi en matière de régale* (1682/1753) by Le Vayer de Boutigny,[5] and the treatise *Les Loix Ecclésiastiques de France dans leur ordre naturel* by Louis d'Héricourt (1719). The essence of this civil tradition is the concept of an equilibrium between three forces, the monarchy, the papacy, and the French clergy; balance is maintained by defining firstly the relations between the State and the Church, and secondly the relations between the French clergy and their spiritual sovereign in Rome.

---

[3] AN F. 19. 6523 and F. 19. 12,428 (Administration des Cultes); AN F. 19. 1865 and 1867 (personal files of senior officials); AN F. 19. 2001, papers of M. de Contencin, Director-general of the ministère des Cultes.

[4] See the summary of *galllicanisme parlementaire* by the Ambassador to the Holy See, Rayneval, Jan. 1853, quoted in Maurain, *Saint-Siège*, 146–170.

[5] Le Vayer's *Dissertation* of 1682 was reprinted in 1753 as one of the pillars of the gallican system, under the title *Traité de l'autorité des rois touchant l'administration de l'Église*.

Since it exists in the natural as well as the supernatural order, the Church is subject both to the purely spiritual government of the Pope and to the temporal government of the civil magistrate, and delimiting the two spheres is the responsibility of the State. In general, when a particular question is a matter of faith, related to some basic point of Catholic dogma, the authority of the Pope is paramount. When the question is not *de la foi*, the civil magistrate has the right to enquire if it has a bearing on the interest or the security of the State; in such cases the Church must accept the maxim that it exists as a body within the State, and is subject to civil authority. The Pope has no right to act in temporal affairs or to undermine civil authority in any way; the first of the Gallican Articles of 1682 declares that 'Kings and Sovereigns are not, by God's command, subject to any ecclesiastical power in temporal matters; that they cannot be deposed, directly or indirectly, by the authority of the heads of the Church; that their subjects cannot be dispensed from obedience, nor absolved from the oath of allegiance'. The civil government, on the other hand, has every right to act in a wide range of religious matters: the 'external manifestations of religion' are, inescapably, political facts, and the government has a duty to control them by legislation.

With regard to relations between the French clergy and Rome, the monarchy and the parliaments had always taken the view that the church was like a useful medicine with awkward side-effects, a guarantee of social harmony and order but also a potentially explosive force within the French nation. Its nominal head, the Pope, was not simply a spiritual leader but a foreign sovereign whose own record in temporal affairs and in European diplomacy did not inspire confidence, and who was ready at any moment to use the French clergy to further Roman interests. The jurists made a clear distinction between religious orders like the Jesuits or the Dominicans whom they saw as an international militia under direct Roman control, and the diocesan clergy, *l'Église de France*, which at all costs must remain French in its personnel, allegiance, and style. It was assumed that a truly national Church, obedient to Rome in fundamental dogma but relying on French traditions when it came to interpretation and practice, would be a moderate Church. Under papal influence the abbé Jekyll could easily turn into Monsignor Hyde; the clergy, therefore, had to be encouraged to remember the many precedents in canon law and ecclesiastical history for resistance by the national Churches to the claims of Rome. The gallican tradition from Pithou to d'Héricourt, summed up in Articles II, III and IV of the Declaration of 1682, insists that although the Pope must be recognized as supreme in spiritual matters his authority over the French Church is indirect, and limited by the canons and rules of Church Councils 'as received and agreed in this kingdom'. In the *mot* of the President de Harlay, 'we must kiss the Pope's feet, and tie his hands'.[6]

Gallican opinion saw no break in continuity between 1682 and the Concordat of 1801. Far from inaugurating a new era of Church–State relations, as ultramontanes believed, Napoleon's treaty with the Church simply reaffirmed the basic gallican principles. In Article I of the Concordat the Pope recognized the absolute right of the State to control the external manifestations of religion; and in Article XVI the First Consul was declared to have inherited 'the same rights and prerogatives which the former government enjoyed in relation to the Holy See'. The other fifteen articles and the seventy-six Organic Articles appended to the Concordat in effect continued the traditional policy of protecting the French Church against papal interference. To complain that the Pope had conspicuously not agreed to the Organic Articles was irrelevant, because they represented no more than a code of practice in an area of legitimate state concern. No papal encyclicals, decrees of the Roman Congregations, or any other communications from Rome were to be passed on to the French bishops unless they had been registered and approved by the ministère des Cultes. Apart from the Nuncio, a purely diplomatic agent, the Pope was not to send any legate or commissioner to disturb the proceedings of the Church in France. The French bishops were to control their own dioceses and clergy; the Four Articles of 1682 were to be taught in the seminaries.

Gallicanisme ecclésiastique

The civil gallicans were inclined to be impatient with the *fainéant* record of the French Church in its dealings with the papacy. Looking back on many centuries of 'cowardice and indecision',

---

[6] Ollivier, *L'Église et l'État*, vol. i, 275.

the diplomat-historian Adolphe de Circourt noted that at the time of the Eastern Schism in 1054 the French had missed an excellent opportunity to set up their own patriarchate; they had failed to take proper advantage of the Council of Constance in 1414; the hierarchy had helped to suppress the Jansenists instead of supporting 'this learned and energetic element in the Church'.[7] When Napoleon had announced in 1808 that the French Church, 'more learned and more truly religious than the Church of Rome, has no need of it', and the ministère des Cultes had invited the bishops to exercise 'episcopal power in its full plenitude', they had been paralysed, Circourt said, by the fear of schism. Dupin remarks in the preface to his *Manuel du droit ecclésiastique* that the French clergy should be grateful to the jurists and *parlementaires* who had defended them in the seventeenth and eighteenth centuries, when the monarchy had faltered and temporized, against the foreign intellectual despotism of the Roman Curia; if the bishops could bring themselves to accept the gallican jurists as allies they could still secure for themselves a fair degree of independence.[8]

The ecclesiastical gallicans always rejected this idea of an open alliance and were extremely careful to distinguish their own arguments from those of the State. Every clerical writer on this question from the 1820s to the 1860s goes through the ritual of dissociating himself from *les exagérations du gallicanisme parlementaire*. Bishops who were themselves strong gallicans wrote pastorals attacking each new edition of Dupin's *Manuel* as it appeared; but in reality, although it began with different assumptions about the nature of the Church, and appealed to different authorities, the gallicanism taught in the seminaries arrived at a position not very far from that of the lay jurists. The gallican revival in the seminaries after 1802 began with the determination of the older clergy not to allow the Revolution to separate them from their history. Speaking with the authority of men who had survived a decade of dispersal and persecution, they encouraged their students to look back with pride on the great luminaries of the French Church from Gerson to Bossuet, and to admire the

---

[7] Notes for an essay on the gallican Church, written shortly after 1870: Circourt/BN 20501. see also Ollivier, *L'Église et l'État*, vol. i, 266 ff.; and the polemic by a learned layman, Jean Wallon, *Jésus et les jésuites* (1879).

[8] Dupin, *Manuel du droit ecclésiastique*, xiii.

generations of learned prelates who had formed the ecclesiastical gallican tradition before 1789. This continuity was best preserved by the Sulpicians and Lazarists because of their veneration for the particular traditions of their own orders. Both drew their ecclesiology from the 1744 edition by the Lazarist Collet of the works of Honoré Tournely, Professor of Theology at the Sorbonne at the end of the seventeenth century; both orders used the same collection of gallican classics: where the jurists had their Pithou and Le Vayer, the ecclesiastical gallicans relied on Bossuet's *Défense de la Déclaration de 1682* and *Sermon sur l'unité de l'Église*, Fleury's *Histoire ecclésiastique* and *Discours sur les libertés de l'Église gallicane*, Bergier's *Théologie* and Bailly's *Theologia dogmatica*. At Saint-Sulpice, Renan wrote, earlier centuries were still alive and vividly present. Bossuet, Fénélon, and the great Sulpician Tronson had preached in the small stone church at Issy where the students prayed. When the order prepared a new edition of Tronson's *Examens particuliers* in 1806 the printer added a note on the title-page to the effect that the work was 'revised and corrected by the abbé Emery'; Emery was horrified at the idea that he had 'corrected' Tronson, and had the whole edition withdrawn.[9] This doctrinal tradition regarding the nature of authority in the Church, which represented the core of ecclesiastical gallicanism, was transmitted to nineteenth-century students by Emery's editions of Bossuet and Fénélon (1797) and of Fleury's *Nouveaux opuscules* (1807), the teaching of Frayssinous later summarized in his book *Les Vrais ·Principes de l'Église gallicane* (1817), Boyer's lectures under the Restoration and the lectures of Icard and Galais under the July Monarchy.[10] The idea of an infallible Pope had not yet developed the ethereal ambiguity of the Vatican Decrees of 1870, and since both gallicans and ultramontanes assumed that infallibility, if ever defined, would

[9] Leflon, *Mazenod*, vol. i. 310; Renan, *Souvenirs*, chap. 14. Because of the way in which Emery and his colleagues understood the idea of 'continuity', Saint-Sulpice was considerably more gallican in the early nineteenth century than it had been in 1789: See J. McManners, *French Ecclesiastical Society under the Ancien Régime* (Manchester 1960), 136–8 and notes 46–60.

[10] On Sulpician gallicanism under the Empire, Mgr Frayssinous, *Les Vrais Principes de l'Église gallicane* (1817); J. Leflon, *Monsieur Emery*, 2 vols. (1946), vol. ii; Leflon, *Mazenod*, vol. i, 287–388 and 496; J. Audinet, 'L'Enseignement De Ecclesia à Saint-Sulpice', in *L'Ecclésiologie au XIXe siècle: Unam Sanctam 34* (1960), 115–39. On the gallican teaching of Icard, Galais and Carrière in the 1840s, J. Pommier, 'Le traité de l'Église' in *La Jeunesse cléricale d'Ernest Renan* (1933), and Montclos, *Lavigerie*, chap. 1.

have clear administrative consequences, it was necessary to establish precisely the relationship between the Pope and the bishops. The Sulpicians were in no doubt that the Church was a monarchy with aristocratic participation and consent, and that there was room for a healthy pluralism within the universal Church. Bishops were of fully scriptural origin: the injunction to 'go and teach' had been addressed to all twelve of the Apostles, and divine certitude was promised to the whole Church, not to an individual; it was not an article of faith that primacy of teaching should reside in the See of Rome. A General Council presided over by the Pope was infallible, and could issue decrees which bound the Pope and his successors, but 'the most probable opinion' was that the Pope alone was not infallible. Following Bossuet and Tournely, Saint-Sulpice taught that 'the consensus of the Church is necessary if papal decrees are to become absolute rules of faith'. Even if we were to allow the ultramontane claim that a papal statement *ex cathedra* is infallible, Frayssinous asks, how would the body of the faithful know if a particular papal encyclical had the quality of being *ex cathedra*? They would know, he says, 'by the subsequent public adhesion of the bishops'; thus, only the universal Church as a whole can make an irreformable statement. Bossuet had admitted that papal decrees which received the tacit approval of the episcopate were 'indefectible', that is, that the Popes enjoyed sufficient divine guidance to ensure that Rome could not *persist in error* over a long period: this was the most reasonable interpretation of texts such as Luke 22: 32 and John 16: 13; it followed of course, that a particular papal judgement—'even the most solemn'—might easily be wrong.[11]

From this point it was possible to argue for a high degree of autonomy, by establishing a general right of Catholic bishops to exercise their functions without detailed supervision from Rome, and by emphasizing that the French Church in particular had always behaved independently, with papal approval or acquiescence. Since the time of the Second Council of Constantinople it had been accepted that when the Church was 'in a state of dispersal', during the long periods between General Councils, the bishops retained the right to judge matters of doctrine and

[11] Frayssinous, *Les Vrais Principes*, 95–102; H. L. C. Maret, *Du Concile général et de la paix religieuse*, 2 vols. (1869), vol. i, chap. 14.

needed to refer a question to Rome only if it had proved impossible to resolve locally, or if it was thought to be of such importance as to deserve the attention of the Church as a whole. In the formula of the University of Paris in 1406, 'the Pope was instituted for the Church, and not the Church for the Pope'. Saint Augustine and the historian Eusebius had cited many cases of heresies being judged and condemned by individual bishops without the necessity of calling a provincial council, and with no reference to Rome. The bishops, moreover, had the right to continue discussing a question of doctrine after the Pope had ruled on it, and could delay acceptance of a papal decree until they had examined it and agreed that it conformed to scripture and tradition; this discretion had been exercised even on so fundamental a matter as a statement on the Incarnation. Fénélon had not been challenged from Rome when he had claimed an ancient right, going back to the Gaulish period, 'to judge with the Pope and even after the Pope'.[12]

In quoting authorities the churchmen sometimes had to overcome their distaste for the civil gallican tradition. Frayssinous, the most historically minded of the *école sulpicienne*, found that the most trenchant statement of the autonomy of bishops had come from the Chancellor d'Aguesseau, and he quoted it in spite of having already gone to great lengths to dissociate himself from the 'excesses' of the jurists:

We know that the power and authority of bishops, inherent in their office, of being judges in causes concerning the faith, is a right as old as religion itself, as divine as the institution of the episcopate, as unchangeable as the word of Jesus Christ ... They can examine separately matters which they have not had the opportunity of deciding in common, and a [papal] decision which is certainly venerable in its own right is stamped with the character of a dogma of faith by the consent, expressed or tacit, of the bishops ... Nothing can shake this incontestable maxim which was born with the Church and will last as long as the Church: that each episcopal see, a depositary of the faith and the tradition of its forebears, has the right to bear witness either separately or in an assembly of bishops ...

Frayssinous had to admit that 'this great magistrate explains the

[12] Maret, *Du Concile général,* vol. i, 520–30. Ollivier, *L'Église et l'État,* vol. i. 254–6 gives several examples.

question as an enlightened theologian . . . Could anything be more precise or more luminous?'[13]

Having set limits to papal authority, the argument went on to emphasize the distinction between extraordinary Roman intervention, which could perhaps be justified in a major crisis, and ordinary Roman jurisdiction, which the old French Church had never admitted. At this point the gallicans had to deal with the ultramontane assertion that since 1801 the old French Church no longer existed: as part of the concordatory settlement the Pope had suspended or transcended canon law by deposing the French bishops, whose titles were as legitimate as his own, and the new French episcopate was in effect a papal delegation whose authority came directly from Rome. The gallican reply was that this episode had been 'rare and exceptional': to avoid a threat of schism the Pope, exercising administrative power on behalf of the whole Church, had done quickly what a General Council would have found it necessary to do after long deliberation; nevertheless, it had been a temporary departure from canon law, not a precedent.[14] It was noted also that the act had been requested by the French government for its own reasons, and that the new bishops had been nominated in the usual way by the State; the ultramontane case would have been stronger if the Pope had appointed his own nominees. There could be no doubt that the French Church in the nineteenth century enjoyed the same rights *vis-à-vis* Rome as it had done before 1789. Where Portalis and Dupin drew this conclusion from the wording of the Concordat itself, the ecclesiastical gallicans preferred to argue from a reading of the Roman documents. The encyclical *Christi Domini* of November 1801 had abolished 'all the episcopal sees of France', but because it had not abolished 'the Church of France' those sees which were immediately re-erected could claim that they enjoyed the full rights of their predecessors; in 1801, to reassure Napoleon himself and those members of the Tribunate who had strong reservations about the Concordat, Cardinal Caprara had formally promised that Rome would respect 'the freedoms, prerogatives, and usages of the French Church'.[15] In

[13] Frayssinous, *Les Vrais Principes*, 97–9.

[14] Frayssinous, *Les Vrais Principes*, 145–6, 185–90; abbé Barruel, *Du Pape et de ses droits religieux*, 2 vols. (1803), vol. ii: *L'Église gallicane sur le Pape*.

[15] Note for the Ministre des Cultes by Archbishop Sibour, 1852, in AN AB XIX. 173 (Ministère des Cultes: Archevêque de Paris.)

1814 the procedure in the diocese of Nantes for nominating a new
bishop had been approved on behalf of the Pope by Cardinal
Pacca 'according to the usage of the Church of France': as there
had been no other similar cases since the Concordat this can only
have meant the usage current before 1789.[16]

The French Church remained, therefore, broadly in the
situation defined by the Declaration of 1682. Emery was
criticized by some churchmen for a lack of tact in reaffirming the
Four Articles and publishing his edition of Fleury's *Anecdotes sur
l'Assemblée de 1682* at a moment in 1807 when the Pope was in
severe difficulties. His purpose, he explained, was to demonstrate
that the Declaration had not been an anti-papal manifesto. He
told the ministère des Cultes that the Sulpicians would give a
lead by continuing to teach the Declaration of 1682 in a moderate
and conciliatory sense, reminding students that these matters
were not *de la foi*—the Assembly of 1682 had not been a General
Council, and the Four Articles were not the Four Gospels.[17]
However, when it came to translating 1682 into a practical mode
of procedure for the nineteenth century the ecclesiastical
gallicans were as firm as the civil jurists. If it was clear that the
Pope's own authority was constrained by the decrees of Councils,
by canon law, and by 'venerable rules consecrated by general
respect', it was even clearer that the Pope's servants could have
no jurisdiction in the Church of France. Everybody knew, wrote
Frayssinous, that there were four 'effective liberties' which were
fundamental to French ecclesiastical law. No Roman documents
could be received until they had been 'examined'; the Papal
Nuncio had no jurisdiction; French subjects could not be
summoned to Rome for any proceedings of the Papal Congregations; and, above all, 'France does not receive the tribunal of the
Inquisition'.[18] Since the sixteenth century this last point had
seemed so obvious that it hardly needed restating. The mechanism
of the Roman Index might be considered useful for discipline and
unity in countries without theological traditions of their own, but

---

[16] Mgr Dupanloup noted this point from the *Praelectiones* of the Sulpician Icard:
S. Sulp/BN 24725: 24–36.

[17] Leflon, *Emery*, vol. ii. 302–18. Sulpician teaching emphasized that although the
papacy had declared in 1690 that the articles of 1682 were null and void, no specific
theological censure had been applied to them: AN F. 19. 3955 (Reception of the
Declaration of 1682.)

[18] Frayssinous, *Les Vrais Principes*, 70–1.

how could it apply in France? The French bishops were quite
competent to make doctrinal judgements, to grant or refuse the
imprimatur to books on theology or canon law and to choose
libraries for their diocesan seminaries, and there could be no
question that their decisions might be overturned by a committee
of Italians in the Congregation of the Index. The French
liturgies, also, were more ancient than the Roman Congregation
of Rites which claimed to supervise them, and ecclesiastical
discipline could be managed perfectly well by the hierarchy with
only very infrequent recourse to the Congregation of Bishops and
Regulars. On this general point the civil and ecclesiastical
traditions were absolutely agreed: in Dupin's *Manuel* 'the decrees
of these Congregations have no authority at all in this kingdom
and are not executed';[19] Fleury puts it that 'we honour their
decrees as the opinions of grave and learned doctors, but we do
not grant them any jurisdiction over the Church of France'.[20]
The principle of indefectibility allowed the Popes themselves to
make occasional mistakes, and even the most ardent ultramontanes
had never so far claimed that the Roman bureaucracy was
indefectible. In a long accumulation of case-law going back at
least to the twelfth century there were many examples of the
Gallican Church flatly refusing to acknowledge, for example,
that a French theologian had been condemned by Rome. 'For
us', Frayssinous said, 'the Holy See is the centre to which all
things tend, but it is not the source from which all things
emanate.'[21]

Gallican doctrine in this sense was taught not only in the
twenty Sulpician and ten Lazarist seminaries but also in the
great majority of seminaries conducted by the diocesan clergy,
whose senior instuctors were frequently Sulpician or Lazarist
graduates;[22] not having the resources of the teaching orders,
however, the ordinary diocesan seminaries could not afford to
turn away competent teachers who happened to be anti-gallican,
and were thus to be less able to resist the ultramontane current
when it began to rise in the 1830s and 1840s.

[19] *Manuel du droit ecclésiastique*, 524 f.
[20] Fleury, *Institution au droit ecclésiastique*, 1767 edn., chap. 25.
[21] Frayssinous, *Les Vrais Principes*, 93.
[22] This estimate is confirmed by Dupanloup's view of Sulpician and Lazarist
influence in his *Lettre à M. le duc de Broglie* (1844).

III

The gallican establishment

WHEN Montalembert said in 1844 that it would be hard to find even four bishops who would publicly endorse the Four Articles of 1682,[1] this was true to the extent that hardly any bishop would have done anything so needlessly provocative and injurious to the papacy; but the great majority of bishops, vicars-general, and seminary directors remained gallican in the Sulpician mode. In the seminaries the Four Articles were explained, rather than taught, as a perfectly legitimate way of understanding the government of the Church, and the hierarchy was generally agreed on the need to remain independent from the jurisdiction of the Roman Curia: 'In France the Pope reigns but does not govern'.[2] A number of episodes in the first half of the century helped to define and reinforce this basic gallican position. The unsettling effect in the seminaries and the parishes produced by Lamennais and the *Avenir* movement, the *exalté* papalism and antirational philosophy of the Mennaisians, their contempt for the concordatory French Church, and the polemical violence with which they attacked anyone who did not share their views, convinced the bishops that ultramontane radicalism could easily destroy the fabric of a moderate and national Church, and this impression was strengthened a decade later when the Allignol brothers revived the Mennaisian theme that priests owed their first allegiance to Rome.

The extraordinary growth of the religious orders in France also represented a challenge. From the 1830s onwards Jesuits, Dominicans, Benedictines, Marists, Redemptorists, and various orders of brothers became very active, opening schools, conducting missions, and soliciting funds for their multitudinous *œuvres*. The bishops were in a dilemma: they needed the schools and

[1] Speech of 16 Apr. 1844, in *Discours de M. le comte de Montalembert*, 3 vols. (1892), vol. i, 206.
[2] A remark by Mgr Affre, Archbishop of Paris 1840–8, quoted by R. Limouzin-Lamothe and J. Leflon, *Mgr Denys-Auguste Affre* (1971), 9.

missions, but were suspicious of organizations whose Fathers-general were in Rome and who claimed to be exempt from local diocesan authority. Bishops who welcomed an order into their dioceses often lived to regret it. The French Jesuits were known to be moderate in their views and were constantly in trouble with Rome for 'liberalism', but as an order they could be hard to manage: in Rouen they bought a house and asked permission to say masses for a small invited congregation; very soon, as the archbishop complained, it became a mark of social distinction to be seen at the Jesuit mass instead of at the cathedral;[3] and the next step was to begin recruiting well-educated boys for their own order, persuading them on occasions to leave a diocesan seminary. Some bishops, like Thibault of Montpellier and Bonnechose of Carcassonne, would not allow a Jesuit within their diocesan boundaries. Even the ultramontane Pie of Poitiers, a keen mariologist himself, refused to admit a Marian order from Grenoble who wanted to collect money for a monument to commemorate the appearance of the Blessed Virgin at La Salette. One bishop had been turned into a convinced gallican by many years of struggling with the missionary orders when he was Vicar-Apostolic in the Far East. In the debate on secondary education in 1849 Adolphe Thiers pointed out that 'an important part of the clergy' had very strong reservations about the international orders.[4] In the 1840s the awareness of these dangers arising from within the Church led the hierarchy towards a closer relationship with the State.

Relations between the Catholic hierarchy and the State had passed through several phases since 1802. At first, churchmen had been grateful not to be living under the Cult of the Supreme Being, or a Napoleonic version of Anglicanism. With all his unprecedented power the First Consul had chosen to restore the old religion; but his brusque treatment of the Church and of the Pope was a warning of problems in the future. The Restoration, by contrast, almost smothered religion with official favour whose only result was to make the Church unpopular; and the government of the Restoration showed no inclination to dismantle

[3] Mgr Blanquart de Bailleul to Mgr Donnet of Bordeaux, 14 May 1845, Donnet/AN 160 AP : dossier 1.
[4] *La Commission extraparlementaire de 1849: texte intégral*, ed. G. Chenesseau (1937), 217.

the Cultes apparatus, which was actually stronger in 1830 than it had been in 1810. Under the July Monarchy a striking paradox emerged. The public picture was of the Church having to fight against the coarse-grained voltaireanism of the official class in a series of bitter conflicts, especially over education, with the State's coercive machinery of *police des Cultes* weighing heavily on the clergy and the Organic Articles preventing the bishops from meeting in councils or synods. Behind this public antagonism, however, the bishops discovered the basic modern principle that while governments of different complexions come and go, government departments remain and constitute the reality of the State; and the ministère des Cultes, being staffed by jurists and historians, had a particularly well-developed sense of continuity. In spite of its difficulties with the July Monarchy the episcopate managed to establish a working relationship with the ministry which was to remain more or less undisturbed through all the upheavals of the Second Republic and the 1850s.

The relationship was almost symbiotic in the matter of appointing bishops, as ministry and hierarchy understood that their interests and their criteria for selection were essentially the same. For every vacancy the ministry sifted through dozens of letters from influential persons putting forward the names of their clerical friends and relatives, to confirm that each candidate had a good reputation in lay society, that his local MP thought him ready for a bishopric, and that he had the qualities required to manage the particular diocese in question. For more detailed *renseignements* concerning a man's doctrinal position and his standing in the Church it was usual to consult the archbishop of the province where the vacant see existed. In forming the episcopate of the late 1840s the government relied especially on advice from five of the archbishops who had very wide contacts and reputations for good judgement: Affre of Paris, Bonald of Lyons, Donnet of Bordeaux, Blanquart de Bailleul of Rouen, and Mathieu of Besançon came to be regarded as an unofficial panel of selectors for vacant sees all over the country. These men represented the core of the gallican episcopate and were themselves very close to the ministry's ideal of a bishop, with backgrounds in *les classes éclairées*, good educations and some experience of the world outside the seminary; all were Sulpician trained. Denys-Auguste Affre, a nephew of the Sulpician Boyer, had joined the order after graduating but had been asked to resign because his gallican opinions were a little too forward even for Saint-Sulpice; he was a tough and resourceful administrator and a prolific writer on Church–State relations, education, and liturgy.[5] Maurice de Bonald was a son of the eminent philosopher. His own views on ecclesiology were very moderate, but he appointed active gallicans as vicars-general and took great pride in the excellent Sulpician seminary of Saint-Irénée at Lyons; by 1850 there were no less than ten old Irénéens in the episcopate.[6] Ferdinand-Francois Donnet, the son of a doctor, had been trained at Saint-Irénée and at the *École des Hautes Études* at Lyons. At the beginning of the July Monarchy he had been called in as a vicar-general to administer the chaotic diocese of Nancy; the bishop, Forbin-Janson, after irritating the middle classes of the diocese by his aristocratic insolence and his ultra-royalist politics, had been forced to flee from Nancy at the Revolution of 1830, and could not return. Donnet had to reconcile factions and restore confidence, and the experience taught him the value of tact in ecclesiastical affairs. As archbishop of Bordeaux he was a great civic notable, a diplomat and a *bon viveur*, and he had many friendships in legal and parliamentary circles in Paris.[7] Louis-Edmond Blanquart de Bailleul was the son of the *procureur général* of Douai and had graduated in law before entering Saint-Sulpice. He was greatly appreciated by the government for his talent and personal integrity; in his early thirties he had declined a bishopric in order to remain as vicar-general to the aged bishop of Versailles who had treated him kindly.[8] Jacques-Césaire Mathieu, archbishop of Besançon, was another law graduate and had been received at the Bar under the Empire; he was ordained at Saint-Sulpice in 1823 and was a bishop within nine years. Mathieu, a gallican in the mould of Emery and Boyer, exercised a powerful influence over appointments: he was chaplain to the Royal household and a close friend of the Papal Internuncio, Mgr Garibaldi, who had confidence in Mathieu's judgement and consulted him regularly between 1832 and 1843;[9] and he kept up

[5] AN F. 19. 2555 (Affre).
[6] *Episcopat* (Lyons); AN F. 19. 2531 (Bonald).
[7] Donnet/AN 160 AP; AN F. 19. 2506 (Donnet); abbé Pougeois, *Vie, apostolat et épiscopat de S. E. le cardinal Donnet*, 2 vols. (1884); Ollivier, *L'Église et l'État*, vol. ii, 13–15.
[8] AN F. 19. 2572 (Blanquart de Bailleul).   [9] *Garibaldi/Mathieu*, chap. 8.

a voluminous correspondence with Saint-Sulpice.[10] The ministry also had its favourites amongst the diocesan bishops: three who were particularly influential were Frédéric de Marguerye, a serious and thoughtful man who was very successful in his own diocese of Saint-Flour and later at Autun,[11] Guillaume Angebault of Angers, the son of a *parlementaire* and a graduate of the Sulpicians at Nantes,[12] and Gaston de Bonnechose of Carcassonne, later archbishop of Rouen. Bonnechose was the son of an *émigré* noble and a Dutch Protestant girl; he had taken a law degree and was an *avocat général* at 27 when he decided to join the Church. Instead of attending a seminary he studied privately for holy orders as a protégé of the philosopher Louis Bautain, and was appointed Superior of the French Seminary at Rome soon after his ordination. His bishopric was conferred in 1847 as a reward for having argued the French government's case in the negotiations with Rome over the expulsion of the Jesuits. Successive ministres des Cultes were impressed by his good sense and his quiet charm: Émile Ollivier, who knew him well, wrote that 'he knew how to conceal his fiery soul behind a majestic serenity', and Hippolyte Fortoul always said that ten minutes' conversation with de Bonnechose made him feel relaxed and co-operative.[13]

These senior men understood that in episcopal appointments they were not looking for saints or prophets. Piety and impeccable conduct, certainly, and some reputation for ecclesiastical learning; but, as Mgr de Marguerye pointed out, 'the government of a diocese has much in common with civil administration', and the first need was for men who had administrative skill without being mere bureaucrats. The best candidates, he thought, were vicars-general who knew the problems a bishop had to deal with and perhaps had carried out some episcopal duties already. Above all, they had to be men who could maintain public respect for religion by their excellent manners, personal dignity, and knowledge of the world: these

---

[10] 220 letters from Mathieu to the abbé Boiteux of Saint-Sulpice are in S. Sulp/AN AB XIX 517, dossier 5; the archives of the archdiocese of Lyons hold over 100 letters from Mathieu to the abbé Carron, 1838–56.

[11] Marguerye's moderate but firm Sulpician-style gallicanism was expressed in a letter to the Papal Secretary of State in 1852: ASV: Francia: 1853: III. His personal file is in AN F. 19. 6178.

[12] AN F. 19. 2489 (Angebault).

[13] AN F. 19. 2572 (Bonnechose); Ollivier, *L'Église et l'État*, vol. ii, 14.

qualities were more likely to be found amongst the higher classes, Marguerye wrote, although he was 'far from wishing to confine the episcopate to any particular caste'.[14] Too much experience as a parish priest was a positive handicap: we must not appoint *curés*, Marguerye wrote, underlining the word, 'whose ideas smell of the parish and who often want to govern a diocese as they ran the sacristy'. Zealots known for their 'medieval excesses in the pulpit' had no chance; even if they were gallicans for the moment, they were temperamentally inclined to sudden conversions and might embrace some extreme doctrine without warning. Great preachers were used to immediate successes and 'wanted to carry every position by frontal assault'. A bishop had to be a man who understood that the role of religion was to add a dimension to human life, but not to control every aspect of it; and to reconcile Frenchmen rather than setting them at one another's throats. The most admired clerical intellectuals and writers were often *esprits à système* and lacked the flexibility to cope with practical problems, although it was admitted that five years' experience as a vicar-general could sometimes turn an intellectual into a formidable bishop.[15] And, as a general rule, no ultramontanes, or at least nobody who made an ostentatious show of enthusiasm for Rome; a candidate with Romanizing tendencies was occasionally endorsed if he was outstandingly good in other respects. 'We do not condemn ultramontane opinions', wrote Mgr Affre, 'but we think them less probable, and less likely to keep people in the Church or to win them back when they have abandoned religion'.[16] With advice of this kind the ministère des Cultes entirely concurred. The harmony of views was so close that in some cases the ministry was asking about a particular candidate, 'Is he pious?' while the man's archbishop was asking, 'Can he understand finance?' Both sides searched for the same ideal candidate, 'serious, ripe in experience, moderate, and conciliatory in manner'—disappointed applicants complained that the policy was *surtout, pas de zèle*—and both sides made occasional mistakes. Neither the hierarchy nor the ministry

[14] Marguerye to Ministre des Cultes, 21 Mar. 1846, *Garibaldi/Mathieu*, 75–7.

[15] The main material on successful candidates is in their episcopal dossiers, AN F. 19. 2479–596, arranged by dioceses. On candidatures, AN F. 19. 2609–46 and F. 19. 6528. See also *Garibaldi/Mathieu*, chap. 6, 'La recherche organisée des épiscopables'.

[16] Mgr Affre, *De l'usage et de l'abus des opinions controversées entre les ultramontains et les gallicans* (1845).

wanted the alliance of Church and State to become too close or too obvious. There was a danger that the system might produce merely 'governmental' bishops, and the churchmen wanted to keep their right to speak freely and attack government policy, as happened in the education dispute of the forties. Equally, the ministry did not expect bishops to follow every political trend, and no action was taken, for example, against those bishops who remained legitimists after the Revolution of 1830.

If we examine the episcopate in 1850, choosing the year in which the most serious conflict between gallicans and ultra-montanes began, we find that sixty of the eighty bishops had been appointed under the July Monarchy, nine bishops from the Restoration still held their sees, and twelve had been appointed since 1848. Forty-two, or slightly over half, could be described as broadly middle-class by origin, and twenty-one came from the nobility, although not from the most socially prominent families; ten came from farming and eight from artisan backgrounds; one was the son of a sailor.[17] Thirty-five had been educated in secular schools, and thirteen had followed adult careers before entering the priesthood: five had been lawyers, three army officers, and five civil servants; Levezou de Vesins of Agen was a widower with five children and had been a sub-prefect before being ordained at forty-three. Perhaps ten could be described as scholars and intellectuals, but the general level of education was high and the majority of bishops had publications to their credit on a variety of subjects from patristic studies to local history. Three had taught in secular universities.

Only twenty-one of the bishops had any substantial experience as parish priests. The typical pattern of a bishop's career before his elevation was an administrative post or a seminary chair immediately after ordination, sometimes four or five years as a bishop's secretary, and then a vicar-generalship; several had also been directors of seminaries or headmasters of *petits-séminaires*. Three had been royal chaplains. Fifty-nine of the bishops, or 74 per cent, were Sulpician graduates, thirty-four from Saint-Sulpice in Paris, ten from Saint-Irénée in Lyons, and fifteen from

---

[17] The figures given are compiled from the published biographies of the bishops; their personal dossiers in AN F. 19. 2479–596; Baunard's *L'Épiscopat français* (1907); Charles Pouthas, *L'Église et les questions religieuses . . . de 1848 à 1877* (Cours de Sorbonne 1961).

other Sulpician seminaries in the provinces. One had been trained by the Lazarists. Four were actually members of the Sulpician Order.[18] The strength of gallicanism in the episcopate cannot be deduced from this fact alone, but it is possible to arrive at a general picture by applying some other criteria whose relevance will become apparent in later chapters of the present study. By looking at the bishops' direct contributions to the gallican–ultramontane debate, their recorded attitudes towards the Mennaisian movement, the opinions they expressed about Roman and diocesan authority in the *inamovibilité* question in the forties, and the parts they were to play in the controversies over the Roman liturgy and the jurisdiction of the Index, we can divide the eighty bishops with a fair degree of accuracy into three main groups. (See table, p. 58.)

Firstly, there were thirty-three convinced and active gallicans who engaged in public controversy. Secondly, there were thirty moderates; most of these were in fact gallicans and privately agreed with their more outspoken colleagues on the gallican side, but they were frequently constrained by local factors or personal difficulties.[19] Thirdly, there were seventeen active ultramontanes. Given the prevailing methods of selection it may seem surprising that there were any at all. Five of the sixteen were appointed quite deliberately, during the brief tenure of the ministère des Cultes by the ultramontane vicomte de Falloux under the Second Republic. The other eleven appointments reflect the willingness of the ministry to take risks: a candidate's ultramontanism was sometimes known but not thought serious enough to outweigh his positive qualifications, and in other cases the man's ultramontane views only became apparent after he had been safely installed in a bishopric.[20] By 1850 the combined efforts of the ministry and the hierarchy had succeeded in placing strong or moderate gallicans in all but two of the fifteen archbishoprics, in all the bishoprics in major centres of population, and in almost all of the dioceses with high levels of religious practice—in the

---

[18] The Sulpicians were reluctant to lose good teachers to bishoprics, and the director of Saint-Sulpice, Carrière, made difficulties about each case.

[19] The three oldest bishops in this group, Philibert de Bruillard of Grenoble and Saunhac-Belcastel, both ordained in 1789, and Devie of Belley, ordained in 1791, had been more active gallicans when they were younger.

[20] See chapter 4, 'Ultramontanism after Lamennais', for further comment on the ultramontanes who reached the episcopate before 1850.

Catholic west, for example, Angers, Le Mans, Nantes, Vannes, Quimper, and Saint-Brieuc; with the exception of Gousset at Reims, the ultramontane bishops held dioceses which were of little importance in themselves.

Only a close examination of each man's personal history can reveal the accidents of background and training which divided the ultramontane bishops from their gallican colleagues, but some generalizations are possible. The obvious social point that the gallicans were mainly middle-class and the ultramontanes were not, will be explored further in the chapter on ultramontanism. About half of the gallicans and moderates, but only a quarter of the ultramontanes, had received their secondary education outside the seminary system. Gallicans and ultramontanes had the same low proportion of men with parish experience. There is a sharp division by age: amongst the thirty-three bishops who had been ordained to the priesthood before 1819 there are only two ultramontanes, Villecourt and Gousset; the fourteen other ultramontanes in the list belong to the generation young enough to have been influenced by the Mennaisian movement.

Perhaps unexpectedly, there was roughly the same proportion of Sulpician graduates amongst the gallican, moderate, and ultramontane bishops. A Sulpician training was not enough by itself to preserve students from the temptation of ultramontane ideas. Some seminarians were inspired by the tradition of Fénélon and Bossuet, others reacted against it. Of the three future bishops who sat together in the final ordination class at Saint-Sulpice in 1823, for example, Mathieu and Alouvry were to keep their allegiance to gallicanism while Gignoux became one of the leading ultramontane activists. It is worth paying some attention to a significant career pattern which helped to confirm and strengthen the opinions formed in the seminary: practically every one of the younger gallicans had come under the personal influence of one of the bishops or seminary directors who had been ordained before the Revolution, or had joined the priesthood in the first decade after the Concordat and received the principles of gallicanism directly from Emery and Boyer; for various reasons the ultramontanes had mostly escaped this influence. These distinguished older men transmitted their own reverence for French ecclesiastical traditions and admiration for 'the old clergy' to their young vicars-general, secretaries, and chaplains: when Guibert of Viviers said that 'the bishops should carry the Pope on their shoulders; but to do that they must stand on their own feet' he was quoting his mentor, Mazenod of Marseilles; and Mazenod had been Emery's favourite pupil, almost an adopted son.[21] 'I began my theological studies at the age of sixteen', wrote Cœur of Troyes, 'under the closest and most fatherly direction of a doctor of the old Sorbonne who had been vicar-general to Cardinal Fesch . . . and the principles I learned will remain with me all my life.'[22] Mgr de Marguerye had been secretary to Cardinal de Rohan and vicar-general to the saintly old bishop of Soissons, Mgr Simony. Jean-Baptiste Bouvier had been one of the first Sulpician graduates after the Concordat, and was director of the Le Mans seminary for fifteen years, writing his own textbooks, before becoming bishop of the diocese; the Papal Nuncio noted with disapproval that almost the entire clergy of Le Mans had been Bouvier's pupils and were tainted with his opinions.[23]

Apart from Paris, to be examined in detail later, the *archevêché* of Lyons was the most notable channel of influence. Cardinal de Bonald had been a pupil of Emery and had helped to carry the great Sulpician's coffin in 1811. One of his vicars-general was the Sulpician Callot who was to organize a fifteen-year resistance against the introduction of the Roman liturgy at Lyons, and the other, the abbé Lyonnet, later bishop of Saint-Flour, wrote admiring biographies of two of Cardinal de Bonald's predecessors.[24] The former students of the seminary of Saint-Irénée at Lyons, a more resolutely gallican establishment even than Saint-Sulpice itself, were spread throughout the hierarchy and included some of the most influential gallican bishops such as Donnet of Bordeaux, Mioland of Toulouse, Cœur of Troyes, Dufetre of Nevers, and Pavy of Alger, and at least twenty prominent vicars-general; and each of these had his own pupils and protégés. There were many other strongholds in the provinces where the *évêché* had been occupied since the Concordat

[21] Follenay, *Guibert*, vol. ii, 274.
[22] Cœur to Rouland, Ministre des Cultes, 28 Jan. 1857, AN F. 19. 2590.
[23] ASV: Francia: 1853: VII.
[24] See Callot's nomination to the see of Oran in 1867, AN F. 19. 1955 and F. 19. 2551; for Lyonnet, AN F. 19. 2484.

44   *The gallican establishment*

by a succession of strongly gallican bishops, assisted by vicars-
general of the same stamp, the seminary was in the hands of the
Sulpicians or the Lazarists, and a young priest-administrator
could hardly avoid being confirmed in a gallican view of the
Church at the beginning of his career. Bordeaux, Rouen, Tours,
Orleans, Clermont, Nancy, Dijon, Metz, and Saint-Flour were
all *foyers du gallicanisme*; Autun was ruled by the energetic gallican
du Trousset d'Héricourt for twenty-two years and by Frédéric de
Marguerye for twenty, and three of its vicars-general, Devoucoux,
Thomas, and Rousselet, were to be leading opponents of
ultramontanism as bishops in the 1860s.[25] Perhaps the most
remarkable provincial centre was Montpellier. The bishop, Mgr
Thibault, had begun his career as secretary to that vigorous old
gallican prelate Mgr d'Astros who had been *chef de cabinet* to his
uncle Portalis under the Empire, and was one of the most
outspoken opponents of Lamennais. Thibault watched his
seminary closely for the slightest sign of Roman influence,
although he need not have worried, since the Lazarists' teaching
was based firmly on Bossuet and Tournely, and under his
patronage the circle of the *évêché* included some of the most
learned and determined gallicans in the French Church whose
influence extended far beyond Montpellier.[26] The seminary and
the Faculty of Theology did their best to preserve the ideal of a
learned clergy in spite of their limited resources. The abbé
Ginoulhiac, who taught philosophy and theology from 1830 to
1839, was one of the leading intellectuals in the Church, much
admired in the secular press for his historical writing on the
development of dogma in early Christianity. German critics
regarded him as one of the few French clerics who could be called
a scientific theologian;[27] ultramontanes thought him 'too cold
and too much the scholar to see the distant horizon where the
star of Roman authority was rising'.[28] Amongst Ginoulhiac's

[25] AN F. 19. 5781–2.
[26] AN F. 19. 2539; E. Appolis, 'Un évêque ennemi des jésuites', *Actes du 81ᵉ Congrès national des sociétés savantes* (1956), 715–20; G. Cholvy, 'Les milieux néo-gallicans du diocèse de Montpellier', *Les Catholiques libéraux au XIXᵉ siècle* (Grenoble 1974), 281–98. The seminary is the one described in Fabre's *Ma Vocation*.
[27] Döllinger to Montalembert, 3 May 1853, in S. Lösch, *Döllinger und Frankreich* (Munich 1955), 425.
[28] L. Baunard, *Un siècle de l'Église de France* (1919), 168–70; Ollivier, *L'Église et l'État*, vol. ii, 15; AN F. 19. 2531 (Ginoulhiac).

pupils at Montpellier were two future archbishops and innumer-
able vicars-general and seminary directors. He was vicar-general
of Aix during the gallican–ultramontane conflicts of 1850 to 1853
and later bishop of Grenoble, and as archbishop of Lyons he was
to be one of the chiefs of the Minority party at the Vatican
Council. The abbé Flottes, who held the chair of philosophy at
Montpellier as well as teaching theology at the seminary from
1838 to 1867, also had a Parisian reputation; Saint-René-
Taillandier wrote in the *Revue des deux mondes* that Flottes's essays
on Pascal, Saint-Augustine, Lamennais, and Daniel Huet
constituted an *œuvre* with the qualities that had distinguished the
best theological debate of the seventeenth century.[29]

From the strength of gallicanism in the middle rank of the
Church, amongst the vicars-general, academics, and headmasters
who were to be the episcopal candidates of the future, it is clear
that gallican principles had been transmitted to a younger
generation with considerable success.[30] A polarization of opinion
was also taking place which will become clearer in the course of
the present study. While many young clerics were moving
towards an authoritarian ultramontanism, the gallican party in
the Church was becoming more liberal. The Restoration style of
churchmanship where gallicanism was often combined with an
ultra-royalist *politique* had almost faded away, leaving Mgr
Clausel de Montals of Chartres as one of its last defenders; for the
younger men gallicanism, because of its emphasis on 'Frenchness',
implied at least a tentative search for ways of reconciling
Catholic doctrine with the principles of 1789, constitutional
government, and a pluralist model of society. This gallican-
liberal style was most highly developed in the archdiocese of
Paris.

Gallican clergy and laity in Paris

In the strict juridical sense Paris was not a primatial see. On
certain points of administrative detail the archbishop exercised a
minor degree of authority over the suffragan bishops of Versailles,
Orleans, Meaux, Blois, and Chartres, but any attempt to extend
his formal influence beyond the archdiocesan boundaries would
have been rebuffed by the rest of the episcopate. Nevertheless, in

---

[29] *Revue des deux mondes*, 15 Apr. 1859.
[30] AN F. 19. 2790–813 and 6530 (Vicars-general).

the nineteenth century Paris was potentially in a strong position to exercise a *de facto* leadership of the Gallican Church. The ancient sees of Lyons and Reims had lost much of their status under the concordatory system; ecclesiastical publishing was more than ever concentrated in Paris, and the Parisian daily press, which took a keen interest in religious controversy, reached almost every part of the country; the head of state and the machinery of government were now firmly situated in the capital, and the senior Parisian clergy had immediate access to the ministère des Cultes, the archbishop and the minister being usually on friendly enough terms to be able to settle many delicate ecclesiastical matters in private conversation. Above all, the powerful magnetic attraction of Paris drew in the talented churchmen along with the ambitious lawyers and civil servants, the writers and the artists. Intelligent young priests who had come from Brittany or the Aveyron to study at Saint-Sulpice, an experience 'like emerging from a room lit by smoky lamps into an explosion of sunlight', as Renan said, were always reluctant to return to their home dioceses and would try to get appointments to metropolitan parishes or to chaplaincies or directorships of religious *œuvres*; and once installed these men were hard to dislodge, even by promotion. It was impossible, for example, to persuade the *curé* of the Madeleine, Deguerry, who enjoyed a *casuel* of 40,000 francs a year and moved in the best Parisian society, to desert the brilliant life of the capital for a silent *évêché* deep in the provinces; Deguerry refused several bishoprics, including Marseilles. The abbé Cœur, who was a professor in the Faculty of Theology at the Sorbonne, did his best to avoid being made a bishop before reluctantly leaving for Troyes in 1848. There were several cases also of bishops declining archbishoprics which would have taken them further away from Paris. Provincial bishops who worked hard in their dioceses and felt that they were entitled to spend some time in Paris by way of compensation eagerly accepted seats on the *Conseil supérieur de l'Instruction publique* and on various government committees, honorific chaplaincies to the Royal Family, and editorships of devotional volumes which had to be seen through the press. Quite minor problems brought the cardinals up from Bordeaux or Tours for personal discussion with the ministre des Cultes. When the *coup d'état* occurred on 2 December 1851 there were nine bishops in temporary residence in Paris. Some very highly qualified seminary instructors in the provinces were willing to apply even for prison chaplaincies in order to get back into the metropolitan current. This concentration of clerical talent raised the temperature of ecclesiastical debate in the capital, and the constant procession of visitors, applicants, and advisers made it certain that any event or any dispute which concerned the *archevêché* would receive the widest possible publicity throughout the Church.

After Archbishop Affre had been killed while trying to mediate on the barricades in June 1848 it was known that none of the cardinals and archbishops was particularly anxious to take the see of Paris at a moment of such political turmoil, but there was a good deal of surprise when the choice fell on the relatively junior bishop of Digne, Dominique-Auguste Sibour. He had a reputation for inconsistency in both theology and politics and was thought to be altogether too insubstantial a figure for Paris. The ministry, however, had some reason to think that Sibour was underrated by his critics, and that he had very good qualifications to be archbishop of Paris in a democratic republic. Sibour was born in the Drôme department in 1792, and studied for the priesthood at Rome. As a canon in the diocese of Nîmes he had come under the influence of Lamennais and had written articles for *L'Avenir* in 1831, but unlike most of the clergy at that time he was more attracted by the liberal and democratic side of the Mennaisian movement than by its apocalyptic papalism. An equally important influence was his friendship at Nîmes with the young Henri Maret, an extremely gifted Sulpician graduate who was later to become Dean of the Faculty of Theology at the Sorbonne. Sibour and Maret became disenchanted with the *exalté* tone of *L'Avenir* and concluded that the real lesson of the Mennaisian episode was the necessity for priests to be better educated, especially in theology and patristic studies. Maret went to Germany and became an academic scholar; Sibour became a diocesan administrator.[31] It was unkindly said that he owed his appointment as

---

[31] AN F. 19. 2555 (Sibour); J.-F. Poujoulat, *Vie de Mgr Sibour* (1857). On Maret in this phase of his career and his relations with Sibour, G. Bazin, *Vie de Mgr Maret*, 3 vols. (1891), vol. i; C. Bressolette, *L'Abbé Maret* (1974); A. Riccardi, 'Alle origini del neogallicanesimo di Henri Maret', *Archivum Historiae Pontificiae*, xiv (1976), 219–64; R. Thysman, 'Le gallicanisme de Mgr Maret', *Revue d'histoire ecclésiastique*, lii (1957), 401–65; Montclos, *Lavigerie*, chap. 2.

bishop of Digne in 1839 to the fact that the ministre des Cultes, M. Teste, was a friend of his family, and Sibour came in for much satirical comment a few years later when M. Teste was convicted for taking a bribe as President of the Appeal Court. Sibour had a very emotional temperament for a bishop; he was inclined to plunge unreflectingly into new enthusiasms and to be badly shaken by small setbacks. In 1840 he was one of the few bishops to sympathize openly with the grievances expressed by the Allignol brothers, and without consulting anyone else in the episcopate he began a series of reforms at Digne to restore the *officialités* and to give priests more say in diocesan government; he also required the parish clergy to take annual examinations in theology. This programme was described in his *Institutions diocesaines* and attracted widespread interest, not all of it favourable. Mgr Garibaldi, the Papal Internuncio, would not agree to a proposal to translate him to the larger and more difficult diocese of Angoulême: behind Sibour's cleverness and ebullience, he wrote, 'he is timid, uncertain, and wavering on every subject, needing a lot of personal reassurance'.[32] In 1848, however, Sibour had two influential sponsors. His cousin Léon Sibour, *curé* of Saint-Thomas-d'Aquin, was a deputy in the *Assemblée nationale*, and his old friend Maret was now Professor of Dogma at the Sorbonne and in considerable favour with the government as an adviser on ecclesiastical matters. Maret recommended Sibour to the ministère des Cultes as a liberal who was sympathetic to scientific and intellectual enquiry; he wrote a series of articles in the radical Catholic journal *L'Ère nouvelle* to the effect that Sibour was the man to bring about a reconciliation between the Church and the modern world, and that his democratic background—in April 1848 he had actually stood for election as a republican candidate, advocating social reform and *ateliers communaux*—would help to make the Church more acceptable to the Parisian working class. The Roman authorities, for their part, were under the impression that Sibour was an ultramontane because of his support for the Allignol movement, and were quite pleased with his nomination.

Sibour, in fact, does not seem to have had any fixed views on the gallican–ultramontane question when he came to Paris in

---

[32] Letter of 28 May 1842, in *Garibaldi/Mathieu*, 351–2, and see also ibid. 65–7.

October 1848; but he was to become more gallican month by
month, impelled by the logic of his position as archbishop of the
greatest Catholic capital in Europe. He had inherited Affre's
entourage, known in the Church as *les africains*, a group of clergy
who held the key administrative and intellectual posts depending
on the *archevêché* and were reserved and sceptical in their attitude
towards Rome. The senior vicar-general, Buquet, the secretary-
general, Ravinet, and Léon Sibour, who was president of the
commission on parish matters, were all Sulpician-educated
gallicans. The abbé Bautain, vicar-general for secondary education, was a former pupil of Victor Cousin and had been in trouble
for almost twenty years with the Holy Office, where he was
suspected of theological errors, or worse. The leading instructors
at Saint-Sulpice, Carrière and Galais, were in very close touch
with the archbishop's household, and the professor of dogma at
Saint-Sulpice, the abbé Delacouture, was official examiner of
books submitted for the imprimatur. Henri Maret acted as a
political adviser and a liaison with the staff of the Sorbonne. In
this circle there were also a number of gallican intellectuals who
had begun to make their names in religious and political
controversy before the 1848 Revolution and who were now
writing even more vigorously in the freer atmosphere of the
Republic. The abbé Gratry, a graduate of the Polytechnique who
had studied German religious thought at Strasbourg in the
1830s, was chaplain of the École Normale and was engaged in a
long public debate with its director, Étienne Vacherot, on the
philosophy of the early Christian church. Two other priests who
were becoming well known to editors and reviewers in the secular
press were J.-R. Prompsault, who published a three-volume
Dictionnaire de droit et de jurisprudence civile-ecclésiastique in 1849, and
Georges Darboy, cleverest of the *africains*, the most brilliant
product of the seminary of Nancy in the nineteenth century.
After ordination Darboy had been an instructor in dogma at
Nancy, but had disturbed his superiors by lecturing on Hegel
and Saint-Simon as well as Saint-Augustine, and by bold
interpretations of the Greek Fathers, whose works he read
fluently. On hearing about Darboy's frustrations at Nancy, Affre
had invited him to a sinecure post in Paris and encouraged him
to write for the ecclesiastical press, where he immediately
scandalized the Papal Nuncio with a detailed criticism of Rome's

favourite theologian, Perrone.[33] The *curés* of the most important city parishes were gallicans to a man, the most outspoken being Martin de Noirlieu at Saint-Jacques who kept dinner-parties amused with accounts of clerical politics at Rome 'where the Pope wears a triple crown, while his boss had to be content with a crown of thorns'; Deguerry of the Madeleine and Lecourtier, archpriest of Notre-Dame, held similar opinions.

The events of the Second Republic presented a significant challenge to the gallican clergy of Paris. After the ambiguous adventures of .1848, when churchmen had at first welcomed the democratic and social republic but then retreated quickly to a more conservative position, the Republic in 1849, under a president who was anxious for the time being to show how devoted he was to the interest of Catholicism, and with an Assembly full of 'men of order', seemed to offer the best opportunity for the Church since the Napoleonic era. Religion, Sibour thought, would be able to 'put its roots down deeply into the nation'; but he and his circle knew that this would depend on a difficult feat of balance. The Church had somehow to understand and share in the development of ideas in France while preserving its dignity and not feebly adapting itself to every nuance of politics; it had to keep clear of party alignments, and avoid any suggestion of fanaticism or theocratic blustering. Even the urban working class might not be irretrievably lost. In spite of the anticlericalism of the political clubs the clergy were not personally unpopular in working-class quarters of Paris. Affre's courageous death was remembered, and Sibour was well received when he made pastoral visits to factories and workshops. Sibour's own speeches on the social question and the articles written by Darboy and Bautain for the semi-official *Moniteur catholique* in 1849 and 1850 show the *archevêché* willing to support fairly radical measures and to consider, for example, the duty of the state to legislate for fair wages and the right of workers to form associations.[34] Converting the urban masses, however, was

[33] 'La théologie du P. Perrone', *Le Correspondant* (25 Nov. 1847); on Darboy, later Archbishop of Paris, AN F. 19. 2555 (Darboy); J. Foulon, *Mgr Darboy* (1889); and the article by J. Gadille, 'Georges Darboy, archevêque de Paris', in *Mélanges offerts à A. Latreille* (1972). P. Poupard, *L'Abbé Louis Bautain* (1961); V. Advielle, *Notice biographique et littéraire sur l'abbé Prompsault* (1862); and on Gratry, B. Reardon, *Liberalism and Tradition* (Cambridge 1975), chap. 9.

[34] Historians have generally been impatient with Catholic social policy in the

not an immediate prospect, nor the most immediate concern. At this point in the middle of the nineteenth century the main problem for the French Church was to gain and keep the respect of the educated political class.

The Parisian clergy could not help being uneasily aware that they were under the constant scrutiny of a large body of well-informed laymen. Since Church–State relations formed so important an element in French politics there were, naturally, a great many experts. Ten past and future ministres des Cultes were MPs under the Republic, but there were perhaps fifty or a hundred other men in Paris who could have managed the portfolio perfectly well. Although not many of them had formal training in theology as such, in the fields of ecclesiastical history and Church–State jurisprudence there were laymen much better qualified than the clergy who passed for professors of the subjects, and always ready to neglect their professional careers for the absorbing pleasure of writing articles on the Concordat or the Roman liturgy.

The educated laity may be seen as a series of concentric circles, beginning with a group of committed activists, *catholiques avant tout*, at the centre and shading outwards through circles of moderates, nominal Catholics, and men whose private beliefs verged on agnosticism; and beyond the Catholic periphery there were further circles where a close interest was taken in religious affairs and there was considerable sympathy for the Church. The most conspicuous of the activists, Charles de Montalembert, Alfred de Falloux, and Frédéric Ozanam, the leading spirits in Mme Swetchine's ultramontane salon since the 1830s, had not lost their belief that the papacy would eventually take the lead in a cultural and political renaissance in Europe; their disillusionment with Pius IX was still some years in the future. They were very

Second Republic, and sarcastic about the shift of clerical support from republicanism in 1848 to Bonapartism in 1851: H. Guillemin, *Histoire des catholiques français au XIXe siècle* (1947); P. Pierrard, *1848: les pauvres, l'Évangile et la Révolution* (1977); M. A. Gabbert, 'Bishop *avant tout*: Archbishop Sibour's betrayal of the Second Republic', *Catholic Historical Review*, lxiv (1978), 337–56. A more complex picture emerges from the first volume of Bazin's *Vie de Mgr Maret*, J.-B. Duroselle's *Les Débuts du catholicisme social* (1951), and from several contemporary sources: *Mandements, lettres et instructions pastorales de Mgr Sibour*, 2 vols. (1853–7), vol. i; AN F. 19. 5604 (Political attitude of the clergy, Second Republic); C. Bressolette (ed.), *Henri Maret: L'Église et l'État: Cours de Sorbonne inédit 1850–52* (1980); Y. Daniel (ed.), *La Religion est perdu à Paris: Lettres d'un vicaire parisien à son archevêque (1849)* (1978).

eloquent in promoting Catholic causes, but their ultramontanism meant that they had only a distant relationship with the *archevêché* in Affre's time, and held themselves even more aloof from Sibour.[35] Their notoriety in parliament and the press should not obscure the point that educated lay opinion in Paris was predominantly gallican. A clearly gallican circle can be identified amongst the Catholics who held posts in the *Université*. Charles Giraud, Professor of Roman Law and Inspector-General of Higher Education, had published a defence of gallican principles in 1847,[36] and other Catholic academics with liberal-gallican views were J.-J. Ampère (French Literature), C. Daremberg (Medicine) and Gaultier de Claubry (Toxicology and Legal Medicine): Gaultier de Claubry in particular wrote frequently for the religious press and was to be an outspoken opponent of ultramontanism in the early fifties.[37] Eugène Rendu, the Chief Inspector of Primary Education, was the son of Ambroise Rendu, one of the founders of the *Université* in 1806 and for many years permanent head of the ministère des Cultes; his uncle was bishop of Annecy and his aunt was mother-general of an order of nuns. Rendu published scholarly monographs on Catholic and secular education in Germany, and a series of reports on papal government in Italy which later earned him a place as an adviser to Napoleon III on Italian Catholic affairs.[38]

Ampère and Rendu had close social links with the more sceptical but still nominally Catholic milieu of the academicians, lawyers, diplomats, and political theorists whose voices can be heard in Nassau Senior's *Conversations* and who included some of the most thoughtful critics of ecclesiastical affairs. Louis Bonjean, the distinguished jurist who was to be President of the Appeal

[35] On Montalembert and Mme Swetchine's circle, see chapter 4.

[36] C. Giraud, *Les Libertés de l'Église gallicane* (1847).

[37] *A.-M. Ampère et J.-J. Ampère: Correspondance et souvenirs de 1805 à 1864*, 2 vols. (1875); Henry James, 'The two Ampères', *French Poets and Novelists* (London 1878); R. P. Jullien, 'Quelques souvenirs d'un étudiant jésuit à la Sorbonne et au Collège de France', *Études*, cxxvii (1911), 329–48. For Gaultier de Claubry, a very interesting figure in the scientific community during the Second Empire, Duroselle, *Les Débuts du catholicisme social*, 621–2; he wrote a good article on the Pagan Classics controversy in the *Ami de la religion* of 11 Sept. 1852, and an attack on ultramontane political ideas, *L'Univers en présence de lui-même*, in 1856.

[38] Eugène Rendu, *M. Ambroise Rendu et l'Université de France* (1861); Rendu, *Conditions de la paix dans les États Romains* (1849); J. Gay, *Les Deux Romes et l'opinion française* (1931); B. Ferrari, *Eugène Rendu e Massimo d'Azeglio 1849–1865* (Santena 1967).

Court and a Senator under the Second Empire, was a specialist on Roman law and papal history, and was commissioned by the government to investigate the financial problems of the parish clergy; he kept in touch with opinion in the hierarchy through his friendships with Maret and Cardinal Donnet of Bordeaux.[39] The *avocat général* at the Appeal Court, Alexandre Freslon, had been Falloux's predecessor as ministre des Cultes and was very sympathetic to the defenders of gallicanism in the clergy.[40] Adolphe de Circourt, ambassador to Berlin in 1849, was for many years at the centre of a circle with strong gallican opinions; he wrote articles on Church history for the press and left others unfinished amongst his papers.[41] One of the most interesting laymen was Tocqueville's old friend Louis de Kergorlay, a profound scholar with very independent views. All the Tocqueville–Beaumont circle thought that Kergorlay had one of the best minds in Europe and constantly urged him to 'come forward', but apart from a brief collaboration with Gobineau on the *Revue provinciale* in 1848/49 he published almost nothing, because of his extreme perfectionism; he followed every turn of ecclesiastical politics, and brought an immense body of learning to bear in writing a long manuscript on 'Le pour et le contre sur le clergé français' which is full of radical suggestions, such as the idea that the Pope should be elected by a kind of ratepayers' franchise in which every layman who contributed to the support of the clergy should be entitled to a vote.[42] Circourt, Kergorlay, and another important gallican layman, Jean Wallon, who was to be one of the leading lay opponents of the Declaration of Infallibility in

[39] Bonjean was executed with Archbishop Darboy as a hostage of the Commune in 1871. There is a small deposit of his papers in AN 303 AP; and see G. Bernoville, *La Vie ardente du président Bonjean* (n.d.). Bonjean's principal work in this field is his edition of documents *Du pouvoir temporel de la papauté* (1862).

[40] Freslon, letter to the abbé Henri Bernier, 26 July 1850, in A. Houtin, *Un dernier gallican, Henri Bernier* (1904), 270–1.

[41] Circourt/BN 20501, including the long essay on the gallican Church quoted in chapter 2 above, and a study of the Eastern Church. On Circourt, R. C. Winthrop, *Tribute to the memory of Count Adolphe de Circourt* (Massachussetts Historical Society 1880); Nassau Senior, *Conversations with Distinguished Persons*, 2 vols. (London 1880), vol. ii, 268–9; and *Conversations with M. Thiers, M. Guizot . . .*, 2 vols. (London 1878), vol. ii, 75–6.

[42] Kergorlay/Arsenal 14107–8; see J.-A. Lesourd's introduction to the Tocqueville–Kergorlay correspondence, vol. xiii of the *Oeuvres complètes de A. de Tocqueville* (1977). On Kergorlay's papers, A. G. Gough, 'French legitimism and Catholicism' (Oxford D.Phil. thesis 1966).

1870, had private libraries of ecclesiastical books far superior to those in the best seminaries.[43] In their turn, these men were conscious of critical opinion further along the spectrum of religious belief, in the Protestant, Jewish, and agnostic milieux of Paris. Rendu, Gaultier de Claubry, Circourt, and Kergorlay knew that as Catholics they could find themselves tainted by association if the clergy behaved arrogantly or stupidly. They worked beside their professional colleagues at the Sorbonne, in the law courts or in the ministries; they sat on the committees of learned societies with agnostic experts on the Church like Dupin or like Adolphe Franck, the author of a *Philosophie du droit ecclésiastique*. They mixed every day with the formidable writers on religious matters in the press: Saint-Réné-Taillandier of the *Revue des deux mondes* had published a study of Duns Scotus and scholastic philosophy in the 1840s, and the *deux mondes* also had Charles de Rémusat, Charles Louandre, Émile Saisset, and Barthelémy-Saint-Hilaire, a distinguished panel of polymaths— Rémusat, for example, reviewing the sermons of the eminent Thomist, Father Ventura, was able to demonstrate that Ventura did not know his Aquinas.[44] In each of the crises of Catholic affairs under the Republic and early Empire the Catholic laymen had to defend and excuse their Church before this critical audience while not always being able to conceal their own exasperation with it.

The debates in the Assembly on the military expedition to restore the Pope to Rome in 1849, and on the education bill which became the Loi Falloux in 1850, indicated—to the great relief of senior churchmen—that after a generation of anti-clericalism the political class as a whole, deeply disturbed by the catastrophes of 1848, was now willing to concede that the Church had a major part to play in French national life;[45] but at the same time there were many doubts expressed about the capacity of the

---

[43] On Wallon, *E. Paul et Guillemin: Catalogue de la bibliothèque de feu M. Jean Wallon* (1911); J. Wallon, *La Vérité sur le Concile* (1872), and *Jésus et les jésuites* (1879).

[44] *Revue des deux mondes* (1 Mar. 1853). See, for example, C. Louandre, 'Du mouvement catholique . . .', *Revue des deux mondes* (Jan.–Feb. 1844), and Émile Saisset, 'La philosophie du clergé', ibid. (Mar. 1844). Catholic affairs were reviewed in the *Journal des débats* by Silvestre de Sacy and Prévost-Paradol. On Rémusat, Michael Roberts, 'The religious thought of Charles de Rémusat', *Journal of religious history*, vii (1973).

[45] The famous and symptomatic change of heart of Adolphe Thiers can be seen in the committee discussions of the Loi Falloux in 1849, *Commission extraparlementaire de*

clergy to rise to the occasion. The laymen who studied clerical
affairs were in no doubt that the basic problem was ignorance.
They knew Sibour and the leading Parisian clergy well enough to
see that they were not theocrats or fanatics, but they knew also
that too many leading churchmen were essentially orators rather
than thinkers. Jules de Lasteyrie told Nassau Senior that 'the
clergy are seldom fit to be our companions'; he meant the
bishops, he said, as well as the humble parish priest. The famous
Dominican preacher Lacordaire, according to Circourt, was 'the
most ignorant man that ever entered the Academy. His history
and theology were absolutely original, for he invented them as he
went on'.[46] Even the best Sulpician graduates and the genuine
scholars like Gratry and Darboy had gaps in their education, and
might be hard pressed either to sustain a serious argument in the
Revue des deux mondes or to resist the arguments of the extreme
ultramontane party within the Church. The laymen knew
something of ultramontanism from its tactical successes in the
education question and the liturgy campaign in the last years of
the July Monarchy, and it filled them with distrust. 'Every new
swarm of priests that issues from our seminaries', Circourt said,
'is more narrow-minded, more bigoted, more mischievous than
the one that came before it. They are utterly indifferent to liberty
or law'.[47] Kergorlay wrote that ultramontanism would have no
chance if the clergy had to follow the original Napoleonic
prescription of taking degrees from secular universities before
beginning their special studies in theology.[48]

The circle of the *archevêché* had good reasons to know that the
secular intellectual world had to be dealt with on a basis of
mutual respect. Gratry, for example, had wide contacts amongst
the laity through his colleagues at the École Normale and
through the salon of the Chevreux family, which was frequented
by Ampère, Circourt, and Léon Say. His debate with Vacherot
on early Christianity was conducted with perfect courtesy,
although Vacherot was Gratry's director and could easily have
dismissed him. Deguerry belonged to a committee for European

1849: texte intégral (1937); cf. F. Ponteil, *Les classes bourgeoises et l'avènement de la démocratie*
(1968), 198–9, 238–41.
[46] Senior, *Conversations with Distinguished Persons*, vol. ii, 64–5.
[47] Senior, *Journals kept in France and Italy 1848–52*, vol. ii, 267.
[48] Kergorlay/Arsenal 14114: 66–7.

peace whose other members included Lamartine, Victor Hugo, the Protestant pastor Athanase Coquerel, and the agnostic Jean Macé. Sibour himself had taken over a long-standing project of the *archevêché* to lead Victor Cousin into the Catholic church. His *Histoire de la philosophie* had been condemned by the Roman Index just at the moment when he had been thought to be on the verge of conversion; Affre had gone to great lengths to keep Cousin's major work, *Le Vrai, le beau et le bien*, off the Index and to make sure that he was not attacked in the Catholic press. At different times under the Republic Cousin was said to be discreetly *pratiquant*: he was going to Mass at the Madeleine, Eugène Rendu reported, and if he could find a formula for avoiding the attentions of the Index he would be virtually converted.[49] This would have been a triumph to balance the defections of Lamennais and Renan; but men like Cousin and Vacherot could be captured only by tact and patience, and by solid argument. Cousin's hesitation was widely regarded as a telling point against the Church.

When Sibour was appointed the archdiocese had already taken some steps towards the creation of a *clergé doctoral*. Since 1815 there had been several tentative plans for a centre of higher education for priests which might eventually restore Paris to the position it had once occupied as an intellectual counterweight to Rome in the Christian Church. In 1840 Victor Cousin himself, as Minister of Public Instruction, had supported Affre in an attempt to revitalize the Faculty of Theology at the Sorbonne, but this project foundered because Rome would not give canonical recognition to the Faculty's degrees. Affre then decided that the Faculty of Theology should be essentially a showcase of clerical talent, where learned clergy lectured on religious topics to audiences of lay students, and that another institution was needed where the ablest younger clergy could receive the best tertiary education.[50] In 1845 an *École des hautes études ecclésiastiques* was finally established in the former Carmelite convent in the rue de Vaugirard, where it became known as the *École des Carmes*.

---

[49] Letter of Eugène Rendu to Gino Capponi, 27 Oct. 1852, in A. Carraresi (ed.), *Lettere di Gino Capponi e di altri a lui*, 3 vols. (Florence 1882–4), vol. iii; J. Barthélémy Saint-Hilaire, *Victor Cousin: sa vie et sa correspondance*, 3 vols. (1895), vol. iii.

[50] Letter of Ambroise Rendu on Affre's plan, in L. Séché, *Les Derniers Jansénistes*, 3 vols. (1891–3), vol. iii, 27 n.

The abbé Cruice, an Irishman with a doctorate of the Sorbonne, headed a mostly lay staff of professors, civil servants, and engineers; Ernest Renan was to have been Professor of Hebrew. The students were nearly all graduates of Saint-Sulpice, with some others recommended by provincial seminary directors. For those subjects which the *Carmes* could not provide they attended regular lectures at the Sorbonne, and at the end of the course they sat the ordinary university examinations in history, literature, or science and took degrees of the University of Paris. The archdiocese saw no need to ask for Roman approval, since the degrees awarded were not in theology.[51] Sibour had always been a strong advocate of better education for the clergy, and one of his first actions in Paris had been to require priests to take regular examinations in dogma, canon law, and history.[52] He was very impressed by the success of the *École des Carmes*, which by 1849 had produced about twenty graduates and its first doctor, the future Cardinal Lavigerie. It would surely do a great deal to answer the most serious criticisms of the intellectual state of the clergy, and create a much better rapport between the Church and the intellectual world; it might also be expected to strengthen the influence of the Paris archdiocese, and generally of the French, within the Church in Europe.

His support for this initiative, however, was to have profound consequences for gallicanism. At the same time as Sibour was issuing his ordinance about examinations for priests, an official of the Roman Curia, Mgr Giovanni Corboli-Bussi, was preparing a confidential report for the Pope 'on certain religious affairs in France'. In his seventh chapter, on education, Corboli-Bussi admitted the necessity of higher learning for the French clergy—but not, preferably, to be given at Paris: the Sulpician influence was bad enough, he said, without exposing priests also to the gallicanism and neo-jansenism of the Sorbonne.[53] Corboli-Bussi's report was presented to the Pope in exile at Gaeta in 1850. Sibour was already well aware of the perennial tension

---

[51] Prospectus and list of staff in 1850, Dupanloup/AN AB XIX 526; Limouzin–Lamothe and Leflon, *Mgr Affre*, 179–87; Montclos, *Lavigerie*, 78 ff., 128–33. The École des Carmes had obvious affinities with the Mennaisian ideal of a learned clergy, with the essential difference that the Mennaisians had wanted their learning to be judged by the Pope rather than by the Sorbonne.

[52] *Mandement* of June 1849, AN F. 19. 4087.

[53] *Corboli Bussi*, articolo vii.

between Rome and the *archevêché* of Paris, and of the rising
challenge of the ultramontane movement in France, but he did
not know that he was shortly to be at the centre of a great contest
between two antithetical styles of Catholicism.

TABLE 1. The French episcopate in 1850

Gallicans	Moderates	Ultramontanes
ARCHBISHOPS		
Blanquart de Bailleul (Rouen)	Darcimoles (Aix)	Debelay (Avignon)
Bonald (Lyons)	Du Pont (Bourges)	Gousset (Reims)
Donnet (Bordeaux)	Jerphanion (Albi)	
Mathieu (Besançon)	La Croix d'Azolette (Auch)	
Mioland (Toulouse)	Mellon-Jolly (Sens)	
Morlot (Tours)	Regnier (Cambrai)	
Sibour (Paris)		
BISHOPS		
Alouvry (Pamiers)	Allou (Meaux)	Baillès (Luçon)
Angebault (Angers)	Bardou (Cahors)	Berteaud (Tulle)
Bonnechose (Carcassonne)	Brossais Saint-Marc (Rennes)	Cardon de Garsignies (Soissons)
Bouvier (Le Mans)	Buissas (Limoges)	Caverot (Saint-Dié)
Clausel de Montals (Chartres)	Cart (Nimes)	Depéry (Gap)
Cœur (Troyes)	Chatrousse (Valence)	Doney (Montauban)
Dufêtre (Nevers)	Cousseau (Angoulême)	Dreux-Brézé (Moulins)
Dupanloup (Orleans)	Croizier (Rodez)	Gignoux (Beauvais)
Dupont des Loges (Metz)	Devie (Belley)	Mabile (Saint-Claude)
Féron (Clermont)	Foulquier (Mende)	Parisis (Langres)
Graveran (Quimper)	Georges-Massonnais (Périgueux)	Pie (Poitiers)
Gros (Versailles)	Jacquemet (Nantes)	Pallu du Parc (Blois)
Guibert (Viviers)	La Motte de Broons (Vannes)	Salinis (Amiens)
Lacroix (Bayonne)	Lanneluc (Aire)	Villecourt (La Rochelle)
La Tour d'Auvergne (Arras)	Le Mée (Saint-Brieuc)	Wicart (Fréjus)
Marguerye (Saint-Flour)	Levezou de Vesins (Agen)	
Mazenod (Marseilles)	Mascarou-Laurence (Tarbes)	
Menjaud (Nancy)	Monyer de Prilly (Châlons)	

Gallicans	Moderates	Ultramontanes

BISHOPS (*cont.*)

Gallicans	Moderates
Olivier (Evreux)	Morlhon (Le Puy)
Pavy (Alger)	Philibert de Bruillard Grenoble)
Rivet (Dijon)	Raess (Strasbourg)
Robiou (Coutances)	Robin (Bayeux)
Rousselet (Séez)	Rossat (Verdun)
Thibault (Montpellier)	Saunhac-Belcastel (Perpignan)
Du Trousset d'Héricourt (Autun)	

IV

Ultramontanism after Lamennais

Rome! Serene amidst the tempests of Europe, thou hast not
doubted thyself, thou hast felt no fatigue. Thy glance, turned to
the four quarters of the world, followed with sublime penetration
the development of human affairs in their relation to the Divine
. . . I did not fail to recognize thee when I saw no kings prostrate
at thy gates. I kiss thy dust with unspeakable joy and respect.
Thou art the benefactress of the human race, the hope of its
future, the sole grandeur now existing in Europe, the Queen of the
world.

> Henri Lacordaire, *Considérations sur le système philosophique de
> M. De Lamennais*, chapter XII.

GALLICANISM was bound to be challenged in a period when the
intellectual current was running so strongly against classicism,
rationality, and moderation. It was inevitable that amongst those
young men who took their Catholicism seriously enough to join
the priesthood or to become active and dedicated laymen, some
would be attracted by the authoritarian elements in Catholic
romanticism. In the first half of the nineteenth century ultramontanism in France was essentially a dissident movement
amongst student intellectuals, bored with the cool pragmatic
view of the role of religion in society put forward by the sober
gallican theorists and yearning for wider horizons and more
exciting programmes of action. Outside the seminaries, papalism
was in the air. In Germany Novalis, Görres, and von Haller had
written of an ideal Middle Ages when the papacy had ruled over
a united and submissive Christendom, and the clergy had been
the unquestioned arbiters of politics and morality—for all the
French and German romantics the medieval period was a kind of
Atlantis about which they wrote copiously without reading the
documents. In 1819 Maistre's *Du Pape* had created an immense
effect with its vision of the Papacy as a gigantic rock standing
motionless while around its base rushed the turbulent waters of
pride and revolution. But for the French the most seductive

appeal was that of Lamennais. Between 1825 and 1834 some of the most exceptional members of the clerical élite of 'honours students' and younger seminary instructors, and some of the brightest young Catholic laymen, were drawn by the great Breton magus away from the Sulpicians and the universities to his counter-seminary of La Chenaie; there they were exposed to an eclectic mixture of the ideas of Maistre, Barruel, and the German medievalists and to Lamennais's own *nouveau christianisme*, embodied in his *Essai sur l'indifférence* (1817) and *Des progrès de la Révolution contre l'Église* (1828), and were encouraged to plan a future society based on the primacy of the spiritual power. Jules Morel's experience was typical: 'An invitation was sent to me while I was on vacation from the seminary. Instead of returning to Saint-Sulpice I rushed to La Chenaie where I found the great man, seconded by the abbé Gerbet. [Gerbet was well known to Morel as a Sulpician graduate of 1822, of legendary brilliance.] These two eminent spirits were ready to explain their plans and their hopes to me; I listened with all the delight and the inexperience of my twenty years.'[1]

The condemnation of Lamennais and his defection in 1834 made remarkably little difference to the Mennaisian movement. Not a single one of his disciples, not even his closest associates at La Chenaie or on the journal *L'Avenir*, followed him out of the Church. By hastily and publicly repudiating those parts of the master's doctrines with which they had never felt entirely comfortable, especially the idea of truth as something perceived and validated by the *sensus communis* of mankind, they managed to preserve more or less intact the principal elements of the ultramontane credo. They avoided having to take a clear stand on the more difficult question of the power of unaided human reason to ascertain divine truth, which Lamennais had appeared to deny, and there was no pressure on them to repudiate the whole ambience of La Chenaie.[2] After a short period of

---

[1] Preface to Morel's *Somme contre le catholicisme libéral* (1872). On the Mennaisian movement, abbé Ladoue, *Mgr Gerbet, sa vie, ses œuvres*, 3 vols. (1872), vol. i; J.-R. Derré, *Lamennais, ses amis et le mouvement des idées à l'époque romantique 1824–1834* (1962); Reardon, *Liberalism and Tradition*, chaps. 4–5; Louis le Guillou, 'Le dossier Lamennais', *Romantisme* ix (1975), 126–30.

[2] To receive permission to be ordained at Rome in 1834 Emmanuel d'Alzon had to sign a statement that he admired Lamennais's early writing on the papacy but rejected the doctrines of *L'Avenir*: S. Vailhé, *Emmanuel d'Alzon*, 2 vols. (1926), vol. i, 189–90.

embarrassment and silence the original Mennaisians were able to resume publication, and enjoyed vast prestige amongst the younger generation of enthusiasts who had not quite been old enough to have experienced the excitement of the movement at first hand.

The *école mennaisienne* which thus continued to grow and to disturb the bishops inherited a potent blend of cultural and political romanticism. In the first place, the movement had concentrated the minds of its followers on an image of Christian Rome itself as the ultimate answer to the cultural influences of the Enlightenment, classicism, and rationalism. The famous visit in 1832 by the editors of *L'Avenir* inaugurated a long series of similar pilgrimages over the next twenty years. As one Mennaisian wrote, Rome was the capital city of the soul; 'it breathes a subtle perfume that only true Christians, with their more exquisite taste, can perceive'.[3] Young men who had been taught by their schoolmasters to admire the austere virtues of Cato and Marcus Aurelius found themselves in tears before the tombs of holy virgins and martyred saints. Where Gibbon had felt the tremendous presence of Republican and Imperial Rome, they looked around them and saw only Christianity, with the classical ruins badly out of focus in the background. Pagan remains in general, Montalembert said, 'make no impression on my anticlassic soul'.[4] The Forum was tedious, the Pantheon a meaningless heap of stones. The mosaics and the Baths of Caracalla were monuments of gross pagan luxury and evil. The fountains of Rome reminded them only of the endless flow of divine grace. They deprecated the Renaissance splendour of Saint-Peter's, and Gaston de Ségur, standing in front of Michelangelo's Moses, wrote in his diary: 'an old goat'.[5] But the chalices, the vestments, the relics, the catacombs . . . In 1832 Montalembert and Rio found that nobody in Rome knew much about the catacombs, and had to explain their significance to the ignorant and apathetic priests who acted as their 'guides'; a

---

[3] Ladoue, *Gerbet*, vol. ii, 148–9.

[4] P. de Lallemand, *Montalembert et ses amis dans le Romantisme* (1927), 249.

[5] Ladoue, *Gerbet*, vol. ii, chap. 7; E. Ricard, *L'Abbé Combalot* (1892), 232–43. On the *Cercle de la rue Cassette*, an influential group of priests who had trained at Rome and shared a distaste for pagan and Renaissance imagery, see B. du Boisrouvray, *Mgr Gay: sa vie et ses œuvres*, 2 vols. (Tours 1921), vol. i, and the early chapters of M. de Hédouville, *Mgr de Ségur (1957)*.

decade later the underground passages were crowded with
pilgrims. Phillippe Gerbet came for a three weeks' holiday and
stayed for ten years. All of them were fascinated by the immense
continuity of papal tradition. 'I looked at the ancient walls of
Rome', Lacordaire wrote, 'and I returned to my solitary room,
happy at having felt myself for a moment far from my century.'[6]
The mood was so strong that ultramontane travellers returning
through northern Italy refused to look at anything but holy relics
and miraculous portraits.

The ultramontane laity

It was evident, however, that there were two different styles of
ultramontanism; devotion to Rome could lead either to liberal or
to authoritarian conclusions, the distinction arising from the
fundamental paradox in Mennaisian doctrine. There had been
great enthusiasm amongst the La Chenaie group and in avant-
garde Catholic circles in Germany and Belgium for the idea of an
intellectual religious revival to reverse the direction of the
Enlightenment. Catholic scholars, scientists, historians, and
astronomers were to conquer the universities by the sheer force of
well-informed argument, and by persuading and converting the
educated classes to establish Catholicism on a secure footing in
the nineteenth century: 'faith will espouse science, and science
will be penetrated with faith.'[7] This grand vision implied a belief
in free debate and a liberal-parliamentary model of society. The
spokesmen of Protestantism and scepticism had to be free to put
their case so that they could be challenged and defeated, but the
Church could hold her own in the free market of modern thought
and need not be afraid of competing ideas. Catholicism,
Lamennais had said, easily became stagnant without the clash of
debate and was healthiest in those countries where it had to
struggle against skilful opponents. The Mennaisians envisaged
the nineteenth-century Catholic renaissance as being under the
patronage of Rome, with a succession of learned and tolerant
Popes of the future encouraging scholarship and restoring the
Church to a central position in European intellectual life; but at
the same time they saw the papacy itself as the ultimate

---

[6] *Lettre sur le Saint-Siège* (1838), 55.

[7] *L'Avenir* (3 May 1831). The theme is fully developed in Lamennais's *Des progrès de
la Révolution* (1829).

repository of truth and the only valid interpreter of the products of the human mind. All Catholic thought—history and science as well as theology—had to pass through the filter of Roman approval. The last issue of *L'Avenir* had declared that 'we shall go to hear our judgement pronounced, prostrate before the Chair of Saint-Peter . . . If one of our thoughts, even one, deviates from those of the Holy Father, we disavow and reject it.'[8]

This surrender in advance was to have unfortunate consequences throughout the careers of the group of laymen who regarded themselves as the heirs of a liberal Mennaisian tradition. Charles de Montalembert, François Rio, Albert and Pauline de la Ferronnays, Louis de Carné, Alfred de Falloux, Frédéric Ozanam, and Félix de Mérode gathered in Mme Swetchine's salon in Paris after the condemnation of Lamennais,[9] and managed to sustain their enthusiasm for a Catholic intellectual revival even in the face of the encyclical *Mirari vos* which lumped the liberal Mennaisians together with Carbonari and revolutionaries whose ideas were described as 'filth vomited into a sewer.'[10] At Mme Swetchine's, Ozanam wrote, 'we avoid those points of doctrine on which Rome has requested silence';[11] but they felt free to continue with their plans for the conversion of the educated classes. The reign of Gregory XVI would come to an end eventually, they reflected, and the Church would 'move out of its political era into its era of learning';[12] they were to experience a moment of intense joy and expectation when Pius IX was elected in 1846. With independent means, and friends and family connections in several European countries, they travelled constantly and were able to discuss their vision of the future of Catholicism with Hungarian aristocrats, English converts, Irish patriots, and Italian philosophers. They spent months at a time in the congenial atmosphere of the German

---

[8] *L'Avenir* (15 Nov. 1831).

[9] On the liberal Mennaisians in the thirties and forties, Pauline Craven, *Récit d'une sœur* (1867); R. P. Lecanuet, *Montalembert*, 3 vols. (1904–5), vols. i–ii; N. Burtin, *Le baron d'Eckstein* (1931); M. C. Bowe, *François Rio* (n.d.); R. Rancœur, 'Falloux de 1835 à 1848', in *Les Catholiques libéraux au XIXᵉ siècle* (Grenoble 1974), 307–36; A. de Falloux, *Mme Swetchine*, 2 vols. (1861).

[10] *Mirari vos*, in *Recueil des allocutions consistoriales, encycliques . . .* (1865), 156.

[11] Letter to Ernest Falconnet, 5 Jan. 1833, in L. Celier (ed.), *Lettres de Frédéric Ozanam*, 2 vols. (1973), vol. i.

[12] Louis de Carné in G. Goyau (ed.), 'Le portefeuille de Lamennais', *Revue des deux mondes* (1 and 15 Nov. 1928), 107.

universities, and studied topics like Oriental languages, monasticism, and Christian architecture which they felt could surely not cause offence at Rome. As historians they were ardent rather than critical and had supreme contempt for the 'pedantry' of Protestant scholarship. Montalembert, as one of his critics remarked, turned his medieval monks into modern academics, and Falloux in his *Histoire de Pie V* disguised the Inquisition as a benign system of paternal correction.

The liberal ultramontanes had a moderate following amongst the educated laity, but made very few friends in the senior clergy because of their endlessly reiterated hostility to gallicanism. Some of the dilemmas and moral crises which were to overtake them later, and which left Montalembert disillusioned at the end of his life, could have been avoided if this group of liberal laymen had taken the opportunity to ally themselves with the gallicans in the episcopate, who were becoming increasingly liberal in the 1840s. Almost everything that Montalembert and his circle believed about the possibility of reconciling Catholic doctrine with the principles of 1789 was echoed in Dupanloup's *De la pacification religieuse* of 1844 and was accepted without difficulty by bishops like Affre, Mathieu, Donnet, or Bonnechose. But the question of the papacy divided them. Montalembert hardly ever spoke in public without making some scathing reference to gallicanism. The concordatory system, 'the creation of that great theologian Napoleon Bonaparte', he said, had transmitted the shallowness and aridity of the eighteenth century into the nineteenth: what could the Gallican Church and its 'sensible accommodation' with the State produce except a meaningless official religion, with cathedrals packed with generals and functionaries on great festival days but no spontaneous religious practice in the country as a whole? Judging gallicanism always by the worst years of Charles X, they took 'moderation' to mean empty parish churches and a bored and cynical clergy; ultramontanism would put Catholics once again in touch with the rich devotional life and mystical exaltation of the Middle Ages, *'le catholicisme avec toutes ses grandeurs et toutes ses délices'*,[13] and defy the vulgar rationality of the modern world. In spite of his own conviction that the clergy needed a higher standard of education

[13] Ozanam, quoted by M. Gontaut, 'Deux camarades du Collège Royal de Lyon, Fortoul et Ozanam', *Cahiers d'histoire* xvii (1972), 324.

Montalembert was profoundly suspicious of Affre's attempts to improve the Faculty of Theology at the Sorbonne and his foundation of the *École des Carmes*, because of 'the narrow gallican spirit of Saint-Sulpice' that he detected in both these enterprises.[14]

Montalembert's ultramontane rhetoric was responsible also for his equivocal position in the parliament of the July Monarchy, where he was recognized as one of the most brilliant orators of the period but won only a few temporary successes, and made no converts. He defended liberty in superb speeches which were applauded like operatic arias, but then spoiled the effect by adding that if it came to a conflict between liberty and papacy he would be *catholique avant tout*. The parliamentarians listened sceptically while he spoke of the historic role of the European clergy, gentle and peaceful men, he said, devoted to scholarship and good works and presenting no possible danger to French institutions; after one of these oratorical triumphs the President of the chamber, Dupin, joined openly in the applause and then passed a note to the next speaker, Emmanuel Arago: 'Emmanuel, skin this priestling for me.'[15] In the eyes of his parliamentary colleagues and of commentators in the secular press Montalembert and all the liberal Mennaisian group were fatally compromised by their submissiveness to Rome; public opinion saw little real difference between 'liberal' ultramontanism and the harsher authoritarian papalism which was becoming more noticeable every day amongst the younger clergy.

The ultramontane clergy

Although many of the clergy were attracted by the cultural aspects of ultramontanism, as they were to show in the campaign to introduce the Roman liturgy, very few of them were interested in the ultramontane liberalism represented by Montalembert and his circle. As Jules Morel said, it was all very well for laymen to follow the liberal mirage, but priests, with the benefit of a proper training in theology, should address themselves to the more serious problem of establishing a secure Christian authority in the post-Revolutionary world.[16] The kind of ultramontanism which was spreading amongst the clergy before 1848 was

---

[14] Limouzin-Lamothe and Leflon, *Affre*, 182.
[15] Séché, *Les Derniers Jansénistes*, vol. ii, 334 n.
[16] Morel, preface to *Somme contre le catholicisme libéral*.

essentially a counter-revolutionary doctrine, as much a part of French political theory as of Catholic ecclesiology. Very little of it came directly from Rome. Major papal encyclicals like *Mirari vos* in 1832 indicated clearly enough the general drift of Roman doctrine, and the bishops gleaned what they could from the hints they received on their occasional visits. The very few French priests who studied at Rome before 1848 did not necessarily come back imbued with *romanità*. The works of modern Italian theologians like Perrone were hardly known in France, and it was not until the late fifties that the French began to be swayed by the neo-Thomism of Taparelli and Liberatore. They had their own models and their own history; they cited biblical and patristic sources and made adroit use of encyclicals, but seldom mentioned any recent ecclesiology or political theology from Rome. Clerical ultramontanism in France developed by the interaction of the Mennaisian movement with legitimist theory, in a period when royalist laymen like Maistre, Donoso Cortès, and Crétineau-Joly achieved a semi-official status as Catholic theologians, and in turn Mennaisian clerics like Combalot, d'Alzon, Pie, and Ségur exercised a powerful influence on the policy of the legitimist party. Lamennais himself, who hated the Bourbons, came to be regarded by his disciples as the greatest theorist of legitimism. The spread of the Mennaisian movement in the Church coincided with a profound change in outlook on the part of legitimists. Charles X died in 1836, and the old royal gallicanism of the Bourbons was replaced by the romantic ultramontanism of the new Pretender, the comte de Chambord (Henry V); politicians who visited the exiled court at Frohsdorf were rather taken aback by the atmosphere of prayer and meditation. In 1839 Chambord tried to establish his court permanently at Rome but this was prevented by French diplomatic pressure. The legitimist concept of monarchy and the ultramontane concept of papcy developed together from the forties to the sixties until there was to be a virtual fusion of ideas at the time of the attempted restoration of Henry V in 1873.[17]

Their common factor was a rejection of the middle-class ideal of pragmatic moderation in both State and Church, in favour of a

---

[17] P. de Luz, *Henri V* (1931); A. G. Gough, 'The conflict in politics', in Zeldin (ed.), *Conflicts in French Society*.

more dramatic analysis of politics. It was a *déformation profession-nelle* amongst Catholic political theorists in general to believe that social disruption was caused by intellectual revolt, and only to a lesser extent by economic and administrative breakdown. In the Restoration period the air was filled with conspiracy theories to explain not only the Revolution of 1789 but the continuing turbulence of political life in the early nineteenth century. The *émigré* generation had been deeply influenced by the statement of the conspiracy theory in the *Mémoires pour servir à l'histoire du jacobinisme* published by the abbé Augustin de Barruel in 1798. In an earlier work of 1789, the *Discours sur les vraies causes de la Révolution française,* Barruel had given some weight to factors like bad harvests and unsound fiscal policy; further study, he wrote in 1798, had convinced him that these were irrelevant. It was all the fault of Voltaire, d'Alembert, Diderot, and Frederick the Great.

> I will not confine myself merely to proving that their writings are those of impious enemies of Christianity; I say that each of them formed the resolution to annihilate the religion of Jesus Christ; that they communi-cated their resolution secretly to one another; that they discussed together the means of realizing it; that they provided the support and the principal impetus for all the secondary agents who joined the conspiracy.[18]

The secondary agents, as Barruel demonstrated in five volumes of charts and secret protocols, had been Freemasons, Protestants, and Illuminists conspiring in the underground lodges just before the Revolution of 1789 to forge those quintessential slogans 'the Rights of Man', 'Sovereignty residing in the Nation', and 'Liberty, Equality, and Fraternity'. Barruel was followed by a dozen writers in the same genre, each with his own favourite villains—the Freemasons, the Martinists, the *Sublimes Maîtres Parfaits,* the Carbonari. By the 1830s, under the influence of Maistre and Lamennais, this confused mass of ideas had settled down into one more or less coherent doctrine which was widely believed even by very sensible men, and was to influence Catholic thought until well into the twentieth century.

Its essence is the belief in an entity called *la Révolution,* a

---

[18] A. de Barruel, *Mémoires pour servir à l'histoire du jacobinisme,* 5 vols. (Hamburg 1798–9), vol. i, 21–2. On Barruel see J. M. Roberts, *The Mythology of the Secret Societies* (London 1972), chap. 6.

perennial conspiracy against Christianity which can be traced back from Barruel's revolutionary élite, beyond the Enlightenment to the Protestant doctrine of private judgement in religion, beyond that again to the neo-pagan philosophers of the Renaissance, and ultimately to the father of revolt, Satan, crying 'I will not serve'. Its purpose in the modern period is to undermine the foundations of European order by destroying the authority of the Pope, the only real force for counter-revolution. In the endless warfare between Rome and *la Révolution* particular outbreaks of revolt, even that of 1789, have been no more than skirmishes. *La Révolution* has survived into the nineteenth century with its vitality greatly increased because all the pernicious influences of the past three centuries and all the secret societies and conspiracies are now for practical purposes unified into one international body. 'Calvinism, Jansenism, philosophism, illuminism', wrote Maistre, '. . . it is all one, and should be considered as a single sect which has sworn the destruction of Christianity and all the Christian thrones.'[19] In Catholic literature from Maistre to Albert de Mun at the end of the century 'the Revolution', *la secte*, was seen as an actual committee co-opted from one generation to the next, a permanent general staff which 'has drawn up a programme', 'brushes aside protest', 'leads by the hand the French gallican Church' and 'stakes all on a final throw of the dice'; 'the Revolution has decided to change tactics', 'the Revolution fears the restoration of Henry V' and 'will try to prevent the proclamation of the doctrine of the Immaculate Conception'. Legitimist and ultramontane writers, borrowing arguments and documents freely from one another, identified the principal members as Mazzini, Eugène Sue, Ernest Renan, Victor Cousin, Lord John Russell, and the Elders of Zion.[20] Even experienced Catholic politicians who were perfectly well aware of the complexity of motives in public affairs and could not bring

[19] Joseph de Maistre, *Quatre chapitres inédits sur la Russie*, written in 1811 but not published until 1859, ed. Rodolphe de Maistre, 66. Maistre had many reservations about Barruel's accuracy but eventually came round to accepting the main Barruel thesis.

[20] For detailed references, Gough, 'French legitimism and Catholicism' (Oxford D.Phil. 1966). The integration of ultramontane and legitimist themes can be seen clearly in the borrowings from Jacques Crétineau-Joly's *L'Eglise catholique en face de la Révolution* (1859) in Mgr de Ségur's very popular *La Révolution* (1862), which was given as a prize in Catholic schools.

themselves to believe in clandestine meetings between Victor
Cousin and the Jewish Sanhedrin found it easy at times of stress
to fall into the rhetorical habit of blaming all social and
intellectual upheaval on the 'atheists, pantheists, rationalists,
Jews, Protestants and Saint-Simonians who unite with a marvellous
accord to try and shatter the angular rock of Catholicism'.[21] The
comte de Montbel wrote to the marquis de Pastoret in 1846 that
'these revolutionaries, whatever their language or their position
or their precise beliefs, are the *provocateurs* of all the disorders
which threaten Europe. It is a struggle between individualism
and law . . . In their general plan the Polish insurrection was
intimately linked with the overthrow of papal authority in Italy
and the success of anti-Catholic liberalism in Switzerland.'[22] The
idea persisted until it merged with the 'Jewish–Masonic conspiracy'
in the 1880s.[23]

The main instrument of 'the Revolution' in the nineteenth
century was the parliamentary model of society, 'Protestant
heterodoxy in action'. The sovereignty of parliament took no
account of the sovereignty of the will of God; it was based on the
concept of law as something arrived at by the clash of rival
opinions and the counting of votes, instead of something deduced
with philosophical certainty from first principles.[24] The practical
corollaries of parliamentarism were disastrous, especially the
implied requirement for a free press: in the free competition
which Montalembert thought so healthy, the Catholic press
might win a few hundred converts while the secular newspapers
led millions into scepticism; pessimistic ultramontanes stood the
argument of Milton's *Areopagitica* on its head and asked 'who ever
saw error put to the worse in a free and open encounter?' But
parliaments, in any case, were inevitably dominated by the
enlightened classes, fellow-travellers of the Revolution, who

---

[21] Émile Keller, *L'Encyclique du 8 décembre 1864 et les principes de 1789* (1866), 14. Jews
were always included after 1832: it was an article of faith that the duchesse de Berry's
rebellion had been betrayed by a Jewish secret agent named Deutz. After the Mortara
affair in 1858 the Jews were usually listed first.

[22] Montbel to Pastoret, 11 May 1846: Papers of Amédée-David de Pastoret, BN
N.a.f. 12946: 157–8.

[23] See Albert de Mun's memoirs, *Combats d'hier et d'aujourd'hui* (1911).

[24] The leading neo-Thomist philosopher Taparelli said that the modern state did
not need a parliament, but a committee of 'great reasoners in the deductive mode':
'I principii dell'Ottantanove esposti ed esaminati', *Civiltà Cattolica*, Series V, viii,
439–44.

insisted on throwing open for debate matters which were the province of the Church and on which divine law was already perfectly clear. As one ultramontane theorist remarked, to allow a parliament, especially one containing agnostics and Jews, to debate marriage or education was like depending on a parliamentary vote to decide whether or not water was composed of hydrogen and oxygen. The Orleanist parliamentary spirit could corrupt even Catholic statesmen; under the Concordat the *budget des cultes* had to be debated each year, creating an opportunity for parliamentarians to make speeches about seminary education or the liturgy, and it was observed that Catholic MPs were amongst the worst offenders. There was complete unanimity between ultramontane and legitimist views on the subject of Orleanism. From the duc d'Orléans to the usurper Louis-Philippe 'that accursed family' of sectaries and crypto-Protestants represented 'the Revolution wearing a crown'. The deputy editor of the legitimist *Gazette de France*, Honoré de Lourdoueix, who coined this phrase, said that the voltairean middle classes of the July Monarchy were affiliated almost to a man with *la Révolution*: with their approval 'crosses were torn down from church steeples by order of the prefects. Everywhere the professors of pantheism, appointed and salaried by the State, sowed amongst youth the seeds of impiety, atheism, and revolt. Everything which . . . cast doubt on the great moral verities which are the basis of civilization was covered by official tolerance'.[25] The leading right-wing Catholics who joined in the general rejoicing over the Revolution of 1848, and were later to be satirized for showing equal enthusiasm for the *coup d'état* of Louis Napoleon in 1851, saw no contradiction. In each case they had believed that they were witnessing the end of parliamentarism. Neither ultramontanes nor legitimists were afraid of democracy, so long as it was guided by Christian principles; they hoped for the eventual disappearance of the middle-class parliamentary barrier which prevented Church and monarchy from speaking directly to the people.

A glance at the ultramontane leadership in the clergy suggests the classic counter-revolutionary alliance of both ends of the social spectrum against the middle. The matter of social origins,

[25] H. de Lourdoueix, *La Révolution, c'est l'Orléanisme* (1851), 81. For the persistence of this anti-Orleanist vein, Alexis Nugon, *Les Grandes Triomphes de l'Immaculée Conception* (Lyons 1901).

of course, must be approached with caution. Eventually, later in the century, the ultramontane movement was to include the great majority of the clergy, from all kinds of backgrounds; and there were many subtle factors of personal temperament which could lead a particular priest or seminarian to reject gallicanism and the Sulpician style of churchmanship. Nevertheless, it is impossible to miss the sharp contrast between the social origins of the leading ultramontane clergy and the predominantly upper-middle-class backgrounds of the leading gallicans. The former associates of Lamennais who went on to be the most influential ultramontane clergy in the thirties and forties included four of the younger bishops, Gousset (Périgueux, later archbishop of Reims), Parisis (Langres, later Arras), Doney (Montauban) and Gignoux (Beauvais); the eloquent and combative abbot of Solesmes, Prosper Guéranger, who had quasi-episcopal status; Emmanuel d'Alzon, founder of the Assumptionist Order; five who could be described as intellectuals and theologians, Antoine de Salinis, Philippe Gerbet, Melchior du Lac, Mathurin Gaultier, and Jules Morel; and two famous preachers, Henri Lacordaire and Théodore Combalot. Not one of them came from the middle or upper ranks of the bourgeoisie. Salinis, du Lac, d'Alzon, and Combalot belonged to the minor aristocracy and shared the belief of many pious young nobles that their birth imposed on them a duty to atone for the irreligious behaviour of the upper classes in the past two centuries. The others came from lower middle-class, farming, or artisan families with *dévot* traditions who had suffered in various ways during the Revolutionary period. Père Mathurin Gaultier, for example, director of studies at the Holy Spirit Fathers' seminary in Paris and a passionate opponent of the gallican bishops, was a farmer's son; when he received his legacy, a horse, he sold it to pay for books on the primacy of Rome. All of these men had come under strong counter-revolutionary influences in their youth and with one exception were either legitimist in politics from the beginning or evolved in that direction during their careers. The exception was Lacordaire, who is perhaps best described as an authoritarian democrat. Lacordaire is usually associated with Catholic liberalism but in the earlier phase of his life was more clearly ultramontane; his celebrated Notre-Dame sermons of 1835 helped to define the mystique of papal Rome. The impression of origins outside the middle class and a legitimist *politique* is strengthened if we look also at the leading figures in the younger generation of ultramontane clergy who drew their ideas and inspiration from the original Mennaisians: the abbés Pallu du Parc, Cazalès, Conny, la Bouillerie, Valois, Eleuthère de Girardin, and Louis-Gaston de Ségur were aristocrats, and Louis-Édouard Pie, vicar-general of Chartres and later as bishop of Poitiers to be one of the most important strategists of ultramontanism and royalism, was the son of a shoemaker.[26]

The distinctive style of ultramontanism developed by this *école mennaisienne* in the clergy amounted to an answer to the problem posed by Maistre and Barruel. If 'the Revolution', working through constitutions, parliaments, press, and universities, had already undermined the structure of European society, how was a total collapse to be averted? Not by Catholic gentlemen admiring stained glass windows, or by waiting for fifty or a hundred years for the slowly permeating effects of some Catholic scientific congress; not by State-appointed bishops making sensible concessions to middle-class opinion; and certainly not through the Sulpician ideal of higher education for priests—the ultramontanes suspected that an 'enlightened clergy' might mean another generation like Sieyès and Loménie de Brienne. The answer lay in a true counter-revolution which would be the absolute antithesis of Sulpicianism. The Roman papacy, the only institution to have emerged from the Revolutionary period with credit, should establish (ultramontanes always said 're-establish') both direct and indirect influence over civil government; and within the Church papal authority should be supreme and unchallenged.[27]

---

[26] Canon Gousset, *Le Cardinal Gousset* (Besançon 1903), and AN F. 19. 2565; C. Guillemant, *Pierre-Louis Parisis*, 3 vols. (1925), vol. i, and AN F. 19. 2493; AN F. 19. 2538 (Doney); AN F. 19. 2502 (Gignoux); Dom Delatte, *Dom Guéranger, abbé de Solesmes*, 2 vols. (1909), vol. i; S. Vailhé, *Emmanuel d'Alzon* (1926); abbé Ricard, *L'École mennaisienne: Gerbet et Salinis* (1883), and AN F. 19. 2494; on Melchior du Lac, the 'Dossier du Lac' in V/BN 24635; P. Baron, *La Jeunesse de Lacordaire* (1961), and Théodore Foisset, *Vie du R. P. Lacordaire*, 2 vols. (1870), vol. i; abbé Ricard, *L'Abbé Combalot* (1892); on Gaultier, M. de Hédouville, 'Romains et gallicans' (Univ. of Paris thesis 1956); L. Baunard, *Histoire du cardinal Pie*, 2 vols. (1886), vol. i, and AN F. 19. 2561.

[27] The following sketch of ultramontane doctrine in the clergy before 1848 is based on Melchior du Lac, *L'Église et l'État*, 2 vols. (1850–1); Mgr Gousset, *Le Code civil commenté dans ses rapports avec la théologie morale* (1829 and eight further editions to 1877); Delatte, *Dom Guéranger*, vol. i; Ricard, *L'Abbé Combalot;* Mgr Pie, *Oeuvres sacerdotales*

In the tradition of Maistre and Lamennais the French were notably less cautious than their Roman counterparts and were inclined to state flatly some propositions which medieval jurists had put forward only with the greatest reservation. Since divine law preceded human law and formed its essential foundation, they argued, there could be no doubt that papal jurisdiction was superior to civil jurisdiction, and not simply in a delimited sphere labelled 'spiritual affairs'. Looked at in the right spirit, everything was *de la foi*, and papal authority was valid in virtually every area of government and administration. Civil governments in Christian countries had a duty to bring civil law into harmony with divine law, using ecclesiastical canon law as a guide; and all legislation ought ideally to be subject to papal veto. Beginning with the proposition that the Church did not have to co-operate with the State if government had fallen into the hands of non-Catholics, the ultramontanes went on to revive the medieval argument that the papacy could release subjects from their allegiance and depose unsatisfactory rulers. It was taken to be a weighty argument in favour of absolute monarchy that the deposing power worked best when relations between the Pope and a king could be severed at a single stroke; deposing a parliament of heterodox individuals representing a multiplicity of interests was admitted to be harder. Ultramontane rhetoric envisaged the papacy controlling many aspects of civil life directly, using the monarch as its agent, and it followed that the king could not be an effective defender of Christianity unless his own power in the civil sphere was absolute, not limited by constitutions or parliaments. 'No cabinet has more ancient traditions', Lamennais had written, 'nor so long an experience of the vicissitudes of politics. From the height of the Vatican the Popes have seen all things begin and end'.[28] Louis-Édouard Pie thought that the Roman Church 'has a certainty and precision of manœuvre which allows her to guide humanity through all dangers, taking account both of the principles which never vary and of the circumstances in which those principles must be applied'.[29]

1839–1849, 2 vols. (1891); Jules Morel, *Somme contre le catholicisme libéral;* C. Louandre, 'Du mouvement catholique', *Revue des deux mondes* (Jan.–Feb. 1844); M. Ferraz, *Traditionalisme et ultramontanisme* (1880).

[28] *L'Avenir* (16 Oct. 1830).

[29] On Pie's political ideas, Gough, 'The conflict in politics', in Zeldin (ed.), *Conflicts in French Society*, 95 ff.

When Pius IX was elected in 1846 the abbé Combalot wrote that the new Pope should be a Lion of Judah, his roar heard throughout the universe; he should revive the combativeness of Gregory VII and Innocent III.[30] Having survived the desperate struggles with Islam, the medieval Empire and the rising European nation-states, the papacy could surely deal with the heirs of the Enlightenment. There could hardly be a more satisfying affront to the enlightened classes of the nineteenth century than to suggest that their parliamentary-liberal age should submit, or be made to submit, to the ancient supernatural authority of Rome; but Rome, as Lacordaire said, was 'never more divine than when crushing human pride'.[31]

The immediate obstacle to any root-and-branch reform, in this view, was the gallican hierarchy. Bishops nominated by voltairean officials in the ministère des Cultes and promoted and decorated by the government of Louis-Philippe were not very likely to put themselves at the head of a programme of national regeneration. There was also the fear, common to ultramontanes in all European countries but most sharply felt by the French because of their historical experience, that State-appointed hierarchies would be incapable of defending the Church if governments should become actively hostile to religion. In a period of rapid political change only a supranational Church whose bishops owed their first allegiance to the Pope could survive; the French hierarchy's insistence on national traditions and gallican independence was in reality, the ultramontanes said, a blind surrender to centrifugal forces which could split the Catholic Church into helpless fragments, at the mercy of anti-Christian governments of the future. Ultramontanes, in any case, found the parliamentary model as repugnant in ecclesiology as it was in politics, and could not accept the idea of a constitutional structure for the Church in which either the teaching authority or the disciplinary jurisdiction of the Pope was limited by the consent of the bishops. The Sulpician view of the Church, they said, was a logical extension of the neo-Cartesian philosophy taught in the seminaries, which began with doubt and tried to reach certainty through elaborate proofs of Catholic dogma; thus the Church itself, in the Sulpician analogy, was a body in which truth emerged after discussion and

---

[30] Ricard, *Combalot*, 350.
[31] *Considérations sur le système philosophique de M. de Lamennais* (1834), chap. 12.

consent. Lamennais and his original followers had considered their critique of Sulpician philosophy to be absolutely central: since truth, they argued, could be reached only by beginning with the great axioms of divine law, and since only the papacy had the power to deduce and interpret with unerring certitude, the idea of 'the consent of the Universal Church' was irrelevant. In the nineteenth-century fashion for accepting simplistic interpretations of texts which had been treated with greater subtlety by the early Fathers, the well-known biblical citations from Matthew 16—'. . . upon this Rock . . .'—and Luke 22 were taken confidently as proof that the institution of papacy preceded the institution of bishops, and that far from being teachers in their own right the bishops had never been more than agents or delegates of Rome; the Pope exercised a universal episcopate, and his jurisdiction in any diocese of the Christian world was not exceptional, but ordinary and immediate.

The bitter polemical tone which the Mennaisians adopted from the first under the influence of Lamennais's own overheated rhetoric reflects their exasperation with French bishops who failed to recognize a great historical opportunity. The gallican arrangements were 'a disgusting *mélange* of absurdity and conceit, stupid nonsense and foolish complacency, small passions, small ambitions, small intrigues and an absolute impotence of mind'.[32] The task of bishops was not to collaborate with voltairean governments but to harass and dominate them, to proclaim the superiority of the spiritual over the temporal, and eventually to inaugurate the reign of Christ on earth; but the French hierarchy were *tranquillistes*—'prudence everywhere', Mgr Pie remarked.[33] The gallican chiefs were hopeless: Angebault of Angers was 'an arch-slacker'; Thibault of Montpellier had 'entirely sold out'. Affre of Paris, called 'Mgr Affreux' in ultramontane correspondence, was 'incoherent' and 'cowardly', 'a nonentity'.[34] The abbé Combalot wrote that the Sulpicians were incapable of training real bishops, 'a *milice* equipped to fight the enemies of the faith'; if Rome did not recover its ascendancy over the gallican Church and if the seminaries were not put in other hands, all would be

[32] Lamennais, *Lettre à Mgr l'archevêque de Paris* (1829).
[33] *Correspondance du cardinal Pie et de Mgr Cousseau* (Tours 1896), 110.
[34] E. Sevrin, *Mgr Clausel de Montals*, 2 vols. (1955), vol. ii, 734, quoting Pie's correspondence with other ultramontanes.

lost. 'We must glorify Rome, demonstrate that it is the source of life, the only salvation for the Church of France.'[35] The Sulpicians, indeed, were as great a problem as the bishops themselves. Saint-Sulpice had led the counter-attack against Lamennais at the time of the *Censure de Toulouse* in 1832, and the Sulpician scholars Boyer, Carrière, and Galais continued to write and lecture against Mennaisianism and the rhapsodic and unreliable history which supported it; but the tide was beginning to run against them. As ultramontane influence spread, dissident seminarians in the younger generation became more sympathetic to the Mennaisian critique. Sulpician lectures on the glories of the seventeenth century were listened to with impatience by students who had glimpsed the dizzying historical perspectives of papal Rome. They teased their instructors by using the Roman pronunciation of Latin, and circulated cartoons showing the Sulpicians defending the French Church from behind a rampart of mouldy gallican textbooks. One drawing showed Galais as Don Quixote on a rocking-horse and his pupils as a rabble of dwarfish Sancho Panzas, assaulting the papacy with goose-quill pens.[36] The Mennaisian celebrities were their models, especially Guéranger, who had begun his campaign to Romanize the French liturgies, and Combalot, who travelled around the country preaching on the theme that 'the sword has rusted in the scabbard of the hierarchy' (he was seldom invited to preach a second time). Combalot's zeal was widely appreciated in the seminaries: calling on a country priest one day and finding him absent, he passed the time by throwing the *curé's* gallican books into the fire.[37]

Year by year, also, in spite of their own suspicion that they were being kept out of the episcopate by a Sulpician old-boy network, more of the leading ultramontanes became bishops.[38] The ministère des Cultes and its advisers in the hierarchy were preoccupied with their search for men of administrative ability

[35] Combalot to Veuillot, 24 Dec. 1843, in *Louis Veuillot*, vol. i, 439.

[36] Abbé Lecigne, *Un père de jeunesse, l'abbé Timon-David* (1923), 51–2, 148.

[37] Combalot is an excellent example of the fusion of ultramontane and legitimist motives. He was related to several families of Vendéean aristocrats, and resented the gallican bishops not only for their doctrines but for having failed to resign in a body after the fall of the Bourbon monarchy in 1830.

[38] Letter of Mgr Doney to Falloux, quoted by A. Latreille, 'Un enquête de M. de Falloux, 1849', *Cahiers d'histoire* v (1960).

and at times seemed almost anxious to be deceived about a candidate's ideas. Mgr Mathieu warned in 1840 that the Mennaisians had not abandoned their views on Church and State, and would create problems if they were given bishoprics,[39] but Mathieu himself supported the candidatures of two ultramontanes, Gousset and Gignoux, on the grounds of their general ability and intelligence: Gousset began publishing works of ultramontane theory immediately after his elevation, and was to be Mathieu's principal opponent in the hierarchy. Mgr Cœur, one of the most convinced gallicans, supported the candidature of Antoine de Salinis as a distinguished literary figure and was then horrified to find that he had 'added one more soldier to Mgr Gousset's troop', and that Salinis was the dearest friend and protector of the abbé Combalot.[40] The promotion of J.-B. Berteaud, who was to become an ultramontane firebrand in the fifties, was supported by several bishops, including Mgr Affre, and by Victor Cousin and a number of MPs; all of them were impressed by his eloquence.[41] The Mennaisian P.-L. Parisis was thought to be a liberal before his elevation to the see of Langres.[42] The old gallican royalist Clausel de Montals of Chartres was willing to overlook the ultramontane views of his brilliant young vicar-general, Louis-Édouard Pie, because he was also a legitimist; Clausel had many opportunities later to regret having endorsed Pie for a bishopric.[43] The Papal Nuncios, who could exercise a limited but distinct influence over appointments, were cautious with regard to the Mennaisians. Mgr Garibaldi, Internuncio from 1836 to 1843, did not like the fanaticism of the movement and had to be reassured in each case that the candidate had repudiated his old connections. His successor, Raffaelo Fornari (Nuncio 1843–50) was perhaps the strongest supporter of papal supremacy in the Roman diplomatic service; his experience in other European capitals had convinced him that the national hierarchies might easily allow the Church to slide into neo-Protestantism and dissolution, and that the fanaticism of the Mennaisians could be very valuable if properly harnessed. He supported ultramontane candidates at every opportunity, although

---

[39] *Garibaldi/Mathieu*, 290 n.
[40] Cœur to Dupanloup, 25 Apr. 1851, Dupanloup/BN 24680.
[41] AN F. 19. 2609, 2591; C. Breton, *Un évêque d'autrefois, Mgr Berteaud* (1895).
[42] AN F. 19. 2493.   [43] AN F. 19. 2561.

he found the Roman Secretariat of State reluctant to accept anyone tainted with the doctrines of *L'Avenir*.[44] The only bishops Fornari could tolerate were those who were ready to abandon all ideas of episcopal autonomy and to concede that they were subordinate field commanders, drawing their strength from their absolute submission to Rome; and this was precisely the attitude taken by the ultramontanes who reached the episcopate, to resolve the ambiguity of their own position. 'The highest duty of bishops', Gousset wrote, 'is obedience to the Pope'.

Individual bishops with ultramontane tendencies, however, could accomplish very little beyond taking the first steps to Romanize their own dioceses: new vicars-general could be appointed, gallican seminary directors could be replaced, pro-papal textbooks like Rohrbacher's *Histoire universelle* could be substituted for 'obsolete' older works, the Roman liturgy could be introduced; Salinis at Amiens stopped the practice of sending gifted seminarians to Saint-Sulpice where they 'imbibed unsuitable ideas'.[45] Gousset at Reims had a wider influence through his textbooks of moral and dogmatic theology and his edition of the eighteenth-century *Dictionnaire de théologie* of Bergier which eliminated most of its gallican propositions; but the ultramontane movement needed the kind of leadership that no single bishop could provide. Even a *bloc* of bishops could not lead effectively, since the Concordat did not provide for a national synod. From the 1840s onwards, ultramontanism in the sense in which the clergy understood it was to receive its decisive impetus from a layman.

---

[44] Article 'Fornari' in *DHGE;* G. Martina, *Pio IX (1846–1850)* (Rome 1974).
[45] Letter of the abbé Follet of Montdidier to M. Boiteux at Saint-Sulpice, S. Sulp/AN AB XIX 518.

V

Louis Veuillot and *L'Univers*

The conversion of Louis Veuillot

IN the well-known photograph by Nadar in the 1860s[1] Veuillot might easily be taken for a successful farmer or a butcher; the square body and the broad pock-marked features suggest the confident and rather brutal style of Catholicism which came to be known as *veuillotisme*. The face of a younger Veuillot, however, looks out from the frontispiece of the first volume of the biography written by his brother Eugène, a thinner, more sensitive face, proud, defiant, and vulnerable. Louis Veuillot was born at Boynes (Loiret) in 1813, the son of a master cooper. He liked to exaggerate his humble origins, claiming that he was the first Veuillot ever to be able to read and write: 'neither my father nor my mother, thanks be to God, knew how to read, which no doubt saved them from many evil thoughts'.[2] In fact his grandparents had been literate, but the families had been disrupted and impoverished in the Revolution. When Louis was five years old his father lost his life savings through the failure of a local business man, and moved his family to Paris where he became foreman for a wine merchant; Louis was left at Boynes in

---

[1] Nadar's photograph is reproduced in Philip Spencer, *Politics of Belief in Nineteenth-Century France* (London 1954); J. Prinet, *Nadar* (Kiosque 1966); Nigel Gosling, *Nadar* (London 1976). The portrait on the dust-jacket of this book shows Veuillot at about 50, from the frontispiece of *Louis Veuillot*, vol. iii.

[2] 'Fragments de mémoires', in *Oeuvres complètes de Louis Veuillot*, vol. x, 532. Unless otherwise indicated, references to works by Veuillot will be cited from the *Oeuvres complètes*, published in 1927–38 in three series (I: *Oeuvres diverses*, 12 vols.; II: *Correspondance*, 13 vols.; III: *Mélanges*, 15 vols.) superseding the nineteenth-century editions of the *Correspondance* and *Mélanges*. The major biography is by Eugène Veuillot, *Louis Veuillot*, 3 vols. (1903–4), with a fourth volume added by François Veuillot in 1913. Other biographical sources are François Veuillot, *Louis Veuillot, sa vie, son âme, son œuvre* (1937); C. Lecigne, *Louis Veuillot* (1913); P. Fernessole, *Les Origines littéraires de Louis Veuillot, 1813–1843* (1922); and the article 'Veuillot' in *DTC*. Veuillot's papers and a great deal of material relating to *L'Univers* are in V/BN N.a.f. 24220–39 and 24617–35. I have made particular use of the following: N.a.f. 24225–8 and 24633–4, Veuillot's incoming correspondence from the later July Monarchy to the Second Empire; 24620, 'Notes intimes'; 24235, correspondence of other members of the staff of *L'Univers*; 24635, 'dossier du Lac': all subsequently cited as V/BN.

the care of relatives and did not rejoin the family until he was
eleven. His parents, realizing very quickly from his progress at
school that he was outstandingly intelligent, wanted him to be a
lawyer, but could not afford to keep him as a student; eventually
they managed to place him as an office-boy in the chambers of
the *avocat* Fortuné Delavigne. This was a lucky choice. Delavigne
had literary tastes and his office was a meeting-place for minor
novelists, journalists and law students with cultural ambitions.
The witty, energetic office-boy became a favourite. The students
lent him books and took him to the theatre; one of them, Gustave
Olivier, encouraged him to write, corrected his grammar, and
convinced him that he had a future as a journalist. In 1831
Olivier was appointed editor of a newspaper in Rouen, and he
took Veuillot, then aged eighteen, with him as a drama critic.
He was a great success, and was wounded twice in duels with
actors.

In 1833 he was invited to be editor of the *Mémorial de la
Dordogne* at Perigueux. The paper was supposed to be an organ of
the prefecture but the twenty-year-old Veuillot insisted on
independence; he wrote from a radical-conservative stance,
urging the government of the July Monarchy to avoid weak-
kneed liberalism, to supress dissent and to tighten up electoral
procedure so as to drive the opposition to despair. He fought
another duel, this time with a liberal, and emerged with credit.
But it was his virtuosity as a writer on literature and drama that
brought him to wider notice. In four years at Périgueux he taught
himself the French classics, reading every major author from the
sixteenth to the eighteenth century, and spending most time on
Rabelais, Mme de Sévigné, and Molière. From this vigorous
programme of self-education and from days and nights of
conversation with the unexpectedly well-read and congenial
circle of friends he found at Périgueux he formed the style that
was to make him one of the most deadly controversialists of the
nineteenth century, a vivid argumentative prose full of unexpected
asides and ingenious metaphors, indiscreet, cruel, and very
amusing. Some of his literary pieces were reprinted in Parisian
journals, and a booksellers' trade paper noted that M. Louis
Veuillot in Périgueux was 'in the first rank amongst those writers
who are working successfully to implant literature in the
provinces'. Behind his confident manner in print he was still

painfully conscious of ignorance. He wanted to write more on politics but knew nothing about political economy or foreign affairs; he tried to study them but gave up, characteristically, when he found that there were no clear answers even to the clearest questions: no two books seemed to agree. A more serious problem was that he was beginning to find that he did not really like the bourgeois life to which his talent had led him. He had acquired an important patron in the new prefect of the Dordogne, Auguste Romieu, a cultivated man who had written for the theatre in Paris. Romieu was delighted with the mordant young editor of the *Mémorial* and introduced him into the best society of the *département*. Veuillot's horizons were widened, he made some lasting friendships and learned a great deal more about politics than he had found in books, but with his strong memories of the decent artisan world of his childhood he was shocked by the licentiousness of provincial society, the corruption, the orgiastic dinners, and the frank sensuality of the conversation. Reflecting later on this period of his life he remembered with particular distaste three dreadful old survivors of the Revolution, an emeritus professor and two former priests, who could recite long and extremely filthy anticlerical poems of the eighteenth century from memory; and the theatre seemed to be occupied entirely with farces about deceived husbands and lost virginity. In upper-middle-class society, also, he was continually reminded of his origins through falling idealistically and hopelessly in love with the daughters of wealthy households where he was welcome as an entertaining dinner guest but not as a prospective son-in-law.

In 1836 Romieu recommended him for a post on a new paper, *La Charte de 1830*, which was being started in Paris to support Guizot, with a distinguished panel of writers including Malitourne, Nestor Roqueplan, Edmond Texier, and Théophile Gautier. At twenty-three Veuillot was in the centre of Parisian journalism, with highly sophisticated and agreeable colleagues and the free run of theatres, salons, and government ministries. When Romieu came to Paris he took Veuillot to dinner with the celebrated Mlle Mars of the Comédie-Française, whose conversation was worse than anything he had heard in Périgueux. He wrote more sharply and brilliantly than ever, and was congratulated by Guizot himself. *La Charte de 1830* ceased publication for tactical reasons, and Veuillot moved to the conservative *La Paix*. He now had friends in the best literary and political circles and was on good terms with notables like Salvandy, Rémusat, and Léonce de Lavergne. From *La Paix* he went to a better post on the *Moniteur parisien*. In an election campaign in 1837 the government sent him to inject some brio into the moribund official newspapers in two doubtful seats. There were flattering offers to join the *Constitutionnel* and the *Journal des débats*, which would have meant changing sides to the liberal cause: and why not? he reflected. He was already disillusioned with political journalism and 'well on the way to becoming one of those condottieri of the pen who are equally happy to fight for one camp or the other'.[3] He wanted to return to literature, perhaps to write a novel, but he needed new scenes, new experiences, fresh faces. He had fallen in love again, with a girl who loved him but was compelled by her parents to marry someone else 'more suitable'; in spite of his comparative success he had made very little money. An affair with a beautiful and talented older woman had reached the point where he had to make a decision. At this critical juncture his old friend Gustave Olivier proposed that he and Veuillot should set out on a voyage to the Mediterranean and the Middle East. Veuillot called on Salvandy at the Ministry of Public Instruction and came away with a substantial grant of money and a commission to study schools and charities in any countries they should happen to visit. They left Paris in March 1838: Olivier, who had recently been converted to Catholicism—'your friend has gone mad', Romieu told Veuillot—suggested that they begin with Rome.

'I went without desire', he wrote. 'People said to me: you will see the Capital and the Vatican, the great tombs and the vast catacombs, the festivals . . . but I hoped for only one thing, not to see myself any longer.'[4] Arriving in this mood, Veuillot was overwhelmed by his first sight of Rome in the clear Mediterranean sunshine, and while he was still in a state of mild intoxication Olivier took him to visit a French Jesuit, Père Rozaven, who acted as chaplain for some of the foreign community. Veuillot found himself talking more freely than he had intended to this courteous, distinguished old man, and after half an hour's

[3] *Rome et Lorette* (1841), *Oeuvres complètes*, vol. iii, 24.
[4] *La Parfum de Rome* (1861), *Oeuvres complètes*, vol. ix, 6.

conversation he admitted to Rozaven that nothing in his life now gave him any real satisfaction, either for his emotions or for his intellect. The Jesuit spoke gravely to him about the need for certainty; he came away very impressed with Père Rozaven but not convinced about Catholicism. Gustave introduced him also to two friends, Adolphe Feburier and his beautiful aristocratic wife Elizabeth, who had been in Rome for some time on a mission of spiritual renewal, and together the four young people went on a tour of churches and shrines in the kingdom of Naples, returning to Rome in time for Holy Week. Veuillot was uneasy in the churches. He looked at pictures and statues while his friends prayed, and sometimes out of politeness went down on his knees beside them; but after a fortnight of their company he had fallen under the spell of the saintly Elizabeth. He was profoundly affected by her demeanour as she came back from receiving Communion, her face shining with peace and joy, two gifts which Veuillot felt he might never hope to possess for himself. Back in Rome, Elizabeth persuaded him to join in their evening prayers, and one evening asked him, in the most delicate and tactful way, to read to them from a volume of devotional texts. As he read Bourdaloue's sermon on 'Penitence' he was seized by a feeling that his former life was over; on the following day, after walking distractedly for hours through the streets of Rome struggling with his doubts and hesitations, he asked Adolphe and Elizabeth: 'Would it make you happy, then, if I were to be converted?' Seeing the glance they exchanged and the tears that came into their eyes, he went straight off to Père Rozaven and asked to make his confession and to receive elementary instruction. A few days later an influential friend arranged for their party to have a private audience with the Pope.

He had led a wandering life, Veuillot was to write later, since being taken away as a child from the small provincial town he had loved. 'I have pitched my tent in one place, then in another, always having to leave just when I had felt my heart putting down roots.'[5] Here at last, in Rome, was a permanent *patrie*; he was a citizen of the Catholic Church—*civis Romanus*. He had found security in the inexorable reasoning of Père Rozaven, and infinite forgiveness in the simple words the Pope had addressed

---

[5] *Rome et Lorette,* chap. 35: 'Vie errante'.

to him on hearing that Veuillot was a new convert. He abandoned his plan for travel in the Middle East, made a pilgrimage to the Holy House of Loreto and a retreat with the Jesuits at Fribourg, and returned to Paris. He had no trouble in finding an undemanding post in the Ministry of the Interior, and began immediately to put his talent to the service of the Church.

Two books appeared quickly, *Les Pèlerinages de Suisse* and *Rome et Lorette*, charting his spiritual itinerary during the year of his conversion, and he started contributing devotional articles to Catholic newspapers. He had to admit that he found the Catholic press unexciting. *L'Ami de la Religion* and the *Journal des villes et des campagnes* in the late thirties were worthy enough journals but handicapped by their moderation, which prevented them from dealing effectively with too many questions. Only one paper, *L'Univers religieux*, seemed to comment on current affairs from a solid basis of Catholic theology. In June 1839 Veuillot had an article accepted by *L'Univers* and went to its offices to correct his proofs. He was surprised by the atmosphere of dank poverty, and even more surprised to find that the editorial staff consisted of one man, Melchior du Lac. *L'Univers* had been founded in 1833 with the collaboration of a number of Catholic celebrities, but had not prospered; at the time of Veuillot's first visit the nominal owner, M. Bailly, was negotiating a loan of 21,000 francs from the comte de Montalembert to enable *L'Univers* to continue. The circulation was about 1500 and almost the entire text of the paper was written by du Lac himself, with some assistance from a Catholic economist, Charles de Coux. Veuillot was greatly taken, and after two or three more visits he had decided that *L'Univers* was to be his vocation: from this tiny apostolic base France could be conquered for the papacy. He asked to join the staff as an unpaid contributor. His first articles were signed only with asterisks; by 1842 he was editor-in-chief, with five assistants, and had turned *L'Univers* into the most powerful organ of the ultramontane movement.

Veuillotisme

Veuillot had written a stream of letters from Rome and Fribourg to announce his conversion to all his friends and colleagues in Paris, and had asked his younger brother Eugène, who had succeeded him on the *Mémorial de la Dordogne*, to pass on the news to their old friends at Périgueux. Most of them were inclined at first to be tolerant, but cynical. Their sharp-witted Louis had simply exchanged one career for another; he would enter the clergy and in fifteen years would be a worldly and popular archbishop, the right-hand man of the ministre des Cultes. Surely, at least, he had adopted the kind of Catholicism suitable for an educated man? They were puzzled by his replies, and absolutely aghast when they saw from the articles he began to publish on his return from Italy that Veuillot had embraced a full-blooded Mediterranean religion of saints, relics, and stigmata: he asserted defiantly that he believed in every miraculous levitation, every bleeding portrait of the Sacred Heart, every appearance of the Blessed Virgin. To one correspondent from Périgueux he wrote that he had 'plunged into an ocean of delights' compared to which his old life was a dreary waste. He wrote a grating reply to his former mistress in Paris who had asked if he could really be serious, and had evidently added some mildly satirical comments on the temptations of Rome: she represented, he said, everything that had been false and sinful about his life; Christianity had liberated him from the bonds in which she had held him, and he would never be so foolish again.[6] Auguste Romieu was sardonic: could this be his friend and protégé, the cleverest young journalist in France, writing about the Virgin Mary? Veuillot's articles

have diminished even the small homeopathic traces of Christianity that remain in me . . . I can admit a God, but a Goddess? One who appears to mortals, who comes to overturn the great physical laws of the eternal geometry; who to make an appearance needs a costume, fingernails, teeth and eyebrows, and must have a certain height and certain measurements?[7]

Veuillot broke off their correspondence.

He had to recognize when he began to write for *L'Univers* that he knew very little about the technicalities of Catholic doctrine

---

[6] *Rome et Lorette*, chap. 49: 'Rêve à Venise'; other letters in *Correspondance*, vol. i, *Oeuvres* xv; and *Louis Veuillot*, vol. i, chap. 7.

[7] Romieu to Veuillot, 29 June 1842, V/BN 24225. Romieu added that his father had been an oficer in the Napoleonic force which entered Naples in 1805, and had been ordered to instruct the Archbishop to see that the miraculous blood of Saint Januarius liquefied as a sign of divine approval. The ceremony was performed, the blood duly liquefied, and Romieu's father gave the Archbishop a receipt.

beyond what he had picked up in a few weeks with the Jesuits at Fribourg, but he wanted to throw himself into front-line combat and felt that he could hardly afford to settle down to three or four years of theology and patristic studies like a seminarian. His Catholic education, unlike his knowledge of literature, had to be acquired very quickly: it came mainly from the works of Joseph de Maistre, which gave a coherent shape to his romantic emotional papalism, and from the personal teaching of Melchior du Lac, whom he was to supplant in the editorship of *L'Univers* but always acknowledged as 'my master'. Melchior du Lac de Montvert came from an aristocratic *émigré* family. He had graduated in law in Paris and then joined the Mennaisian circle at la Chenaie; after Lamennais's defection he decided to join the priesthood, but had to leave the seminary and take up journalism in order to support his father, who had lost the family fortune in speculation. He wore a soutane in *L'Univers* office and most people assumed that he had been ordained. Du Lac was an impressive man, learned, friendly and modest, and totally absorbed by ultramontane theory.[8] Reading the proofs of du Lac's articles and listening to his conversation, Veuillot, who had been a sceptical young journalist at the time of the Mennaisian drama and had dismissed it as a squabble taking place in a shabby world of priests and *dévots*, now eagerly grasped the Mennaisian themes, the concept of *la Révolution* and its lineal descent from Protestantism and the Enlightenment, the feeble compromises of the Gallican Church—du Lac cautioned him against Bossuet and the Sulpicians—and the need for total submission to the papacy.

In his exalted mood in the years following his conversion Veuillot was convinced that the hand of Providence had led him to Rome, and then to *L'Univers*, just at the historic moment when the Church was about to confront the very incarnation of the modern bourgeois spirit, *le monopole universitaire*. As he saw it, the education conflict of the 1840s revealed a failure of leadership on the Catholic side. Not only was Montalembert largely unsuccessful

---

[8] The only substantial information about du Lac is in his dossier in V/BN 24635, and in the sketch by Veuillot in *D'après nature, Oeuvres* x, 448–51. For more than thirty years du Lac lived alone in a miserable rented room; during one whole year after a wall of his building had collapsed he was 'living virtually on a balcony in the open air'.

in parliament on the education issue, in spite of brilliant speeches and a great deal of effort expended in fighting elections and forming coalitions of deputies, but he did not have the unequivocal support of the hierarchy. In their anxiety to secure at least the legal right to conduct their own secondary schools alongside the state system, the bishops were ready to make compromises. They protested with varying degrees of dignity against each of the main provisions of the government's four education bills between 1841 and 1847—the requirement that headmasters of Catholic schools should have university degrees and three years' experience in preparing candidates for the baccalaureat, the *brevet de capacité* for teachers, the exclusion of 'unauthorized' orders from the schools, the need for curricula to be approved by the *Université*—but in each case the hierarchy seemed willing to discuss a watered-down formula.[9] Officially, the Church was not asking for the *Université* to be abolished or even seriously weakened, although churchmen had many grievances against the state system, but only that there should no longer be a state monopoly. The moderate gallicans, anxious not to lose the sympathy of educated Catholics or to provoke the ministère des Cultes to reprisals, tried to restrain the violence of ultramontane controversialists like Combalot and Desgarets who were claiming that the Collège de France was full of satanists and that the lycées were teaching sodomy and incest from classical texts. Veuillot's sympathies were with the extremists, but he recognized that their tactics were clumsy. His own superiority as a polemicist lay not only in his compelling style but in the bitter verve and immediacy that he brought to the attack on the voltairean bourgeoisie. Unlike Combalot and Desgarets he knew *les classes éclairées* at first hand, and saw them with the unforgiving eye of a working-class intellectual who had experienced a religious conversion. When he thought of Victor Cousin or Michelet his mind went back to a scene he had witnessed many

---

[9] On the education conflict, which lies outside the scope of this study, G. Weill, *Histoire de l'enseignement secondaire en France 1802–1920* (1921); C. Louandre, 'Du mouvement catholique', *Revue des deux mondes* (Jan.–Feb. 1844); A.-J. Tudesq, *Les grands notables en France 1840–1849*, 2 vols. (1964), vol. ii, 695 ff.; J. N. Moody, 'The French Catholic press and the education conflict of the eighteen-forties', *French Historical Studies* vii, (1972), 394–415; Anita M. R. May, 'The challenge of the French Catholic press to episcopal authority 1842–1860' (University of Pittsburgh thesis, 1970).

times as a child, etched on his memory with the sharpness of a Daumier cartoon: his father, a strong, dignified man, standing cap in hand in his workshop humbly taking orders from an arrogant bourgeois client, 'a puny, snivelling, thieving creature with doubtful morals'. His father had died in 1839 without ever having known Christianity; the bourgeoisie, Veuillot said, bullied the honest worker and then their intellectual leaders, 'those self-styled sages', deprived him of the religion which might have given his life some meaning. 'If I had not already been a Christian at the time of my father's death, I would have joined the secret societies.'[10]

It seemed appropriate that of all his old friends in Parisian journalism the only ones who had greeted his conversion with genuine sympathy had been the socialists. Victor Considérant and Alphonse Toussenel had told him that they could understand his sudden revulsion from the modern world but felt that logically he ought now to turn to socialism. It was close to the mark, he had agreed, but he had tried to explain to them that Catholicism provided a surer and more lethal way of undermining bourgeois modernity. 'Professors, writers, legislators, bankers, gentlemen of the Bar . . . as a Catholic and a son of the people I am doubly their enemy.'[11] It was a waste of·time for the Church to argue with these pygmies, or to try to distinguish between good and bad elements in modern thought: Veuillot adopted the stance of the plain bluff Christian who has 'seen it all' and can sweep away the entire apparatus of press, parliament, and universities with great shouts of laughter and derision. Knowing as an experienced journalist that his opponents enjoyed reasoned argument but could be thrown off balance by a well-written personal attack, he used his Catholicism as a distorting mirror in which individuals and institutions were reflected in a series of cruel caricatures. The conscientious men who were Ministers of Public Instruction in the forties found themselves lampooned as egotistical careerists. Salvandy, who had treated Veuillot very kindly after the fiasco of his Mediterranean travels, 'does everything with breadth and majesty. He loves to quote the weightiest and most authoritative sources; above all, he loves to quote himself'.[12] Salvandy was 'honest in finding ways to

---

[10] Preface to *Les Libres-Penseurs, Oeuvres* v.
[11] Ibid.   [12] *L'Univers* (10 Mar. 1847).

deceive, and courageous against justice . . . He has a naturally diffuse mind, full of gaps and patches of fog . . . M. Villemain, *universitaire* to the depths of his soul, tells lies by the book; M. Salvandy lies quite naturally, by sheer talent'.[13] The great scholars and scientists of the *Université*, Cousin, Jouffroy, Nisard, Gaultier de Claubry, Jules Simon, emerged in the pages of *L'Univers* as an awkward squad of pedants and buffoons. A professor of chemistry was described as being so short-sighted that he could not see the equipment in his laboratory, and probably had to fake his results. One lecturer was so boring that his classroom was deserted; another was obviously a charlatan because the students crowded in the aisles to hear him. A professor of literature had 'a style like a stagnant disused canal; if one fishes in it one brings up pieces of discarded clothing and dead cats'.[14] On Saint-Marc Girardin's fifteenth anniversary in his professorial chair Veuillot conceded that he had 'lost none of his enthusiasm and popularity: he had none in the first place'.[15] Veuillot was particularly amused with a government project to erect statues of the leading scholars of the epoch: it was a risk, surely, to expose Michelet and his colleagues to the light of day? 'M. Génin lacks grandeur . . . and nobody would have the slightest pleasure in contemplating M. Gérusez.' The annual *concours de l'Académie* when 'the mandarins of the West' walked in procession in their multi-coloured robes and uniforms, was a ludicrous spectacle, the Holy Week of an upstart false religion.[16]

Veuillot was as ready as the gallican liberals to reassure fellow Catholics that there was nothing to be feared from science, history, or philosophy, but for a rather different reason: they were all garbage. It was a favourite saying in *L'Univers* office that the Persians should have won the battle of Marathon and spared the world from the pernicious influence of Aristotle, Demosthenes, Socrates, and Plato: hardly a single one of the ancient Greek philosophers, Veuillot said, would escape prosecution for moral offences if he lived in the modern era.[17] The century of the Enlightenment from which French intellectual culture claimed

---

[13] *L'Univers* (13 Mar. 1847).
[14] The 'Galerie des professeurs de la Sorbonne et du Collège de France', *L'Univers* (Jan.–Feb. 1852), contains much material first used in the forties.
[15] *L'Univers* (10 Dec. 1846).
[16] *L'Univers* (16 Dec. 1846).   [17] *L'Univers* (19 Jan. 1847).

descent had been 'a wretched period which produced virtually no
saints . . . and whose coat of arms could well be a guillotine
standing on the trash-heap of the Encyclopaedia'.[18] Modern
science was a huge confidence trick, especially those aspects of it
which were supposed to threaten religious belief. Christians
should hold fast to the miracles of God, and turn their backs on
so-called triumphs of science like the discovery of the planet
Neptune in 1846 by mathematical prediction. The newspapers
were full of talk about a famous jawbone found in Gascony, one
of the evidences for early man: Veuillot remarked that two of the
government ministers came from Gascony 'and one can easily see
the resemblance to that jawbone'. He wrote a song to be
performed at Catholic concerts: 'the astronomer, peering myopi-
cally into his telescope, catalogues the worlds of the sky, but
doesn't see God; get stronger lenses, my poor fellow. The
archaeologist announces a crazy system from the bottom of a
deep hole; he chips away in search of fossils, but doesn't find
God; get a sharper pickaxe, my poor fellow.' There were several
more verses about poets, journalists, and deputies.[19]

Montalembert and the aristocratic liberals in Mme Swetchine's
circle had at first welcomed Veuillot as a valuable ally, but by
1844 they had become so weary of apologizing to Catholic
academics like Ozanam and Saint-Marc Girardin for what
L'Univers had said about them that they made an unsuccessful
attempt to buy the paper and install another editor. After this,
Veuillot was from time to time on quite good terms personally
with Montalembert, although he was always aware of the social
awkwardness between the comte de Montalembert and Monsieur
Veuillot, but he never trusted the liberals again. Catholic
liberalism was 'a heresy of the rich'; it was hopeless to expect
these upper-class intellectuals to lead the attack on the *Sorbonnards*
with whom they dined and played cards twice a week.[20]
Veuillot's rhetoric establishes him in the bloodline of modern
Savanarolas and prophets from the desert, of both Right and

[18] *L'Univers* (19 July 1852).
[19] Manuscript in 'Notes intimes', V/BN 24620.
[20] *L'Illusion libérale, Oeuvres* x, xxxii–xxxvi; A. de Falloux, *Le Parti catholique: ce qu'il a
été, ce qu'il est devenu* (1856). V/BN 24633 contains a most interesting batch of letters
from Montalembert to Veuillot during the forties; and see also Lacordaire to
Montalembert, 18 Jan. 1855, in J. Gadille (ed.), *Charles de Montalembert: Catholicisme et
liberté* (1970), 58.

Left. His list of scourges of modern civilization: 'philosophy, science, the railway, the telegraph, *la brute polytechnique*, Judas, Coquelet . . .'.[21] Coquelet was Veuillot's invention, the typical reader of the Parisian intellectual press. Everything that Veuillot hated was summed up in the editor of the *Revue des deux mondes*, François Buloz, and his readers, *les embulozés* (from *embu*, something dulled and tarnished), and in the *Journal des débats*, 'the newspaper of the Jews, the Protestants, the *universitaires*, the voltaireans, the most deceitful and persistent enemies of the Church'.[22] Buloz and Coquelet saw beauty only in science; they prayed to the microscope and the telescope and had no time for the Virgin Mary and the saints. Thomas Aquinas, Veuillot said, had never felt the need for a microscope; the Angel needed no telegraph for the Annunciation to Mary.[23] In his black vision the newspapers themselves represented the most sinister aspect of the modern machine culture which he saw as the direct result of the Enlightenment: their steam presses poured out hundreds of thousands of copies a day, and the railway—'there are no more distances', Coquelet liked to say—carried the thoughts of the ideologues of Paris to every corner of the provinces, to the puffed-up lawyers, *instituteurs* and petty savants like those Veuillot had known at Périgueux. The official classes, creatures of the voltairean press, never set foot inside a church: 'I feel that I have been conquered, that I am held in contempt, that a foreign doctrine has come and taken root in France to dominate us, that the soil of the *patrie* does not wholly belong to the true race of the *patrie*.'[24] The idea that the true race must seek asylum in the international *patrie* of Christendom belongs clearly to the romantic medievalism of the nineteenth century, but like all ultramontane thought it has strong links with the *émigré* generation of Maistre and d'Antraigues. The Emigration had accustomed a large number of French conservatives to thinking of themselves as citizens of a homeland which had no fixed geographical location. *Où sont les fleurs-de-lys, là est la patrie*: 'the *patrie* is a word devoid of sense if it does not mean the body of laws under which one has lived . . . To love one's country when it

[21] *Le Parfum de Rome, Oeuvres* ix, 500.
[22] *L'Univers* (7 Aug. 1853).
[23] *Le Parfum de Rome*, 16 ff.
[24] *Le Parfum de Rome*, 224.

has lost its laws and its customs is an absurd idolatry'.[25] While keeping a heavily qualified allegiance to the France of Guizot and Louis Philippe the more serious ultramontanes were ready to be loyal subjects of a supranational Catholic polity; in Mgr Pie's phrase, 'Oh God: Thou art my king, my party . . . my home, my *patrie*'.[26]

The idea that decayed, dilapidated, medieval, Rome should take command of the modern European world of steam power and steel bridges, newspapers, bicameral legislatures, and scientific institutes struck Veuillot as a piquant and delightful paradox. He takes Coquelet to Rome, and imagines him gazing with horror at the Eternal City: where are the railways? Where are the Chamber of Deputies and the Academy of Science? Where is the free press? How can I make this fool understand, Veuillot asks, that Rome was planned to be a deliberate affront to everything he stands for? The voltairean bourgeoisie and their treasured institutions count for nothing here; Rome's gentle, maternal power rests on certainty instead of enquiry, 'Revelation instead of Revolution'. It is 'the place of incomparable conversations', not about astronomy or electoral reform but about the conversion of Russia, the recovery of the Holy Places, the decisions of the Sacred Congregation of the Index.[27] He was always ready to concede with the utmost frankness that papal rule, direct or indirect, would indeed mean complete theocratic absolutism. 'There is only one truth, and if men stray into the thousand paths of error the Church must have the power to bring them back into line: *voilà la Charte de Dieu!*'[28] *L'Univers* applauded Charlemagne's forced conversion of the Saxons, and called for the Inquisition to be revived to deal with Protestant and Jewish philosophers. 'The word "liberty" comes to us from the slave nations; it has no meaning in a Christian society.'[29] True liberty was something acquired by baptism; it conferred on the individual the right to obey the laws of God. If those who were not baptized Catholics failed to understand this, so much the worse for them. When he had to serve a month in Saint-Pélagie

[25] D'Antraigues, quoted by F. Baldensperger, *Le Mouvement des idées dans l'Émigration française*, 2 vols. (1924–5), vol. i, 299–300.
[26] E. Catta, *La Doctrine politique et sociale du cardinale Pie* (1957), 332.
[27] *Le Parfum de Rome*, 207.
[28] *Rome et Lorette*, 184.   [29] *L'Univers* (17 Dec. 1855).

prison in 1844 for having supported the abbé Combalot in a particularly offensive attack on the *Université*, Veuillot wrote that 'on the other side of the wall there is only liberty, the liberty of dogs without masters, liberty that I regard as a whore. As for the liberty of the soul, of prayer, I have never been better off than I am here, not even on retreat at Solesmes.'[30] He enjoyed the cries of rage and horrified amusement in the rest of the press when he declared that the Church in power would rigorously control all public life, emasculate bourgeois political institutions, and sentence *universitaires* to long terms of imprisonment; he expounded these blasphemies in such excellent prose that the other papers could not resist quoting him, and thus gave the editorials in *L'Univers* the widest possible circulation. Émile Ollivier thought him one of the best polemical stylists of the age: his writing had 'marvellous suppleness and rich variety: the earnest tone of indignation, the piercing point of irony, broad flaming eloquence . . . and in the middle of a passage of grand and stately prose he can place an interlude written with simple harmonious words and gentle humorous notes, like a sunlit clearing in a dark forest'; but, as Ollivier noted, Veuillot had unsurpassed power both to charm and to frighten. He was implacably hard towards his opponents; each controversy was treated as a fight to the finish.[31] Charles de Mazade remarked that 'Veuillot's bow is always drawn for the kill'.[32]

By the end of the July Monarchy it was clear that *L'Univers* had been the real beneficiary of the education debate. The parliamentary Catholics had achieved nothing very substantial, but Veuillot was so well established that he could dictate the tone of Catholic debate on almost any subject. To the dismay of the moderates, and especially of the bishops, public opinion had come to accept *L'Univers* as the real voice of the *parti catholique*;[33] it could destroy the effect of a dozen conciliatory speeches and pastoral letters with one editorial on the Inquisition. More significantly, however, *L'Univers* was now in a position to exert a

---

[30] *Louis Veuillot*, vol. i, 462.   [31] Ollivier, *L'Église et l'État*, vol. i, 304–5.

[32] 'Les satires de M. Veuillot', *Revue des deux mondes* (15 July 1863). Cf. the series 'Louis Veuillot et la critique' in the *Revue augustinienne*, vols. iv–v.

[33] On this recognition of Veuillot's dominance in the education debate, Jules Simon, *Notice historique sur la vie et les travaux de M. Michelet* (1886). Veuillot had been able to take advantage of Montalembert's long absence from Paris for family reasons at a critical phase of the conflict.

powerful influence within the French Church because of the
enthusiastic reception Veuillot received from the parish clergy.
His success in the presbyteries was assured from the moment of
his first article on higher education. The sense of inadequacy that
priests felt in dealing with the educated classes melted away as
they read Veuillot on godless mathematics or modern philosophy,
and absorbed the message that there was no need to be afraid of
bourgeois critics whose degrees and diplomas were worthless.
For a great many parish priests Veuillot's contempt for intellectuals
and his crusading militancy were like a new gospel. Their
gratitude was immense. 'God alone knows', one priest wrote to
Veuillot many years later, 'how much good you did for me, the
support, the consolation, the holy joys your words brought me
. . .'.[34] Priests read *L'Univers* to put themselves into the right
mood for preaching sermons, and sometimes read Veuillot's
editorials aloud from the pulpit.[35] Tattered copies were passed
from hand to hand amongst priests too poor to subscribe; two
priests trained their dogs to carry a rolled-up copy from one
presbytery to the other, like the baton in a relay race.[36] Apart
from its editorial content *L'Univers* had the practical advantage of
being the first daily newspaper to be filled with Catholic news
and columns of extremely well-informed gossip and speculation
about the ecclesiastical world. Not everyone who read the paper,
as Lacordaire pointed out, agreed with everything Veuillot and
du Lac wrote, and other reservations might be made about its
direct influence:[37] in many dioceses the clergy were firmly
discouraged from buying it, and the distribution in the provinces
was uneven; nevertheless, it easily eclipsed the other religious
press and the print run of 8000 in 1848, with most copies going to
the provinces, probably meant that at least half the clergy saw
L'Univers two or three times a week.[38] All over the country there

[34] Abbé Gay to Veuillot, 18 July 1877, V/BN 24231.
[35] Le Sueur, *Le Clergé picard*, vol. ii, 59–60. There are *police des cultes* reports to this
effect from almost every diocese.
[36] Sevrin, *Clausel de Montals*, vol. ii, 415.
[37] Lacordaire to Montalembert, 18 Jan. 1855, *Charles de Montalembert: Catholicisme et
liberté*, 61.
[38] 'Dossier du Lac', V/BN 24635, and the breakdown of *L'Univers* accounts in
Dupanloup/BN 24712: circulation rose from about 6000 to 8000 when the business
manager, Taconet, reduced the subscription from 60 to 40 francs in March 1848, after
many requests from the provincial clergy.

were priests who were 'happy to declare ourselves *Universitaires*'.[39]

Veuillot and du Lac in effect re-educated the parish clergy, giving them a daily course in simplified theology and political doctrine, supported by a highly tendentious précis of Church history. In Veuillot's prose the complex ideas of Maistre's *Du Pape* and Lamennais's *Essai sur l'indifférence* became clear as crystal. Priests were especially defenceless on the subject of ecclesiology, where their seminary training had left them with nothing but the memory of half a dozen lectures in Latin and some incomprehensible quotations from Bossuet learned by heart. Veuillot explained that the clergy could forget about Bossuet, Pascal, and the Sulpician tradition. They should reject the concept of the Church as a delicate structure of conciliar checks and balances, in favour of the more exhilarating model of an army in battle. The neo-military flavour of *L'Univers*, which priests enjoyed, owed something to an earlier episode in Veuillot's career. Like many other religious controversialists he gave a distinct impression at times that he might have been happier as a soldier. In 1841, when he had been only a part-time contributor to the paper, he had been commissioned by Guizot to join Marshal Bugeaud's staff in Algeria as an observer; Guizot wanted to be kept informed on the African campaigns so that he could answer his critics in parliament. Veuillot was given a horse, a uniform, and honorary commissioned rank, and had privileged access to Bugeaud's staff conferences without being in any way under military command. He saw some actual combat against the Islamic tribes and found the whole experience fascinating, but after a few months he wanted to return to 'the real war, against ideas'.[40] He came back to Paris with an armoury of military rhetoric and from that time he wrote more than ever in terms of bombs, ambushes, advance guards, sentries, and deserters. Every editorial was a cartridge fired, every *évêché* a fortified camp to be taken by surprise. This vocabulary was perfectly suited to his ideas about authority in the Church. In military ecclesiology it seemed obvious that the Pope as commander-in-chief must exercise day-to-day surveillance

---

[39] The phrase was coined by Louis-Gaston de Ségur in a letter to Auguste Roussel, V/BN 24235.

[40] *Louis Veuillot*, vol. i, 248.

over his subordinate generals, and that the commanders in the
field, the gallican bishops, could hardly claim a right to adapt his
orders to suit the traditions of their own regiments; in any case,
from Veuillot's point of view the gallican commanders themselves
had a dismal record of lost battles and ignominious surrenders.
By contrast, Veuillot introduced the clergy to the great ultramontane warriors in the episcopate, Gousset of Reims, Parisis of
Langres, Gignoux of Beauvais, Rendu of Annecy, and de
Villecourt of La Rochelle, who were praised every day in
L'Univers both for their superlative qualities of leadership and for
their total submission to Rome. For this small group of
ultramontane bishops *L'Univers* provided an unprecedented
means of spreading their influence to the remotest presbyteries.
Without a national synod they had received very little public
notice and had been almost powerless, but from the mid-forties
onwards Veuillot gave them a forum; *L'Univers* became the
continuous seminar of the ultramontane movement, reprinting
pastoral letters on the day they were issued and inviting the
leading activists to harass the gallican establishment in letters to
the editor. Anti-episcopal feeling was always simmering amongst
the lower clergy, whose view of the hierarchy was coloured by
memories of the prizes and favours showered on clever middle-
class seminarians; priests could remember only too clearly the
occasions when their instructor had given them a perfunctory
half-hour lecture before going off to spend two hours teaching
history or Greek to some privileged swot, who was perhaps now
one of the candidates to be bishop of their own diocese. They
were easily persuaded that the French bishops on the whole were
bureaucrats and compromisers, incapable of subduing civil
society, and that the only bishops whose leadership was worth
following were the ultramontanes.

Veuillot and L'Univers *in 1848*

In later years Veuillot was ashamed of having been carried away
by the euphoria of February 1848; the fall of Louis-Philippe had
seemed providential, and he had welcomed the democratic
republic as 'the logical extension of the doctrines of Calvary'. By
the time of the June Days he had recovered, and was pouring
scorn on the naïve Catholic idealists of the *Ère nouvelle* group for
being taken in by demagogues who preached democracy, as he

said, with the Gospel in one hand and a gun in the other, and by posters like the one he noted of Christ as a carpenter, with the caption 'Jesus-Christ, premier représentant du peuple'. Where the liberal gallicans at the *archevêché* saw great opportunities for the Church provided civil order could be guaranteed, Veuillot saw something more apocalyptic, the approach of 'the grand assizes of the bourgeoisie'. Orleanism was not dead; the ideologues of the educated classes were still busy in the press, and, inevitably, their critique of traditional authority was being picked up and garbled by the uneducated into a revolutionary creed that would destroy the whole fabric of society. His own experience as a member of the National Guard in the June Days led to the brilliant pamphlet *l'Esclave Vindex*. During the fighting Veuillot had spent some time stationed beside the group of statuary in the Tuileries Gardens representing Spartacus and his slave-valet Vindex, and he imagined their dialogue: Spartacus, whom he saw as a revolutionary of the privileged class, the analogue of those modern gladiators and popular favourites the radical journalists, declares in magnificently florid language that he means to overthrow the tyranny of kings and priests; Vindex, the ultimate proletarian, looking up at his master with simple admiration, says, 'Hurrah! then *we* can go on to abolish property, marriage, morality and order'.[41] It was clearly the moment for the Church to throw itself into the struggle, but Veuillot knew that he could expect no support from Orleanist-appointed bishops, saturated in the neo-Protestant parliamentary ethos. *L'Univers* would have to represent the Church Militant in the Republic; and its first task would be to purge the gallican episcopate.

By the end of 1848 Veuillot was enjoying a considerable personal success. His articles and pamphlets in the vein of *L'Esclave Vindex* were being reprinted and paraphrased in the Catholic press of several countries. On *L'Univers* he now had a staff of eight contributing editors. The main specialists on ecclesiastical matters and religious history were Melchior du Lac, who had entered the monastery of Solesmes in 1845 but returned to *L'Univers* shortly after February 1848, still not ordained although still wearing clerical costume, and the former

---

[41] *L'Esclave Vindex* (1849); this is a rather summary version of a long and very well written dialogue.

Mennaisian Jules Morel, indubitably ordained but dressed like a romantic poet. Veuillot's brother Eugène, Charles de Coux, Pierre Roux-Lavergne, J.-B. Coquille, and Léon Aubineau wrote on education and current affairs. Gustave de la Tour, who specialized in international relations, was a heavy, gloomy man who had been exiled for his part in the duchesse de Berry's rebellion in 1832 and had served in the Austrian army; he was now a legitimist deputy for the Côtes-du-Nord, and famous as the most boring speaker in the Assembly—his aim, he explained, was 'to achieve the amplitude of a Guizot'. Most people who had to deal with *L'Univers* thought that beside this team of zealots Louis Veuillot himself seemed positively reasonable; the others often pushed him further than he was inclined to go. On the other hand the business manager, M. Taconet, was always afraid that Veuillot would go too far and kept reminding him that the printing workers would lose their jobs if the paper had to close because of a lawsuit, or suppression by the government; as if their precious jobs counted, Veuillot wrote, against the defence of the Catholic church.[42] The principal editors held nearly identical views, and at one point they published a joint declaration that they would be happy to sign one another's articles; certainly the other editors would have been delighted to sign Veuillot's articles.[43]

Radiating from the *Univers* office was an extraordinary network of correspondents and admirers; each of the editors had his own contacts, and Veuillot alone wrote ten letters on an average day. Most of these correspondents were clerics, but *L'Univers* did have a noticeable following by 1848 in the one group of the Catholic laity which was neither gallican nor liberal, the provincial legitimists. Amongst the more devout, and for the most part more remote minor aristocracy, and the editors of small legitimist newspapers in the provinces, there was a core of strict believers who did not agree with the policy of the legitimist

[42] 'Notes intimes', V/BN 24620. The principal sources are the papers and correspondence of the assistant editors of *L'Univers*, V/BN 24235; AN F. 18. 423: Ministry of the Interior press reports; Morel, *Somme*, xxxvii–xlvii and 49–60; on Gustave de la Tour, C. Guyho, *Les hommes de 1852* (1889), 145. Jules Gondon wrote part-time on English affairs but Veuillot doubted 'if he was really one of us': *Louis Veuillot*, vol. ii, 429 n. Charles de Coux fell out with Veuillot and left the paper after 1848.
[43] *L'Univers* (19 Feb. 1852).

politicians like Falloux and Berryer of planning for an early
restoration of Henry V through negotiation and parliamentary
voting. They preferred the harder line, favoured by Chambord
himself, that a restoration would have to wait until there had
been a thorough re-Christianization of *la France pervertie*. They
found Veuillot's attacks on the Orleanist bourgeoisie and his
articles about the intellectual contagion spreading outwards from
the cities very congenial and timely, they greatly enjoyed
L'Esclave Vindex, and they had their own reasons for sharing his
contempt for the gallican bishops, some of whom were known to
have abandoned legitimism for the sake of promotion. Although
Veuillot made it clear from time to time that he belonged to no
party and looked on French politics 'from the point of view of a
spectator who hasn't placed a bet', it was obvious that *veuillotisme*
was close to the essence of legitimist theory and that *L'Univers*
might be a powerful supporter of the Bourbon cause in the
future. After expressing some reservations, men like Emmanuel
de Curzon at Poitiers, Theodore de Quatrebarbes at Chanzeaux,
and Louis de Loverdo at Orleans came during the Second
Republic to be staunch admirers of Veuillot and subscribers to
L'Univers; Loverdo said that he was 'happy to accept this
cooper's son as a leader and a colleague'.[44]

The network in the clergy began with the circle of ultramontane
bishops, who were becoming known as the *école de l'Univers*, and
spread outwards into the second rank of the clergy, amongst
vicars-general, seminary instructors, and priest-secretaries in
diocesan administration, some of them old admirers of Lamennais,
others younger men who had been attracted by the ultramontane
movement in the seminaries, and others again who perhaps had
not given a thought to ultramontanism until they found
themselves at odds with their bishop over some administrative or
pastoral matter. *L'Univers* was able to follow a great deal of
diocesan business in detail, and on occasions an informant could
supply actual letters extracted from a bishop's private correspondence. Reports and documents arrived from sources within the
gallican *archevêchés* of Lyons and Bordeaux. The abbé Bernard, a
canon of Avignon, the abbé Savin, Archpriest of the Cathedral of
Viviers, who had been one of the candidates for that bishopric

---

[44] The position of the leading Chambordists is examined in Gough, 'French
legitimism and Catholicism' (1966).

himself, and Canon Victor Pelletier, perpetual leader of the
opposition in the chapter of Orleans, kept Veuillot abreast of
developments in their respective dioceses. Jules Morel and
Melchior du Lac had several excellent contacts, including for
example the vicar of Saint-Herblain at Nantes who sent du Lac
an acid pen-portrait of his cautious bishop Mgr Jacquemet.[45]
L'Univers became much better informed than the Papal Nuncio.

Veuillot had succeeded also in practical terms. Although
L'Univers was still run at a loss the list of 8000 subscribers was not
far short of the circulation of the *Journal des débats*, and unlike any
other religious paper it attracted a healthy volume of advertising.
Taconet felt that he could afford to pay Veuillot 6000 francs a
year, which put him in the aristocracy of journalism in Paris.[46] In
1845 he had married Mathilde Murcier, the daughter of a
middle-class family at Versailles, who had brought him a dowry
of 40,000 francs. Following his usual instinct to conceal the better
side of his character he used his marriage to tease the upper-class
Catholic intellectuals and to dispel any impression that he might
be softening. He had simply decided, he told everybody, that at
the age of thirty-two a decent ordinary Christian like himself
ought to think about making a sensible and advantageous
marriage; there was no romance about it; Mathilde was a plain,
pious, humble creature who would be a Christian wife and
mother and 'has never been troubled by the itch to read and
write'. Most of this was nonsense. Mathilde was intelligent and
charming, and of course perfectly literate. Their honeymoon in
the mountains of Savoy was the happiest memory of his life, and
he was to be desolated when she died in 1852 at the age of
twenty-eight.[47]

In 1848 they moved from small uncomfortable lodgings in the
rue de Babylone to a much larger apartment at 44 rue du Bac, a
place of rather bizarre grandeur, Eugène said, 'the attic of a
palace . . . but it suited Louis, who was really a grand seigneur at

---

[45] V/BN 24225–6, 24235, 24633–4.

[46] Taconet's summary of costs, Dupanloup/BN 24712. See T. Zeldin, *France
1848–1945*, 2 vols. (Oxford 1973–7), vol. ii, 500–4 on the salaries of journalists. The
Journal des débats had a circulation of about 9500 in 1848; *La Presse* and *Le Constitutionnel*
each sold over 25,000.

[47] On Mathilde Veuillot, *Louis Veuillot*, vol. i, 522–7; the 'Sylvestre et Marianne'
dialogues in *Cà et là*, *Oeuvres* viii; and the 'Notes intimes', V/BN 24620.

heart' and found it amusing to entertain bishops in these archaic surroundings, sitting at the head of his dinner-table while the great ultramontane luminaries talked about Aquinas or the miracle of La Salette; and as an unexpected bonus he discovered that he had a view of Montalembert's garden at number 40.

VI

Some mistakes of Archbishop Sibour

THE extraordinary misadventures into which Sibour and the gallican circle of the *archevêché* of Paris stumbled between 1849 and 1853 were to make it easy for Veuillot and the ultramontane party not only to win a number of local and tactical advantages, but to succeed in their major enterprise of persuading the papacy to take a firmer grip on the French Church; prompted continually by the ultramontanes, Rome became more and more convinced after 1849 that Paris was a serious problem, the focal point of opposition and potentially a source of outright schism.

Almost from the beginning of his episcopate Sibour was drawn into a comedy of errors in which each of his well-meaning communications with Rome was taken by the Holy See as a deliberate provocation. He began with a hopeless gaffe over the question of the temporal power of the papacy. Since the election of Pius IX in 1846 Catholics had generally believed that the new Pope was a liberal, struggling against the influence of reactionary advisers left over from the reign of Gregory XVI, and that the minor administrative changes he had introduced into the Papal States were only the first instalment of a sweeping programme of modern reforms. Under the influence of this misleading picture they were deeply sympathetic when the revolution in Rome forced the Pope to take refuge at Gaeta in November 1848. Opinion was divided, however, on the temporal power itself. Although ultramontane laymen like Montalembert and Falloux felt that it had to be restored as a symbol of legitimate authority, many French churchmen had reservations. There seemed to be no very compelling arguments in ecclesiastical history or canon law for the Pope's direct rule over the states of central Italy being an essential element in the church; Mgr Thibault of Montpellier had written in a pastoral of 1847 that the Popes would divest themselves of the temporal power without regret if this ever became necessary. Apart from a few specialists in Italian affairs like Eugène Rendu, French Catholics did not understand the passions aroused at Rome by any implied questioning of the temporal power, and at this time they could not have predicted how absolutely central an issue it was to be throughout the long pontificate of Pius IX: at the moment of Italian unification in 1860, indeed, support for the temporal power was to be used as a criterion of Catholic belief, supported by the full weight of encyclicals and excommunications. In March 1849, while Montalembert and Falloux were doing everything possible to convince Louis Napoleon and the Barrot cabinet that a French military force should be sent to restore the Pope to Rome, Sibour wrote a letter to the Pope which he felt expressed a widespread view amongst liberals and gallicans. He urged Pius IX to leave Gaeta, where he was surrounded by self-interested and reactionary Italian courtiers, and come to liberal France: the temporal power could be left in abeyance to be recovered later, if the occasion arose, by patient diplomacy and the promise of genuine reforms.[1] Sibour clearly thought that the Pope would welcome this advice. The Nuncio, Fornari, who despised Sibour almost as much as he had detested Affre, went on reminding the Holy See of the incident in many subtle ways, but in any case Pius IX would not have forgotten it. He claimed later to have forgiven Sibour, and forgiven him also for another letter in August 1849 advising the Pope to put himself at the head of the movement in Italy towards free political institutions, but, as the French Ambassador noted, 'everything that comes from the Archbishop of Paris is suspect';[2] and the suspicion deepened when it appeared that Sibour was unsound also on the Immaculate Conception.

The idea that by a special divine dispensation the Virgin Mary had been conceived without the taint of original sin had been debated in the Church since the early councils. Several Popes had condemned it: Leo I, in the letter which moved the Council of Chalcedon to declare that 'Peter has spoken from the mouth of Leo', plainly stated that Mary was subject to original sin like other mortals. By the end of the Middle Ages, after centuries of argument over the precise meanings of 'generation', 'conception', and 'sin', and in spite of a great deal of ingenuity applied to biblical and patristic texts, the weight of opinion seemed to be against the Immaculate Conception; Duns Scotus and the

[1] ASV Francia 1849 (II), correspondence of March–April 1849.
[2] Comte de Rayneval's report, 4 Aug. 1852, in Maurain, *Saint-Siège*, 106–7.

Franciscans were for it, but Bernard, Albertus Magnus, and
Aquinas had declared it to be no more than a pious belief without
any substance that could be defined. In 1476 Sixtus IV inserted
an office of the Immaculate Conception into the Roman
Breviary; in 1568 Pius V abolished it. In 1588 Jesuit scholars
produced documents which were said to prove an unbroken
tradition going back to the Apostle Saint James; Dominican
scholars denounced them as forgeries. After examination of the
matter by a papal commission in 1682 Innocent XI stated that
the Immaculate Conception was a corruption of orthodox belief
based on forged evidence, and forbade any further enquiry; but
the Jesuits, who preferred not to think about the decisions of
quasi-Jansenist Popes like Innocent XI, did not give up.
Eventually the favourable moment came with the election of Pius
IX. The new Pope had a strong personal devotion to the Virgin
Mary as protectress of the Church in times of trouble, more
reliable, as he often said, than the treaties and guarantees of
secular powers, and wanted a dogmatic definition of the
Immaculate Conception to be one of the landmarks of his
pontificate, a defiant gesture of faith in the supernatural order.
With his very active encouragement the leading mariologists in
the Jesuit order prepared a synthesis with a distinctly political
flavour, crude by the standards of the medieval debates but
suitable for the needs of the Church in the mid-nineteenth
century. The Immaculate Conception was declared to belong to
the secret tradition of Christianity. The objection of Aquinas that
there could not possibly be any human creature who did not need
redemption by Jesus Christ was answered by reviving the
argument, already rejected many times in the past, that Mary
was in some sense a divinity in her own right, virtually co-
Redeemer.

An important new element, however, was the emphasis placed
on the role of Mary in exterminating heresy. The distinction—first
made, as it happened, by the heretic Nestorius—between Eve,
through whom sin and error were brought to the human race,
and Mary who brought benediction, salvation, and truth, was
elaborated to show that there was 'a real and necessary nexus'
between a definition of the Immaculate Conception and a
systematic condemnation of modern intellectual and political
errors. To declare that Mary was exempt from original sin drew

attention to the sinful state of the rest of mankind, and the corollaries were obvious: civil governments could not escape their duty to curb the innate evil in the human character; and so-called 'free institutions', the freedom of philosophical and scientific enquiry and the parliamentary system of government, were inadmissible because of the strong tendency of the unaided human reason, flawed by original sin, to deviate into error. The first drafts of the dogmatic definition were meant to include a comprehensive list of modern errors, but this plan was found too difficult to manage.[3]

The manner of the definition was intended to demonstrate the Pope's right to define a dogma without having to summon a General Council. As a gesture towards consultation Pius IX conducted what was in effect a Council by mail. On 2 February 1849 the encyclical *Ubi primum* invited bishops, religious orders, and interested laymen to give their views in writing on the desirability and timeliness of declaring the Immaculate Conception an article of faith. Pius IX was expecting a resounding chorus of agreement rather than any expressions of niggling doubt, and in the event the overwhelming majority of bishops appeared to be favourable, although there were many nuances and reservations. The most enthusiastic response came from the bishops of southern Italy and Spain, heavily over represented in the episcopate, who spoke from long experience of how devotion to the Virgin Mary stimulated piety and preserved the masses from rationalism and materialism. In Ireland the bishops were favourable but the professors at Maynooth were not. Forty-eight of the forty-nine American bishops did not reply at all. The Austrians were mainly in favour but the Germans feared that it would alienate Protestant opinion just at a moment when the conservative forces in European society needed to be united: 'In the whole history of the Church', one of them wrote, 'there could hardly have been a worse time to define such a dogma.'[4]

[3] The list of errors was put aside for further examination, and after passing through many modifications it emerged as the Syllabus of Errors in 1864. On the Immaculate Conception dogma, R. P. Perrone, *De Immaculato B. Mariae Conceptu* (Rome 1847); R. P. Calvetti, 'Congruenze sociali di una definizione dogmatica sull'Immacolato Concepimento della B. V. Maria', *Civiltà Cattolica* (14 Feb. 1852); X. le Bachelet, 'Immaculée Conception', *DTC* xiii, 845–1218.

[4] The German theologian Forster quoted in Martina, *Pio IX*, 523. The replies to *Ubi primum* are in *Pareri dell'episcopato cattolico, di capitoli, di congregazioni, di università, di personaggi, regguardevoli sulla definizione dogmatica . . .*, 3 vols. (Rome 1851–4).

In France the ultramontanes, predictably, were enthusiastic, and Dom Guéranger's long *Mémoire sur l'Immaculée conception* actually had some effect on the drafting of the definition.[5] The gallicans and moderates were more restrained, but there was a general disposition to please the Pope in his exile at Gaeta. There might have been a livelier debate if the encyclical had been more candid about the political implications of the dogma, but the text of *Ubi primum* stressed only the devotional aspects. The 'nexus' between the sinlessness of Mary and the errors of modern society was never made clear to the episcopate; the article in Italian explaining this interpretation, drafted jointly by the Pope himself and the Jesuit theologian Calvetti, appeared in the *Civiltà Cattolica* on 14 February 1852, at a time when the French bishops were preoccupied with other controversies.[6] For the time being, in 1849, most of the French could see no harm in the new dogma and only a few of the most determined gallicans lodged serious objections. Mazenod, Guibert, and Bouvier followed the teaching of the Sulpicians that a case could be made out for the Immaculate Conception from first principles even if there was no clear warrant in scripture, and that it was essentially a matter of piety, better without a dogmatic definition but fundamentally acceptable. Olivier, Blanquart de Bailleul, Robiou, and Clausel de Montals sent dissenting votes, Clausel writing that Rome had 'momentarily gone astray'.[7]

Sibour, evidently imagining *Ubi primum* to be a genuine request for a theological opinion, spent six months drawing up a list of thirty-eight reasons against a definition. He had always been devoted to the Virgin Mary, he explained, and as a bishop of Digne he had encouraged ceremonies in honour of the Immaculate Conception, but he felt it would be disastrous for the Church to insist on making such a doctrine binding on consciences under pain of eternal damnation. The result of an opinion poll, he wrote, could not hide the fact that it was neither scriptural nor

---

[5] G. Frénaud, 'Dom Guéranger et le projet de bulle Quemadmodum', in *Virgo Immaculata: Acta congressus Mariologici-Mariani* (Rome 1956); G. Robert, *Dom Guéranger chez Pie IX* (1960).

[6] Calvetti, 'Congruenze sociali . . .'. The political corollaries of the Immaculate Conception were more widely discussed at the time of the Temporal Power crisis in 1859–60, and became a commonplace of seminary teaching later in the century.

[7] Covering letters by Fornari forwarding the replies of the French bishops: ASV: Parigi vols. 75–6; Sevrin, *Clausel de Montals*, vol. ii, 739.

properly traditional, or that the patristic sources were contradictory; it was not a legitimate extension of any revealed truth,
and it gave rise to glaring anomalies in theology and logic, which
he explored at some length. A formal definition would create a
disgruntled minority whose perfectly respectable opinions, based
on the work of some of the greatest theologians in history, would
now be declared anathema: they would be driven into clandestine
opposition and might easily lapse into heresy. Worst of all, he
wrote, a new dogma on the Virgin Mary proclaimed in the
middle of the nineteenth century for no very clear or pressing
reason would bring Catholic theology into disrepute amongst the
educated classes—especially, Sibour added in his 'doubt number
35', in the archdiocese of Paris—and the church would lose more
souls than it hoped to gain.[8]

According to ultramontane sources the Curia was cynically
amused that Sibour should have taken so much trouble to thwart
the Pope's wishes.[9] His offence was badly timed, because within
a few days of sending off his memorandum on the Immaculate
Conception on 25 August 1849 he was to become involved in a
controversy over episcopal authority and canon law, from which
he might perhaps have had some hope of emerging with success if
he had been in favour with the Holy See: this was the question of
provincial councils. Under the July Monarchy the ministère des
Cultes had been obsessively strict in enforcing the rule (Organic
Article number 4) against the holding of councils or synods.
Bishops were not supposed to meet even in small groups, or to
issue joint pastoral letters in case they implied that meetings had
taken place. After the Revolution in 1848, with the ministère des
Cultes temporarily disoriented and the republican government less
committed to the Organic Articles, the obstacles in the way of
holding a council seemed to have disappeared. In July 1848 the
bishops of Angers, Blois, and Le Mans circulated a memorandum
on the problems the episcopate needed to resolve; sixty-two
bishops indicated their support, and Sibour, Morlot of Tours,
and eleven other senior men were deputed to write jointly to the
Pope asking permission to hold a national council. They were
astonished to receive a flat refusal from Gaeta, accompanied by
'a variety of specious excuses' about the difficult and dangerous

---

[8] *Pareri dell'episcopato* . . ., vol. ii, 26–46.
[9] Delatte, *Dom Guéranger*, vol. ii, 110–11.

times and the undesirability of bishops being called away from their dioceses. Similar refusals went at the same time to the bishops of Bavaria, Austria, and Tuscany.[10] Rome did not like councils; the Curia was still dealing with the errors of the synod of Pistoia in 1786. National episcopates meeting and passing resolutions might easily have created a new Conciliar Movement in the nineteenth century, and the French were thought likely to be the most troublesome of all. After some months' delay Rome grudgingly agreed that each archbishop could hold a provincial council with his four or five suffragan bishops, and the French immediately announced plans for councils to be held on various dates in 1849 and 1850.

Both parties in the Church looked forward to gaining some benefit, the gallicans believing that even at the provincial level councils would create solidarity amongst the bishops and encourage them to resist the ultramontane pressure coming from the parish clergy and *L'Univers*; the ultramontanes, although they expected to be in the minority in every province except Reims, knew that so long as at least one ultramontane bishop was present at each council he might be able to embarrass the gallicans into making competitive declarations of loyalty to the Holy See, by raising issues where open resistance to Roman policy would seem outrageous. With this in mind Mgr Fornari, Mgr Gousset, and several others lobbied the ministre des Cultes to have ultramontane candidates nominated to the sees that fell vacant in 1849, taking advantage of the accident that the minister happened to be the vicomte de Falloux, a leader of the legitimist party and the most convinced ultramontane in Mme Swetchine's circle of ex-Mennaisians.[11] The *école de l'Univers* were not sure if they could rely on Falloux, who had always struck Veuillot as 'not exactly one of us, not what we would call a Catholic first and last . . . basically a man of compromises and transactions',[12] but they found him ready to keep gallicans out of the episcopate if he could—'the abbé Lyonnet, neither for

[10] On the annoyance of the French bishops over this episode, Dupanloup, 'Rapport au Pape', Dupanloup/AN AB XIX 524. Cf. Martina, *Pio IX*, 498–502.
[11] Despatches from Fornari in ASV: Parigi vol. 75, e.g. 15 Aug. 1849; letters of bishops to Falloux, 1849, in S. Sulp/BN 24718; A. Latreille, 'Nominations épiscopales au XIXe siècle: une enquête de M. de Falloux', *Cahiers d'histoire* v (1960).
[12] Veuillot to the bishop of Annecy, 2 Aug. 1849, *Correspondance* vol. iii, 61.

Cambrai nor for anywhere else!'[13]—and easily persuaded if the candidate had a legitimist background. By the end of the year Falloux had nominated four ultramontane-legitimists, two of them very forceful and articulate men, Louis-Édouard Pie (Poitiers) and Pierre de Dreux-Brézé (Moulins), and amongst some other moves promoted the Mennaisian scholar Salinis to the important diocese of Amiens. When the councils began, ultramontanes held all the sees in the province of Reims; in Bordeaux the arrival of the brilliant young Mgr Pie at Poitiers greatly encouraged the ultramontane bishops of Luçon and La Rochelle and stimulated the latent Roman tendencies of the three other suffragans, so that Cardinal Donnet was suddenly beset with problems; and new bishops had been introduced to be irritants in the Besançon, Albi, and Sens provinces where previously there had been a gallican consensus.

Paris was to hold the first council. The suffragans included two strong gallicans, Fayet of Orleans and Clausel de Montals of Chartres, and three moderates with gallican inclinations, Allou of Meaux, Gros of Versailles, and Fabre des Essarts of Blois; Mgr Fornari gloomily expected that the Council of Paris would be a gallican orchestra conducted with panache by Sibour. On 4 April 1849 Fayet died in a cholera epidemic. Without wasting a moment on regrets and condolences Fornari proposed a successor, but here he made a remarkable mistake. At this point in 1849 the abbé Dupanloup, headmaster of Saint-Nicolas and a member of the commission preparing the Loi Falloux, was regarded as the leading spokesman for Catholic education. It was known also that as a theological student he had once written a thesis on papal infallibility; and he was often assumed to be a legitimist because he was confessor to some of the best Parisian society. Fornari thought that he would be ideal for the vacancy at Orleans, and urged Rome to approve his nomination without delay so that he could take his seat at the Council of Paris and thus neutralize the gallican vote of Chartres.[14] The nomination went through; but Dupanloup was as far as possible in spirit from the new ultramontanism of the mid-century. He had great respect for Rome but at least equal respect for the Sulpician tradition and 'the old clergy of France', and although he was on

---

[13] A. de Falloux, *Mémoires d'un royaliste*, 2 vols. (1888), vol. i, 582.
[14] Fornari to Antonelli, 9 Apr., 15 Aug., 16 Sept. 1849: ASV Parigi vol. 75.

good terms with some of the leading ex-Mennaisians like Montalembert and Lacordaire he found the whole Mennaisian current repugnant, and deeply distrusted the harshness and exclusiveness of the *école de l'Univers*; in the education debate he had several times had the experience of being attacked by Veuillot with the usual personal venom. Over the next decade Dupanloup was to fight a running battle with the ultramontanes, sometimes on three or four issues at once, while never ceasing to proclaim his devotion and obedience to the Holy See; eventually the Bishop of Orleans would come to be seen by the Roman Curia as one of its most intractable problems, worse even than the Archbishop of Paris.

The Council was to begin at Paris on 18 September 1849. During August it became generally known that decrees were likely on such awkward subjects as the right of bishops to resolve theological questions in their own dioceses and a possible code of conduct for the Catholic lay press. Fornari knew that Rome's reaction might well be slow and hesitant and that it would be more effective if a critique of the Council's proceedings could be mounted by a French theologian. He found his man in the militantly ultramontane circle led by R.-P. Gaultier at the Saint-Esprit seminary, which trained priests for the foreign missions. There were not many French experts in conciliar procedure, as it was well over a century since the last provincial council had been held, but one of Gaultier's group, the abbé Bouix, happened to be a specialist.[15] Fornari commissioned Bouix to write a study of conciliar practice to dampen the enthusiasm of the gallican bishops in all provinces by reminding them that their freedom of action was strictly limited by canon law and precedent. Significantly, although Bouix was a more learned and substantial figure than the amateur theologians of *L'Univers*, and was himself deputy editor of the small Catholic journal *La Voix de la Vérité*, he and Fornari both recognized that their effort would be wasted unless it was printed in *L'Univers*. Bouix approached Veuillot and arranged to publish a series of articles under the general heading 'Des Conciles provinciaux'. The first two, on 3 and 7 September, dealt mainly with the membership of councils and showed that it was quite normal, historically, for the bishops to be outnumbered

---

[15] On Fornari's relations with the Saint-Esprit circle, Hédouville, 'Romains et gallicans'; E. Naz, 'Bouix', *Dictionnaire de Droit canonique*, vol. ii, 970.

by theologians, mitred abbots, and certain office-holders of dioceses who had a canonical right to attend. Sibour was already in difficulties over the membership. He had intended to invite the Archbishop of Sens and his two suffragans to Paris, as their own province was too small to hold a proper council, but Fornari had pointed out that this would be irregular. Since there had to be theologians and representatives of the diocesan clergy Sibour made sure that he invited mainly gallicans: three Sulpicians, three senior metropolitan *curés*, and the advisers to his own household; the only ultramontanes were two very moderate Jesuits, Ravignan and Rubillon, the latter a consultor to the Roman Index but a model of tact and conciliation. The meetings were to be held in the seminary of Saint-Sulpice.

On 9 September *L'Univers* published a leaked report that regardless of the nominal membership only the bishops would vote on the decrees. Bouix replied in his next article, only four days before the Council was to assemble, with an awe-inspiring mass of citations from Pope Sixtus V and the learned canonists Reiffenstuhl and Schmalsgruber to show that all decrees of councils had to be submitted to Rome, not simply for confirmation but if necessary for revision by the Curia. The Council, he wrote, should expect to receive its decrees back with insertions, amendments, and even outright reversals.[16] A fourth article, timed to coincide with the Council's first debate on 20 September, laid down the limits of discussion: the bishops, it said, should not even mention the possibility of making decisions on matters of theology or discipline which might have wider implications and therefore came under the jurisdiction of Rome, and must confine themselves to purely local and diocesan matters.

At the *archevêché* these lectures from a newspaper on the limited competence of bishops were received with absolute fury and contributed to making the Council more defiant in tone than it might otherwise have been. Its decrees amounted to a manifesto of gallican churchmanship. The clergy were urged to accept all reasonable forms of government, including republicanism, but to remain aloof from active politics. It was decided in principle that

---

[16] D. Bouix, 'Des Conciles provinciaux', *L'Univers* (3–20 Sept. 1849, and an addendum on 28 Sept.) These articles were the basis for his more detailed book *Du Concile provincial*, published in Rome in 1850.

more effort should be made to recruit university graduates and
that priests should study for a bachelor's degree in theology and
canon law, and receive better training in parish management. A
committee was set up to examine the proliferation of superstitious
practices and dubious miracles like those of Rimini and La
Salette; the Council resolved not to discuss the Immaculate
Conception. The Catholic press was warned to leave theological
matters to the hierarchy and not to try and lead the Church of
France in arbitrarily chosen directions. In the plainest decree the
bishops were declared to be perfectly competent to judge
intellectual and theological affairs in their dioceses, and to have
the power in their own right to absolve from heresy. Although a
good deal was said about the Church, Rome was scarcely
mentioned except for a vague promise 'to obey the dogmatic
authority of the Holy See', and a very cautious statement
accepting the introduction of the Roman liturgy at some
convenient time in the future. Sibour's opening address paid a
formal compliment to Rome which 'deserves our subordination,
love and respect . . . it is the foundation-stone without which the
whole edifice would crumble', but compared to the fulsome
language expected when referring to the Holy See this was
almost a snub, the foundation-stone metaphor carefully chosen
to suggest motionless weight and permanence rather than
energetic activity. At the closing ceremony Sibour announced
that the decrees of the Council would be 'laid at the feet of the
Holy Father' but did not add 'so that they can be amended.'[17]

At the end of March 1850 the decrees were returned after
having been passed through the fine Curial mill. Sibour's
omission was repaired, and the bishops were now quoted as
having submitted their resolutions to the Holy See 'in order that
they be examined and revised'; a decree about the duty of the
Church to be above parties and forms of government was deleted
altogether; the bishops were instructed that they did not have the
power to absolve from heresy, and by implication that they were
not the arbiters of theological questions in their dioceses; and the
statement of obedience to the 'dogmatic authority' of Rome was
said to be sufficient: the members of the Council of Paris were
asked to sign an addendum that they would obey the 'disciplinary

[17] *L'Univers* (19–30 Sept. 1849).

constitutions' of the Holy See, or in other words the decisions of the Roman Curia. It was known that at the same time the Pope had written to congratulate Archbishop Gousset on the extremely ultramontane decrees produced by the Council of the Reims province.[18] Sibour told Fornari that he would protest formally to Rome at the insulting treatment given to Paris. Fornari warned the Holy See that to make even the slightest concession in this case would encourage the gallicans to think that 'by resisting one can obtain anything from Rome'. The ministère des Cultes declined to support a protest. Eventually Clausel de Montals persuaded Sibour to swallow the Roman amendments in the hope that it was a question of form rather than substance; but Dupanloup and some of the other bishops were inclined to be more pessimistic.[19]

The difficulties of the Council of Paris convinced Sibour's circle about the urgency of a project already in the air to start an alternative Catholic newspaper which might challenge the dominance of *L'Univers*. There had been two attempts to do this since the Revolution of 1848. The short-lived *Ère nouvelle*, directed by Lacordaire, Maret, and Ozanam, had tried to appeal to left-wing opinion by embracing republican democracy and preaching a social gospel, but it became increasingly confused during 1848 and had lost its momentum by the time of the June Days. In 1848 Dupanloup bought the old liberal-royalist weekly the *Ami de la religion* with the idea of turning it into an intellectual journal; he hoped to have regular contributions from German and English Catholics and to capture a broad lay readership. The editorial staff were old-fashioned men with fixed ideas and Dupanloup had not really succeeded in giving the paper a new identity or in raising its circulation, in spite of some very good individual articles, when he was made bishop of Orleans in August 1849. He was reluctant to give up the *Ami* and continued to direct it by mail from Orleans, which added to the paper's problems.

In the middle of 1849 Sibour himself decided to start a daily newspaper aimed in the first instance at the better-educated

[18] The Councils of Besançon, Lyons, Tours and Toulouse, whose decrees were cautious to the point of ambiguity, received equally cautious replies from Rome.
[19] Dupanloup, 'Rapport au Pape', Dupanloup/AN AB XIX 524; Fornari to Antonelli, 20 May 1850, *Bettoni*, 72–4; Martina, *Pio IX*, 503; Sevrin, *Clausel de Montals*, vol. ii, 552–3.

clergy, to be called the *Moniteur catholique*. His first choice as editor was the abbé Gerbet, who had recently returned from a ten-year residence in Rome to be one of the vicars-general of Paris, and had a considerable literary reputation for his writing on early Christianity; Thiers once said that Gerbet was the only member of the clergy whom he would consider proposing for the Académie française. Sibour was impressed with his talent and thought that it might actually be a tactical advantage to have an ultramontane editor for the paper, especially one of Gerbet's gentle and unassertive temperament, since he meant to have most of the writing done by gallicans. Darboy was to deal with social questions, Bautain with education, and Sibour invited the abbé Gabriel, one of Ginoulhiac's best pupils from Montpellier, to the vacant city parish of Saint-Merri so that he could write for the *Moniteur catholique* on theology; the other contributors were to be two moderate laymen, Bailly, an architect who worked for the ministère des Cultes, and Poujoulat, an experienced journalist and reviewer. Gerbet, however, lasted only long enough to write the prospectus. His closest friend, Mgr Salinis of Amiens, who had been Gerbet's 'guardian angel' at Saint-Sulpice,[20] was disturbed to see him being led into an enterprise where he would have to fight the battles of the *archevêché* and would fall under suspicion at Rome, and be savaged by Veuillot. He spirited Gerbet away to be consultant theologian to the Council of Reims and vicar-general of Amiens,[21] and the editorship of the *Moniteur catholique* passed to Darboy.

Just before the first issue was to appear on 1 January 1850 Sibour invited the editorial staff of *L'Univers* to a reception at the *archevêché* in order to explain that there should be no animosity between the two papers. Veuillot remained ironically silent for most of the evening, and did not reply when Darboy made some complimentary remarks about *L'Univers*. Sibour tried to lighten the atmosphere by telling the story—he told it well, Veuillot had to admit—of how the new ministre des Cultes, Lanjuinais, had given permission for the Council of Paris to be held, and on being told that under the Republic the Church was not obliged to ask for permission said: 'Oh well, I give permission *quand même*'. He

---

[20] Each senior student was made responsible for the welfare of a first-year seminarian; many lifelong friendships began in this way.

[21] The episode is described in Ladoue, *Vie de Mgr Gerbet*, vol. ii, 253 f.

then described the purpose of the *Moniteur catholique* more or less in the terms of Gerbet's prospectus: it would discuss the history and the achievements of Catholicism in such a way as to appeal to the educated mind, and deal with broad political and social questions 'on a high level, dissociating ourselves from all passionate polemic and from all personal discussion'. Veuillot could not resist: 'I understand perfectly, Monseigneur. The *Moniteur* will be Mary and entertain in the salon while *L'Univers* will be Martha and do the rough housework'. He told the Nuncio afterwards that Sibour spoke about Catholicism with an irritating lack of simplicity, his sentences being a maze of qualifications and subordinate clauses 'in which he entangled himself like a silkworm in its cocoon'; he was well-meaning but foolish, not nearly intelligent enough to succeed as Archbishop of Paris. 'You should not complain about that', said Fornari.[22]

If the *archevêché* had persevered with the *Moniteur catholique* it might have done a great deal to improve the confidence of the clergy. The paper printed very impressive articles, conservative in tone but well researched, on education, the democratic franchise, the problems of the working class, and other social questions, and it began to issue special supplements which were in effect refresher courses on ecclesiastical matters like the Concordat, Church–State jurisprudence, European religious history and the management of Church property. With regard to Rome the policy was subtle but clear enough. Sibour had learned his lesson on the temporal power and the *Moniteur* treated the papal restoration with deference, only occasionally dropping a hint about the need for reform and modernization at Rome. A review of a book on Bossuet was taken as an opportunity to stress the traditional devotion of the French Church to the papacy;[23] but whenever the disciplinary structure of the Church was discussed there was a firm rejection of the idea that the decisions of Roman congregations had any authority in France. The *Moniteur* wrote that the Roman Index, for example, could perhaps be excused for banning a book by the Protestant theologian Athanase Coquerel, *Le Christianisme expérimental*, from circulation in the Papal States, but to attempt to ban it also in

---

[22] Veuillot, *D'après nature*, *Oeuvres* x, 487–90; *Louis Veuillot*, vol. ii, chap. 15; J. A. Foulon, *Histoire . . . de Mgr Darboy* (1889), 107.

[23] *Moniteur catholique* (24 Apr. 1850).

France was not only beyond the competence of the Index but a stupid and provocative act, 'a failure of intelligence and Christian charity'.[24]

The sudden end of the *Moniteur catholique* in June 1850 is something of a mystery. Circulation was small but promising, and Veuillot had refrained from attacking it directly. But on 10 May Darboy resigned as editor, evidently after a dispute over policy,[25] and on 14 June Sibour announced that he now 'recognized the disadvantages of episcopal patronage given to one journal in particular', and that in future he would 'protect with equal benevolence all religious newspapers which show themselves worthy of the name'. The *Moniteur* was absorbed into the abbé Migne's *La Voix de la Vérité*, whose line was very close to that of *L'Univers*. This left only the *Ami de la religion* to struggle against Veuillot's ascendancy over the Catholic press. Dupanloup continued to direct the *Ami* from Orleans, even after he had formally sold the paper to the abbé Debeauvais and Charles de Riancey in August 1850 and had appointed the abbé Sisson as editor; and over the next two or three years he received all the incoming correspondence, including complaints from some bishops that the *Ami* was too ultramontane and from others that it was too gallican, advice from one well-wisher that the paper should try to be more lively—'it is no use if the truth is wrapped in the shroud of a glacial style as if on its way to its own funeral'—and from another that the *Ami* should be 'a grave, weighty journal' like the *Civiltà Cattolica* in Rome.[26] The essential point, the distinguished Sulpician Galais told Dupanloup in June 1850, was that there should be at least one journal to express a moderate attitude towards Rome, avoiding the temptation of parliamentary gallicanism on the one hand and 'the yelpings of the Mennaisians' on the other. Dupanloup's editor Sisson was too junior, Galais said, to command respect in the clergy;[27] but the problem of the *Ami* was more fundamental. Everybody

[24] *Moniteur catholique* (31 May 1850).

[25] Internal evidence suggests that he may have wanted to comment more trenchantly on the ultramontane Council of Reims but was told by Sibour to confine himself to summarizing its decrees: *Moniteur catholique* (6–10 May 1850).

[26] Letters in Dupanloup/BN 24712: dossier *Ami de la religion*, especially from Cognat, Méthivier, Valroger, and Place.

[27] Galais to Dupanloup, 13 June 1850 (letter approved by two other senior Sulpicians, Gosselin and Renaudet), Dupanloup/BN 24712.

connected with it, from Dupanloup downwards, was anxious to remain in favour with Rome; its gallicanism had to be very discreet, and this meant that it was engaged in a hopelessly unequal contest with *L'Univers* whose editor could put the Roman case as trenchantly as he liked.

The momentum of the ultramontane current was increasing. As the *Moniteur catholique* episode was coming to its disappointing end the Gallican Church was being challenged by two important ultramontane initiatives, one concerning the adoption of the Roman Liturgy, and the other concerning the power of the Index in France.

VII

The campaign for the Roman liturgy:
the first phase

BOTH gallicans and ultramontanes understood that the characteristic liturgical style of the French Church was an important
element in its identity, and that a successful attack on the
gallican liturgies in the nineteenth century would undermine the
gallican position on matters of doctrine and discipline. The
essence of the French style was regional diversity: there had been
liturgical variations between dioceses at least since the Carolingian
epoch, and some regions could trace their prayers and rituals as
far back as the fourth century. There were many points of
difference from the Roman liturgy, some of them perceptible only
to keen Latinists but others quite substantial, changes in the
order of Mass, different readings from the Epistles and Gospels,
different saints commemorated; the prayers at weddings and
funerals contained many local variants; and the music was
clearly French. The papacy had made efforts in the eighth
century, and again in the eleventh, twelfth, and sixteenth
centuries to introduce some uniformity but without ever insisting
on this as a matter of discipline. In the seventeenth and early
eighteenth centuries, the golden age of power and dignity for the
Gallican Church, the most important dioceses codified their
liturgies, preserving the ancient gallican rite as far as possible but
adding many new prayers in the rather florid Latin style of the
time.

In the general revision of diocesan boundaries at the Concordat
some of the new bishops found that they had inherited as many
as six different liturgies; one diocese had nine. Article 39 of the
Concordat of 1801, prescribing 'only one liturgy and one
catechism for the entire Church of France', represents Napoleon's
own view that national unity required a uniform style of religious
observance, but the First Consul uncharacteristically neglected
to follow the matter through to a conclusion, and the project

foundered for want of a single liturgy that would have been acceptable to the whole of the new episcopate. One solution put forward at the time was that France should adopt the missal and breviary currently in use at Rome. The bishop of Orleans, Mgr Bernier, who had been very active in the negotiation of the Concordat, made a surreptitious attempt to introduce a Roman-style liturgy; he proposed to Cardinal Consalvi that if Rome would draw up a liturgy based on its own observance he would undertake to have it adopted by the Gallican Church without revealing its origin. Consalvi declined this offer out of prudence, but in any case Bernier's initiative had no hope of success because the *rit romain* was repugnant to the majority of French bishops.[1] The mosaic of texts which made up the Roman liturgy constituted a direct affront to gallican opinion in its deliberate choice of scriptural and traditional readings which emphasized the power of the Holy See—the council of constitutional bishops in 1801 had drawn attention to several points where the Roman liturgy even altered the meaning of texts by the judicious omission of key words, leaving out the word *animas*, for example, from the phrase *animas ligandi atque solvendi pontificium tradidisti* in a Collect of Leo IV—and an indirect affront to the French in that the 'rubbish-heap of apocryphal legends' in the Roman breviary, devotions to dubious saints like Aldobrand and Theodoric 'whose miracles cannot decently be repeated', left no room in the liturgical calender for heroes of the national churches of Europe, More and Fisher, Gerson, Palafox, Gault of Marseilles, or Alain de Solminhiac.[2] The liturgy of Paris was agreed to be excellent, but a general adoption of the *rit parisien* would have implied recognition of the primacy of Paris which the rest of the episcopate was not prepared to concede.

There were persuasive arguments, however, for retaining the old diocesan liturgies as symbols of the continuity of the Gallican Church after the hiatus of the Revolutionary period, and the break in Catholic practice gave an opportunity to make a general assessment of the worship in each diocese, to prune away meaningless excrescences, and to decide that the Church should certainly keep those liturgies which were either of great antiquity

---

[1] J. Leflon, *E. A. Bernier, évêque d'Orléans*, 2 vols. (1938), vol. ii, 54–6.
[2] H. Grégoire, Constitutional Bishop of Blois, *Traité de l'uniformité et de l'amélioration de la Liturgie* (1801), 26–8, 37–8, 78–9.

like the beautiful archaic rituals of Lyons and Besançon, or distinguished examples of seventeenth- and eighteenth-century gallican piety.[3] During the Empire and Restoration periods only eighteen dioceses out of eighty adopted the Roman missal and breviary. Thirty-five created liturgies of their own by reconciling the various elements that survived in their regions, and the remaining twenty-seven agreed to copy the rite of some other diocese which had a particularly distinguished liturgical tradition. Most of them followed Paris, Lyons, or Chartres; and this was how matters stood in 1840.[4]

The movement which was to sweep away the gallican liturgies began in the Mennaisian circle of La Chenaie. Amongst the young men in Lamennais's entourage studying various aspects of ecclesiastical history and religious art, Prosper-Louis Guéranger had been commissioned especially to prove by documentary research that the Roman liturgy represented the original form of worship surviving from apostolic times, or at least from the times of the great reforming Popes, and was therefore the basis of unity to which all the national churches should conform. He published a preliminary statement of his findings in the *Mémorial catholique* in 1830,[5] but then had to keep silent for a few years after the disaster of the *Avenir* episode and the defection of Lamennais from the Church. During the 1830s Guéranger was able to raise money to buy the Benedictine abbey of Solesmes which had been deserted since the Revolution, and established himself in it with three companions. In 1837, when the community had grown to twenty-five, it was given canonical recognition as the restored Benedictine Order of France, and Guéranger was made abbot;

---

[3] Chartres and Saint-Denis, for example, decided to keep the custom of saying mass in Greek on Holy Thursday, which had persisted since the early Middle Ages. Local congregations would not give up ancient ceremonies which 'commemorated in perpetuity' the deliverance of their city from plague or foreign invasion. Some of the peculiar rites which disappeared after 1802 were worthy of Beachcomber: at Laon the priests who chanted the Epistle and Gospel were supposed to receive an immediate cash payment from the bishop before leaving the altar. In another cathedral the celebrant at high mass was kissed on the shoulder by the deacon, and then in turn kissed the bishop on the shoulder; nobody was quite sure what this symbolized.

[4] AN F. 19. 5434: *Livres liturgiques, rituels, bréviaires et imagerie pieuse;* Dom H. Leclercq, 'Liturgies néo-gallicanes', *Dictionnaire d'archéologie chrétienne et de liturgie* ix, cols. 1636–1729; R. E. Balfour, 'Note on the history of the Breviary in France', *Journal of Theological Studies* xxxiii (1932); Olivier Rousseau, *Histoire du mouvement liturgique* (1945), chaps. 1–2.

[5] *Mémorial catholique*, four articles from 28 Feb. to 31 July 1830.

and in 1840 he issued the first volume of his *Institutions liturgiques*. Guéranger's *Institutions* is one of the monuments of Catholic romanticism, embodying all the yearning of the Mennaisian generation for a revival of medieval Christendom and their distaste for the Enlightenment and the classical tradition. When Guéranger looked at the French liturgies he saw the products of a neo-classical age, a period of spurious intellectual brilliance which in the end had almost brought the Catholic Church to ruin. The 'impious' bishops who had drawn up the gallican liturgies, he said, had been influenced not only by Jansenism, which was bad enough, but by classicism and the temptations of essentially pagan eloquence. Even laymen in the eighteenth-century parlements had claimed the right to supervise the amendment of sacred texts. To make room for exercises in their impeccable Latin they had discarded verses by the Popes Saint Leo and Saint Gregory. The prayers and hymns in the gallican breviaries were humanistic rather than religious, and treated God as the Greeks had treated their deities, with casual familiarity. Some of the breviaries had been provided with illustrations in the style of the eighteenth-century pastoral, and Guéranger noted especially the Paris breviary in which the Virgin Mary, he said, looked like a lady with whom one could strike up a conversation. Religious imagery should be solemn and hieratic, or, in his own phrase, 'trans-human'. Guéranger and the *école de Solesmes* believed strongly in the idea of apostolic origins: according to this hypothesis, Christianity had been brought to Gaul by missionaries sent personally by Saint Peter and the second Pope, Saint Clement, and Gaul had thus depended on Rome for ritual as well as doctrine from the very earliest centuries. In that simple age of austere uniformity before local variants and impurities had appeared, all the scattered Gaulish dioceses had followed an original Roman liturgy; it was the plain duty of modern bishops to return to it.[6]

The *Institutions liturgiques* provoked a fierce resistance. Throughout the next decade, as Guéranger pursued his campaign, he was attacked by Cardinal d'Astros in a pamphlet of 1843, *L'Église de*

---

[6] The first volume of the *Institutions liturgiques* (1840) contains the burden of Guéranger's argument; the two later volumes in 1850–1 provide mainly additional examples and illustrations, and a discussion of ecclesiastical music. Cf. A. Houtin, *La Controverse de l'apostolicité des églises de France au XIXe siècle* (1903), chaps. 1–4.

France injustement flétrie, a *Lettre aux curés de Paris* by Archbishop Affre, a particularly well-written *Humble remontrance à Dom Guéranger* by the influential vicar-general of Angers, the abbé Bernier, and in dozens of pastorals, open letters, and editorials. The educated laity were sceptical. Circourt told Nassau Senior:

The gallican liturgy is not a pure kind of worship, but it is a tolerable one; some parts of it are excellent and there are very few that are objectionable. The Roman liturgy assumed its present form in the sixteenth century, when the Council of Trent was stereotyping the abuses that during fourteen hundred years had been encrusting Christianity. It is full of the most childish legends, absurdities, and indecencies . . . We are relapsing into paganism.[7]

The debate within the clergy revealed itself as a contest between two aspects of the romantic movement, the ultramontanes putting forward their vision of a supranational Christendom, and the gallicans arguing for a Chateaubriandian romanticism in which religion was intimately linked to *le pays*. Any national church, the gallicans said, had to have its roots deep in the national history, and its liturgical practices should reflect the national character. Guéranger and the ultramontanes were inclined to laugh at the diocesan liturgies because they contained devotions to local saints and local miracles: they were missing the point that Christianity in France had to be an organic growth in French soil. The clergy of Arras, for example, were reluctant to give up their missal which commemorated ten local saints, 'a tribute to the supernatural fertility of the soil of Artois', as one priest remarked; 'we have only to stoop to gather a rich harvest of saints'.[8] The liturgy of Tours could be traced back to Saint Gregory of Tours, and was so beautiful and historically interesting, the archbishop claimed, that even the sceptical bourgeoisie of the city came to mass for aesthetic reasons.[9] The older gallican liturgies went back to the ancient forests of Gaul, to the Church of Charlemagne and Saint Louis; and the more recent liturgies of the seventeenth and eighteenth centuries were the legacy of the age of Bossuet and Mabillon, expressing the French genius in Latin prose of great beauty and distinction.

[7] Senior, *Conversations with M. Thiers, M. Guizot*, vol. ii, 76–7.
[8] Guillemant, *Parisis*, vol. iii, 90.
[9] Paguelle de Follenay, *Vie du Cardinal Guibert*, 2 vols. (1896) vol. ii, 234–5.

Guéranger was 'an arsonist' who wanted to make a bonfire of French religious literature;[10] 'always the same pretentions and presumptions that characterize the Mennaisian', wrote Mgr Bouvier of Le Mans: '. . . altering, falsifying, and exaggerating the facts in order to arrive at his goal of discrediting the French episcopate'.[11]

In its first few years the liturgical campaign made little headway. More than sixty bishops had declared themselves publicly against the *Institutions*, and the opposition was so vigorous that Guéranger became dispirited. By the mid-forties, however, there were enough ultramontanes in the episcopate to give a lead, and one by one Parisis of Langres, Gousset of Reims, Depéry of Gap, Wicart of Fréjus, and Georges-Massonnais of Périgùeux announced that their dioceses were adopting the *rit romain*; and once this movement had begun it received enthusiastic support from the Nuncio in Paris. Mgr Fornari, more forward than Rome on this as on so many subjects, understood the political importance of the liturgy and was ready to send to Rome the most flattering reports on bishops who showed the proper spirit, and to describe as 'neo-jansenist' and 'anti-Roman' anyone who wanted to preserve his diocesan rite; it became known that the warmth of one's reception at the Nunciature depended on one's attitude towards the breviary. But the real turning-point came when *L'Univers* began to take an interest in liturgy. In 1845 Melchior du Lac entered Solesmes as a postulant and began to work closely with Guéranger on liturgical research. He kept in touch with his old colleagues in Paris and in November 1846 *L'Univers* printed the first of a series of his articles on the Roman breviary, the decisions of the Congregation of Rites, and the heretical doctrines implicit in 'the liturgies of the Enlightenment'.[12] Veuillot himself was content to leave the technical details to du Lac but he saw that it was the ideal issue for embarrassing the gallican hierarchy. From 1846 onwards *L'Univers* turned the liturgical question into a referendum in

---

[10] The *curé* of Saint-Martin-Église (Nord), quoted by A. Houtin, *Un dernier gallican, Henri Bernier*, 451.

[11] A. Ledru, *Dom Guéranger et Mgr Bouvier, évêque du Mans* (1911), 121.

[12] 'Détails historiques et statistiques sur les liturgies', *L'Univers* (3 Nov.–15 Dec. 1846). The articles appeared in book form in 1849 and were reviewed by the abbé Darboy in *Le Correspondant* (6 Mar. 1849). Some of du Lac's correspondence on the liturgy question is in V/BN 24633.

which the bishops were invited to declare themselves for or against the Roman style, a marvellous spectacle for the lower clergy. Using his network of correspondents Veuillot was able to report that the diocese of X . . . was on the verge of 'returning' to the Roman missal and breviary; that the bishop had received encouraging letters from clergy in the neighbouring diocese of Y . . . which had recently gone over, to universal joy and acclamation; that local resistance was weakening; and eventually that a decision had been taken. In each case it was treated as a symbolic surrender of gallican independence, celebrated with pages of rhetoric about 'the spirit of unity and submission to the See of Peter' and 'the great family of Christians united in obedience to its loving Father'. *L'Univers* had no difficulty in creating the impression that on the liturgy issue the gallican bishops were struggling against an irresistible groundswell of opinion in the lower clergy. There were indeed many genuine enthusiasts in the parishes who had been influenced by the Mennaisian current, like the abbé Haigneré of Arras who recalled in his memoirs forty years afterwards that 'the wind of change was blowing towards a renovation of all things in the French Church'; it was a great moment in the history of religious art, a return to the true sources of Christian inspiration: 'we dreamed of nothing but Gothic architecture, medieval vestments, Roman plainchant of the thirteenth century, the restoration of the religious orders and of the ancient diocesan boundaries';[13] but the liturgy served also as a focus for many discontents. In every conflict between an *évêché* and its seminary, a bishop and his cathedral chapter or a vicar-general and a group of dissident *curés* the underdogs would sooner or later make a point of declaring their enthusiasm for the *rit romain*. The ministère des Cultes noted with disquiet that parish priests who knew very little about medieval history or literature were using the issue to harass their superiors, and that *L'Univers* was giving wide publicity to dioceses like Evreux, Tarbes, Nevers, and Pamiers where there had been petitions from the lower clergy in favour of Romanization.[14] The degree to which it was a matter of anti-

---

[13] Quoted by Guillemant, *Parisis*, vol. iii, 71.

[14] *L'Univers* (26 Sept. 1849) on Nevers; AN F. 19. 2585 (Tarbes); Fornari to Prefect of the Congregation of Rites, on the Tarbes diocese, 27 July 1849, ASV Parigi vol. 76; AN F. 19. 2522 (Evreux); AN F. 19. 2554 (Pamiers).

episcopal feeling became clear when in those dioceses where the bishop himself was an ultramontane and wanted to introduce the Roman liturgy the agitation was mostly in the opposite direction: one of the complaints in a petition of the clergy against the bumptious Dreux-Brézé at Moulins was that he 'displayed tactless haste in introducing the Roman rite in the diocese',[15] and Doney, Berteaud, and Pie had to struggle for years against tenacious opposition.

Fornari and the French ultramontanes knew, however, that their main problem might be to persuade Rome itself to support the campaign. The Popes in the nineteenth century had taken a relatively moderate line on liturgical matters. In 1842 Gregory XVI actually tried to dissuade Mgr Gousset from abolishing the diocesan liturgy of Reims: the Popes, he said, had always accepted any local liturgy which had been used for more than two hundred years, and 'it would be in any case a difficult and embarrassing task to uproot these customs implanted in your region for so long a time'.[16] As late as 1846 he told the vicar-general of Nevers: 'I would be very pleased, certainly, to see all the dioceses in France return successively to the unity of the Roman liturgy, but I understand the difficulties in the way and I would never order it; I will never order it.'[17] Pius IX thought that variations in the liturgy were a minor problem compared to the more serious symptoms of gallicanism in French textbooks of ecclesiology and canon law. He surprised Guéranger by saying that while he approved the return of the French to the Roman liturgy he had 'no wish at all that rites and prayers consecrated by long practice should be proscribed'.[18]

When Mgr Corboli Bussi dealt with the liturgical question in his confidential report to the Pope in 1849, he had to admit that the French were exasperating. On the one hand, he said, they claimed to be following traditions lost in the mists of antiquity, the diocese of Carcassonne, for example, justifying its adoption of the Parisian rite in 1843 by citing the canons of a provincial council in the fifth century, while on the other hand appealing to the 'two hundred year rule' to validate liturgies introduced in the

[15] AN F. 19. 2541 (Moulins).
[16] Papal Brief of 6 Aug. 1842, in *Corboli Bussi*, articolo vi.
[17] Martin, *La Nonciature de Paris*, 89.
[18] Robert, *Dom Guéranger chez Pie IX*, 39.

age of scepticism. The permeation of Jansenist influence could be
seen, he said, in the way the archbishops of Paris and other
prelates in the eighteenth century had struck out of their
breviaries any mention of the primacy of Rome or of Roman
devotion to 'The Great Mother of God'. Nevertheless, there were
practical problems. Unlike Fornari, who liked to give the
impression in his reports of a generally submissive hierarchy with
only a small minority of troublemakers, Corboli Bussi estimated
realistically that about twenty bishops were in favour of
Romanization; perhaps another twenty would stand up for their
local liturgies, and the rest would do whatever was opportune
and convenient. They would obey a direct command; but how
embarrassing it would be, he wrote, if it proved impossible to put
the command into practice. Most of the French clergy disliked
the Roman liturgy because it was too long, and would have to be
learned, and their congregations would be very reluctant to give
up prayers and ceremonies they had known for generations.
Neither the government nor the municipalities would pay for
tens of thousands of missals and breviaries to be reprinted. In the
face of these difficulties, he concluded, it would have been more
sensible for Guéranger to have addressed the argument of the
Institutions liturgiques privately to the bishops instead of publishing
it as an open challenge. The whole campaign in future must
proceed with tact and patience; Rome should leave it to the local
bishop to decide the opportune moment in each diocese.[19] Pius
IX, who received Corboli Bussi's report early in 1850, appears to
have given exactly this advice to those French bishops who
visited Rome soon after the papal restoration.[20]

Patience was certainly required in dealing with the Congregation
of Rites, which as it happened was one of the most lethargic
departments in the Roman administration, a by-word for
infuriating delay. It was used to a very slow pace of business;
there had been only eighteen communications with France in
three hundred years.[21] Its committees met very infrequently;
octogenarian cardinals dozed through important debates; papers
were lost, or taken away by interested parties; all work came to a

[19] *Corboli Bussi*, articolo vi.
[20] For example to Mgr Rivet of Dijon: Chevallier, *Mgr Rivet*, 81–2.
[21] F. X. Marette, Introduction to the *Dictionnaire des décrets* in the series edited by
the abbé Migne (1852), 51.

standstill in the Roman summer vacation. After the upheavals of
the Roman Republic, and with the main administrative buildings
in Rome taken over as 'strategic points' by the French
occupation army, the Congregation was in even more of a chaotic
mess than usual. Bishops who had convinced themselves of the
need for the Roman liturgy and had managed to overcome the
resistance in their dioceses found that they had to fight a fresh
battle with the Congregation of Rites. Mgr Meirieu of Digne,
badgered by his clergy to introduce the Roman ritual, agreed
that he would do it if he received a formal letter from Rome
approving the change. Fornari urged the Congregation to give
special attention to this matter; but there was no reply.[22] The
Bishop of Blois wrote a similar request in January 1849, adding
that if Blois went over to the Roman rite the example would have
a great effect in the neighbouring diocese of Orleans. Fornari
wrote on his behalf in May, twice more in August, and twice in
December 1849, each time adding fresh reasons: the clergy were
in favour of offering the seminary of Blois to the Jesuits, who were
known to use the Roman liturgy; the diocesan breviary had gone
out of print and the publishers wanted to know which version
they should provide; and so on.[23] Nothing at all came back from
the Congregation of Rites. Corboli Bussi included a summary of
the Blois case in his report, and urged Rome to act without delay.
In 1852 Fornari's successor Garibaldi was still sending reminders
about Blois; eventually the diocese adopted the *rit romain* in 1853
without having received any clear instruction from Rome.[24] The
breviary of Quimper was sent for approval in May 1848, and had
not reappeared three years later.[25] A large part of Fornari's
correspondence was taken up with reminders and requests for
action, mostly without result. The momentum might have been
lost altogether had it not been for the constant pressure kept up

[22] Mgr Meirieu of Digne to Fornari, 12 Dec. 1849, and Fornari to Antonelli, 19
Dec. 1849: ASV Parigi vol. 75 (1797) and vol. 76 (1449); also AN F. 19. 2519 (Digne:
dossier Meirieu).
[23] ASV Parigi vol. 75 (1521–1797).
[24] Garibaldi, 24 Apr. 1852, ASV Francia 1856. A good deal of correspondence
from 1848 to 1852 on the liturgical question has found its way into the archives for
1855 and 1856.
[25] Garibaldi, 2 Apr. 1851. Some similar cases: letter of the bishop of Tarbes to
Fornari, 16 Oct. 1849; Fornari to Antonelli, 28 July 1848 and 16 Oct. 1849; Antonelli
to Mgr Frattini, Promoter at the Congregation of Rites, 5 Nov. 1849; also the case of
Montauban in Garibaldi's dispatch of 13 Mar. 1852: all in ASV: Francia 1856.

by *L'Univers*. By the time of the provincial councils in late 1849 and 1850 Veuillot and du Lac had created an atmosphere of conflict and impending crisis over the liturgical issue, and every bishop felt that his attitude was being assessed both at Rome and in the presbyteries. Some of the leading gallicans were inclined to give way on what could be interpreted as a relatively harmless point. Rome might very well be satisfied by this symbolic gesture of loyalty, they thought, and might leave the French in peace to hold their traditional opinions on the deeper question of authority in the Church; but there was also an argument for preserving the gallican liturgy precisely because it was symbolic. At the councils, however, nobody wanted to make a speech that could be construed as being disrespectful to Rome. Unanimous resolutions were passed that all dioceses would examine the feasibility of introducing the Roman missal and breviary at some suitable time in the next few years, not, it was implied, because the *rit romain* was admitted to be superior but because the change would please Pius IX; but some bishops who voted for these resolutions had no intention of making any change.

The resolution of the Council of Paris in 1849 that the province would 'move towards' the adoption of the *rit romain* was the only one of its decrees that Mgr Fornari liked. Although the suffragans of Paris were not enthusiastic about it he knew their dioceses well, especially Blois, and expected that all of them would have been Romanized within four or five years.[26] The problem was Paris itself, because it was well known that Sibour was prepared to use all kinds of delaying tactics to keep the archdiocesan rite. The Parisian liturgy was perhaps the most irritating of all to the ultramontanes, being not even two hundred years old, the work indeed of Guéranger's *bête noire* Archbishop de Vintimille, the very paradigm of those courtier-prelates who had classicized the liturgies in the eighteenth century, and it was followed by sixteen other dioceses, so that anything done to discredit the *rit parisien* would have had an incalculable effect throughout the entire Gallican Church. An opportunity arose in April 1850. The last action of Falloux before retiring from the ministère des Cultes had been to fill the See of Moulins by nominating the abbé de Dreux-Brézé, an extreme ultramontane-

---

[26] Fornari to Antonelli, 29 Sept. 1849, ASV: Parigi, vol. 75.

legitimist who had been a fellow student of Fornari in Rome. Dreux-Brézé asked if he could be consecrated by Fornari, and in Paris instead of in his metropolitan cathedral of Sens. Sibour said that rather than having the Papal Nuncio performing ceremonies in Notre-Dame, which would have given the impression that Rome had already taken over the archdiocese, he would consecrate Dreux-Brézé himself. The occasion chosen was the rather melancholy gathering of the suffragan bishops to receive from Rome the amended and bowdlerized version of the Council of Paris decrees; several other distinguished visitors were invited, and Sibour began the ceremony in the presence of three archbishops, eight bishops, the heads of five religious orders, and a large assemblage of laymen. At the culminating point, when the oath of consecration was read out to Dreux-Brézé, he claimed not to recognize the wording: it was not Roman. One of the celebrants explained to him in a whisper that the formula had been used by the French Church for many centuries. Dreux-Brézé insisted: it was not the Roman formula. To avoid a scene before the high altar of Notre-Dame, Sibour had to send a vicar-general off to find a copy of the Roman ceremonial. Dreux-Brézé later made a considerable fuss over donating a beautifully bound Roman missal to the archdiocese of Paris.[27]

The Moulins consecration may be seen as the end of the first phase of the liturgy conflict. A second phase after 1850 was to be linked with the use of the Roman Index in France.

---

[27] AN F. 19. 2541 (Moulins); F. Laroque, 'Mgr de Dreux-Brézé et la restauration liturgique', *Ephemerides liturgicae* lxxvii (1963); *L'Univers* (14–15 Apr. 1850); Delatte, *Dom Guéranger*, vol. ii, 18.

VIII

The Roman Index

The école de L'Univers *in 1850*

THROUGHOUT 1850 Veuillot was more provocative than ever. Ten years of religious polemic had hardened his opinions about the duty of a Catholic journalist: 'I believed', he wrote towards the end of his life, 'that I was at the same time a soldier and a judge, and that I had no business making myself likeable, because my authority was not given to me for that'; he added that in the circumstances it was never too much trouble being unpleasant.[1] 'When it comes to doctrine I would fight my own brother, and love the man who murders me.'[2] He did not hate moderate Catholics, he explained: 'hatred has never entered my soul at all, but contempt has never left it. Contempt is clamped and screwed tightly there.'[3] Contemptible behaviour was to be expected from parliamentarians and professors, but surely the greatest disappointment for real Catholics was the cowardly verbiage of the French bishops who were talking, for example, about an epoch of transition in modern society when it was useless to try to impose religion by coercion: as he wrote of Sibour, 'political calculation and the ambiguities of human weakness just where one ought to find shining courage, perseverance, and candour'.[4] Whenever he had to face the awkward point that membership of the Catholic Church entailed obedience to the hierarchy he stepped easily into his habitual role as the privileged outsider. As editor of governmental newspapers before his conversion he had managed to avoid being controlled by prefects, and as Guizot's special emissary to Algeria he had been in the heart of the military establishment without having had to obey the orders of generals and colonels; having joined the Church to be the Pope's crusader against the Enlightenment he had no intention of being harnessed and bridled by diocesan bishops. Catholic journalists, he told Theodore Foisset, were

---

[1] *Louis Veuillot*, vol. iv, 754.   [2] *Correspondance* vol. v, 369.
[3] *Les Odeurs de Paris, Oeuvres* xi, xv.   [4] *D'après nature, Oeuvres* x, 490.

really like the orders of friars, not subject to the bishops of particular diocese but acting as an international papal militia, 'asking only to serve the truth in humility and poverty'.[5] *L'Univers* was 'lay, proletarian, and Roman'[6] and had nothing to do with bishops, although it was always extremely respectful and complimentary towards ultramontane bishops who understood their function as papal agents. The paper was not impressed by the general agreement that the Church should welcome the Loi Falloux in 1850. In spite of some reservations about co-operating with the *Université* the hierarchy knew that the Law represented a more favourable settlement than could have been expected at any time since the Revolution, and gave the Church a high degree of autonomy in conducting its own school system. Veuillot, du Lac and Roux-Lavergne, taking the absolutely intransigent line that it was a disgraceful compromise which only weakened the State educational system instead of dissolving it altogether, attacked every aspect of the Loi Falloux and did everything possible to affront bourgeois-liberal ideas on education. *L'Univers* renewed its satirical articles on the professors of the Sorbonne and the Collège de France, especially Victor Cousin whose teaching was described as lightweight, contradictory, and dishonest, and in April 1850, just after the Loi Falloux had passed the Assembly, printed a series of articles by Jules Morel on the Inquisition as the real answer to intellectual heterodoxy; Veuillot said defiantly that *L'Univers* was not trying to convert unbelievers but to prevent them from doing any further damage:[7] 'the greatest service that one can do for stupid people, in all charity, is to frighten them'.[8]

Observing the angry reaction in the secular press many leading churchmen, including even some of the ultramontane bishops, felt that *L'Univers* was prejudicing their cause at a moment when Catholics should have been united to exploit the advantages offered by the Loi Falloux. Veuillot and Morel were undermining the Church's claim to be a stabilizing element in

[5] Veuillot to Théodore Foisset, 12 Oct. 1850, *Correspondance*, vol. iii, 251.

[6] Veuillot used this phrase to several correspondents in the late forties.

[7] C. Lecigne, *Louis Veuillot* (1913), 163–4. Cf. Veuillot's letter to Mgr de Marguerye, 15 Feb. 1850, *Correspondance*, vol. iii, 122–6; Guillemant, *Parisis*, vol. ii, chaps. 15–17; J. K. Huckaby, 'Roman Catholic reaction to the Falloux Law', *French Historical Studies* (Fall 1965), 203–13.

[8] Veuillot to M. Terret, 12 Sept. 1850, *Correspondance*, vol. iii, 215.

society: in *L'Univers* each day catholicism was presented instead as a disruptive force, subverting French institutions and setting conservatives of different shades at one another's throats. Dom Guéranger had already warned Veuillot that his incessant abuse of the middle classes and their ideals might be taken by naïve readers as an attack on property and order, with unpredictable results.[9] Reading Veuillot and Roux-Lavergne on the Loi Falloux, du Lac on Church–State relations, and Morel on the usefulness of inquisitors, Louis de Kergorlay noted the essential similarity between the *école de l'Univers* and the extreme socialists, both groups believing in 'sudden Islamic conquests' followed by the use of force to suppress dissent.[10] Dupanloup's friend Albert du Boys, a historian of medieval law, wrote that one of the necessary conditions for reconstituting society after great upheavals like the fall of the Roman Empire or the Revolution of 1789 was public respect for Christian bishops; and 'here is Veuillot, terribly on the nose if you will excuse the expression . . . saying every day that the French bishops are no more than the prefects of the Holy See'.[11]

The ultramontanes and Rome in 1850

When the ultramontanes began their campaign in 1850 to persuade or provoke the Roman Index into acting against gallican theologians they could not have been completely confident of success. The potentially devastating weapon of the Index was effective only if everyone concerned agreed about the force of its decrees, and the gallicans were certain to raise all the old arguments against accepting decisions of Roman congregations; but it did not seem likely that they would have the steadiness of nerve to resist a direct challenge from the Index. A more serious problem was Rome itself, where the state of affairs since the Revolution of 1848 was seen by foreign ultramontanes as both highly encouraging and profoundly frustrating. It was clear enough, certainly, that Rome was now more hostile than ever

[9] Guéranger to Veuillot, 31 Dec. 1848, V/BN 24633.

[10] Kergorlay's notes on *veuillotisme* and socialism: Kergorlay/Arsenal 14091: 12 and 14094: 1–72.

[11] A. du Boys to Dupanloup, 5 Sept. 1850, Dupanloup/AN AB XIX 526; some letters in the same vein from Achille Lauras, Secretary-general of the Orleans Railway Company, who held some shares in *L'Univers*, are in this collection. See also J. Gadille, *Albert du Boys: ses souvenirs du Concile du Vatican* (1968).

towards liberal tendencies in politics and Church–State relations. The restored Roman government, although well aware that it could hardly survive for a day without the protective shield of the French military garrison, rejected all the advice offered by the French about the need for reform, and moved determinedly in the opposite direction. The theocratic constitution imposed on the Papal States by the *Motu proprio* of September 1849 made no clear distinction between sin and crime, and placed public affairs even more firmly in the hands of the clergy than had been the case in the time of Gregory XVI; it was said to be a model of Christian society which other Catholic states should try to imitate, but more thoughtful conservatives at Rome like Mgr Corboli Bussi could see that it was likely to give Catholicism a bad name.[12] There was little chance that the papacy would be prepared to understand the subtle intellectual problems of liberal and gallican churchmen in the modern European states. The papal court was surrounded by a close-knit Roman nobility and by Spanish and Austrian diplomats, pious grand dukes, Breton legitimists, aristocratic English converts, and *clercs nationaux* and Auditors of the Rota whose ancestors had fought in the Crusades; the senior·prelates were mostly men who had risen through the Curial bureaucracy and had never had the experience of governing a diocese or dealing with a middle-class laity; very few of the people who came to Rome in the mid-nineteenth century, even as tourists, had any firsthand knowledge of liberal parliamentary institutions. In this atmosphere it was easy for a priori systems of thought to flourish.

Much depended on the personality of the Pope. Pius IX was a charming and impulsive man, not a trained theologian but a strong believer in divine guidance, portents, and miracles. He relied on personal diplomacy and intuition to find his way through most difficulties. He was much more interested than his predecessor had been in the problem of gallicanism and centrifugal tendencies in the Church, and shortly after his election, when it was still being said that the new Pope was a liberal, he had rebuffed the gallican bishop of Montpellier who had written in a pastoral letter that Pius IX would surely follow the lead of previous Popes in respecting the customs of the

---

[12] A. Ghisalberti, 'Una restaurazione "reazionaria e imperita" ', *Archivio della Società Romana di storia patria* lxxii (1949); Martina, *Pio IX*, chaps. 14–15.

French Church and the intellectual tradition of the ancient Sorbonne. The Pope quoted this to a consistory of the Sacred College and expressed surprise that a bishop could be so far astray: he did respect traditions, he said, so long as they were in full accord with the traditions of Rome and had not 'deviated from the sense of the Catholic Church'.[13] Behind everything he said and did lay this conviction of the need for unity and centrality—although in this early phase of his pontificate he was always personally courteous to the great decentralists of the European Church, indeed so affable and even affectionate in his manner that many a prominent gallican bishop returned from a visit to Rome convinced that in some mysterious way he had become the Pope's favourite.

At Gaeta, badly shaken by the experience of revolution and exile, Pius IX was inclined to be easily impressed by ideologues who presented themselves as champions of papal authority, and he gave a particular welcome to a group of neo-Thomist philosophers within the Jesuit Order who had been developing a new philosophical method since the 1830s: neo-Thomism, as it was explained by Taparelli d'Azeglio and Carlo Curci at Gaeta, was a steely construction of deductive logic designed to provide the Church with a coherent philosophical reply to liberal propositions in both theology and politics, an intellectual weaponry likely to be far more effective in the nineteenth century than the exhausted traditionalism currently taught in the Roman seminaries and colleges.[14] Pius IX provided the funds and encouragement for this group to set up the fortnightly journal *La Civiltà Cattolica,* overruling the Jesuit General, Roothaan, who was afraid that his order might provoke reprisals by committing itself to open controversy, and for the next two decades the Pope was to be in close touch with the editors, taking part personally

[13] Houtin, *Un dernier gallican, Henri Bernier,* 221–4.

[14] There is an extensive literature on the success of neo-Thomism and the decline of traditionalism at Rome after 1848. The following are especially informative: R. Jacquin, *Taparelli d'Azeglio* (1943); *Miscellanea Taparelli: Analecta Gregoriana 133* (Rome 1964); T. Mirabella, *Il pensiero politico di P. Matteo Liberatore* (Milan 1956); Carlo Curci, *Memorie* (Florence 1891); Cardinal G. d'Andrea, *La Curia Romana e i jesuiti* (Florence 1861); G. di Rosa, introduction to *La Civiltà Cattolica,* 4 vols. (Rome 1971), vol. i; A. Kerkvoorde, 'La formation theologique de M. J. Scheeben 1852–1859', *Ephemerides theologicae lovaniensis* xxii (1946), 176–84; F. M. Berlasso, 'Il pensiero del Padre Bonfiglio Mura (1810–1882) intorno alla società contemporanea', *Studi storici dell'Ordine dei Servi di Maria,* ix (1959), 18–58.

in drafting some important articles. From 1850 onwards the neo-Thomists exercised a powerful influence on papal policy, urging it away from the comparative reserve of the forties and towards a confrontationist style in which every aspect of Protestantism, liberalism, and parliamentarism was subjected to a harsh critique; and the ecclesiology of the *Civiltà Cattolica*, emphasizing the centralization of power in the Church and the irresistible force of Roman jurisdiction, helped to stiffen Roman resistance to gallicanism and to prepare the ground for the eventual declaration of papal infallibility.

The establishment of the neo-Thomists in the papal entourage was a stroke of good fortune for Louis Veuillot, because Taparelli and Curci were subscribers and admirers of *L'Univers* which they regarded as 'a work of Catholic apostolate'.[15] Curci had visited Veuillot in Paris in 1849 to ask his advice about starting a journal, and kept Veuillot informed of the progress of the *Civiltà* project. Some of the discussions of European politics in its early issues were based on articles that had already appeared in *L'Univers*, and in turn *L'Univers* began translating articles from the *Civiltà* for French readers; some friendly correspondence was exchanged, and by the end of 1850 Veuillot knew that he could rely on sympathy and support from this influential quarter.

In spite of the many factors in their favour, however, the ultramontane activists knew that it would not be easy to exert direct influence at Rome. The more convinced they were about the paramount role the papacy should play, the more impatient they became about Roman caution and ambiguity. Would the papacy be equal to its responsibilities? None of the French had a high opinion of Roman intellectual life. As the abbé d'Alzon noted, one had only to remember the lectures given by Salinis to the Mennaisian circle twenty years earlier, and indeed to remember Lamennais's own conversation, and to contrast those supreme experiences with the naïve and pedantic teaching at the Gregorian University and the Collegio Romano, to see where the Catholicism of the future would come from;[16] the introduction of neo-Thomism in the fifties did not entirely convince the French. And even the greatest *exaltés* found it hard to imagine the Roman

---

[15] Taparelli to Veuillot, 23 Feb. 1849, in P. Pirri (ed.), *Carteggi del Padre Luigi Taparelli d'Azeglio* (Rome 1933).
[16] Vailhé, *Emmanuel d'Alzon*, vol. i, chap. 7.

administration exerting firm control over a militant and centralized Church. The Secretariat of State under Cardinal Antonelli pursued a consistent line of cynical pragmatism and seemed devoted mainly to avoiding extra responsibility. There was a distinct strain of tolerance and moderation in the Sacred College, represented by men like Amat, Mai, De Angelis, and D'Andrea. The tendency in the Curia to take a very long view occasionally led to a decision to support the gallican status quo, as happened when Sibour instructed the abbé Combalot to stop writing ultra-royalist articles in the Parisian press: Combalot appealed to Rome on the grounds that as a temporary visitor to Paris he was not subject to Sibour, but a senior Curial official ruled that the structure of the Church would be damaged by allowing a priest any latitude whatever to disobey a metropolitan archbishop.[17] When they encountered this degree of caution the ultramontanes generally put it down to laziness and to defects in the Italian national character. 'We who love the Church', Dom Guéranger said, 'know how to judge the Congregations as they deserve.'[18] The abbé Lacroix, *clerc national* in the Curia, complained to Louis Veuillot about the unfortunate historical accident which had delivered the papal machinery into the hands of Italians, 'not the most moral race to have charge of the Christian Church'.[19] The only way to accomplish anything at Rome, in Mgr de Mérode's opinion, 'would be to hang four monsignori, one at each corner of the city'.[20]

Some French ultramontanes held positions at Rome: Lacroix and the abbé de Villefort as *clercs nationaux*, Mgr de Mérode, Montalembert's brother-in-law, at the Papal War Ministry, Mgr de Falloux, brother of the French cabinet minister, the Franciscan theologian Trullet, R. P. Rubillon at the Index; they were all supporters of the *école de l'Univers* and sympathizers with the extreme right of European politics, but they were in relatively junior posts without the power to make significant changes. In their different ways, ultramontane visitors and permanent residents did their best to introduce an atmosphere of urgency

[17] ASV Francia 1851 (I); and *Correspondance de Rome* (24 July 1851).
[18] Ledru, *Dom Guéranger et Mgr Bouvier*, 301.
[19] Lacroix to Veuillot, 24 May 1851, V/BN 24633.
[20] Falloux, *Mémoires d'un royaliste*, vol. ii, 404. Mgr Pie said after an *ad limina* visit that the survival of Catholicism in such conditions was a proof of its inherent vitality.

and bustle into the sleepy committee-rooms of the Curia, and consoled themselves by making a mental distinction between 'the Holy See', a concept of mystical perfection, and what they sometimes called *l'écurie romaine*. One group did succeed in manipulating the Curial apparatus very effectively and was to exercise an extraordinary influence at the height of the gallican–ultramontane conflict. In June 1848 the abbé Ludovic Chaillot, a former pupil of Saint-Nicholas-du-Chardonnet and a graduate of Saint-Sulpice who was now established at Rome as a canonist, began to publish a French-language journal called *La Correspondance de Rome*. It had to suspend publication during the period of the Roman Republic, but when it reappeared as a fortnightly paper from 24 June 1850 it created a sensation; nothing like it had ever been seen in the Church. The *Correspondance de Rome* was, in effect, a newsletter based on privileged access to the day-to-day business of the Curia, especially the Congregations of Rites and the Index, and containing very extensive quotations from archival documents and confidential correspondence between French bishops and Rome, with learned and deadly commentaries which could only have been dictated by highly-placed officers of the Curial bureaucracy. It carried the imprimatur of Mgr Buttaoni, Master of the Sacred Palace (a post which ranked with the Prefects of Congregations), Official Theologian to His Holiness and Consultor to the Index.[21] The bishops were horrified to find their supposedly secret negotiations and requests for rulings on matters of canon law, liturgy, and clerical discipline revealed in the press, either disguised as 'a problem in the diocese of N . . .' or flatly identified by name. By a calculated indiscretion the Roman decision, with a magisterial commentary, sometimes appeared in the *Correspondance de Rome* before it had reached the bishop who had asked the question.

From June to December 1850 the *Correspondance de Rome* was an irritant; towards the end of the year it became a menace. Mgr Fornari was made a cardinal on 30 September 1850; he retired from the Paris Nunciature and came to Rome as Prefect of the Congregation of Seminaries and Universities, a piquant appoint-

---

[21] Comments on its own credentials in the *Correspondance de Rome* (14 Apr. and 14 Dec. 1851); and cf. the abbé Delacouture, *Observations sur le décret de l'Index* (1851), 24: documents were passed to the editors of the *Correspondance* 'at least semi-officially, by the surest hands'.

ment for a man who hated intellectuals, bringing with him a
fiercely hostile account of Sibour's administration in Paris, partly
compiled by Louis Veuillot,[22] and ready to give his patronage to
any project that would weaken the spirit of resistance in the
French hierarchy. The French Embassy believed that he was
protecting and encouraging the *Correspondance de Rome*.[23] At some
time late in 1850 Chaillot began to receive regular help from
Veuillot's two agents in Rome, Henri Lerouge de Maguelonne
and the abbé Bernier (not to be confused with the abbé Henri
Bernier, vicar-general of Angers, mentioned below). They made
sure that the best items from the *Correspondance* were transmitted
to *L'Univers* for wider circulation. In November a formidable
recruit arrived: the abbé Bouix, finding himself *mal vu* in the
archdiocese of Paris after the affair of the provincial council, took
refuge at Rome and joined Chaillot as a consultant canon lawyer;
his first article, a study of the documents on conciliar procedure,
appeared on 4 December 1850. The *Correspondance de Rome* now
began to take a serious interest in the application of the Index to
French textbooks, a process which had already been set in
motion with two important cases during 1850.

The Index

The Congregation of the Index was a much more efficient and
conscientious body than the Congregation of Rites, but for over a
century it had been reluctant to interfere in French intellectual
life. The rules laid down by Benedict XIV in 1753 advised
moderation: consultors to the Index were to

bear in mind that there exist a great many opinions which seem certain
to one particular group of scholars, to one institute, even to one nation,
but which are rejected and attacked by other Catholics, without there
being the slightest disturbance to faith or morals. The Holy See knows
and permits this divergence of opinions, and recognizes . . . that there
may well be degrees of probability.[24]

The Index had been especially cautious with regard to books
used in French seminaries. In 1842, for example, it declined to
act against a doubtful book by the director of Saint-Sulpice,

[22] ASV Francia 1851 (I).
[23] Maurain, *Saint-Siège*, 227–33; L. Chaillot, *Souvenirs d'un prélat romain* (1895).
[24] Constitution 'Sollicita ac provida' of 9 July 1753, cited in all nineteenth-century
editions of the *Index Librorum Prohibitorum*.

Carrière, for the sake of avoiding a scandal amongst the French clergy. The *école de l'Univers* knew from their Roman correspondents, however, that in the atmosphere of the papal restoration of 1850 the disciplinary Congregations had become considerably more alert and that the Index in particular, alarmed at the proliferation of errors since 1848, was now willing to go beyond the tolerant spirit of Benedict XIV's rules. The secretary of the Index, R. P. Modena, was said to be reluctant to act on his own initiative but ready to receive suggestions. By making a careful choice of targets it might be possible, therefore, to use the Index to deal, one by one, with the most vexatious gallicans; and the ultramontanes began with the abbé Bernier.

Bernier was vicar-general of Angers and a very active controversialist of the Sulpician school, with many audacities to answer for. In 1845 he had criticized Veuillot and Jules Morel in a *Lettre sur le journalisme religieux*. In a widely discussed pamphlet in 1848, *l'État et les cultes*, he had rejected the *veuillotiste* position that the Church had the power of physical coercion against heretics and Protestants and that it could use the power of the civil arm to prevent Catholics from changing their religion. The fact that some Popes had done this in the past, Bernier wrote, merely proved that 'the Pope is not the Church', and that the papacy had often been ill-informed about civil affairs: 'France and its real needs are usually little appreciated and badly judged at Rome'. Bernier was best known as an opponent of Guéranger, a critic of the monastic enterprise at Solesmes from its beginning and one of the leaders of resistance against the advance of the Roman liturgy. In his *Humble rémontrance à Dom Guéranger* of 1847 he had gone to the heart of the liturgical conflict by treating it as an attack by 'reformers without a mandate' against the fundamental, original centre of unity in the Christian Church, the diocese; the *Humble rémontrance* had drawn letters of approval from many of the senior gallican bishops and was quoted and misquoted in every subsequent discussion of the liturgy.

In November 1849 Bernier attended the Council of the Tours province as theologian to the bishop of Angers, and was chosen as vice-president of the committee of faith and doctrine, and promoter or in effect leader of discussions. Guéranger, invited as abbot of Solesmes, was annoyed to find his old adversary Bernier sitting amongst the bishops and treated with deference as an authority on technical matters, even commissioned to draft some of the main resolutions; he blamed Bernier for the remarkably non-Roman flavour of the council's decrees, and especially for the fact that there was no mention whatever of the liturgy.[25] Guéranger had already spent some time arguing with Bernier in print and he felt now that argument was clearly not enough; in any case, as he told du Lac on another occasion, he was by temperament 'one of those who carries on his back the faggots to burn heretics'.[26] He complained to the Nuncio, and Fornari asked the invaluable abbé Bouix to prepare a brief on Bernier's publications for the Congregation of the Index. A list of twenty of his erroneous propositions was sent to Rome in April 1850,[27] and on 29 June the Index condemned both the *Humble rémontrance* and *L'État et les cultes*; the decree was published in Rome on 11 July after having been countersigned by the Pope. *L'Univers* had been forewarned by its Roman correspondent, and on 16 and 23 July it printed two articles describing Bernier's 'quasi-Protestant' views. The final paragraph of the second article quoted Bernier as having several times dismissed the Index as a weapon of doubtful effect in France: 'would it have no effect on him, then, if he himself were to be condemned?'; and on the next day *L'Univers* printed the Index decree, drawing attention to the point that Bernier was listed alongside Vacherot's *Histoire de l'École d'Alexandrie* and some works by prominent rationalists. Veuillot added the comment that 'the piety of this respectable ecclesiastic is too well known for there to be the slightest doubt of his submission'.[28]

Bernier had expected a certain amount of negotiation and compromise from Rome, and was stunned by this suddden execution of his work. After only one day's reflection he realized that he was not in a sufficiently strong position to defy the Index, as his gallican principles might have suggested; he would have caused grave embarrassment to his bishop, Angebault, who was a close friend, and to some other members of the hierarchy who had supported him through many past battles with the ultramontanes. He prepared an open letter which was printed in both

---

[25] Houtin, *Henri Bernier*, chap. 15.
[26] Guéranger to du Lac, 6 Sept. 1856, V/BN 24633.
[27] Houtin, *Henri Bernier*, chap. 16.
[28] *L'Univers* (16–23 July 1850). The articles were not signed but were written by the abbé A. C. Peltier.

the *Ami de la religion* and *L'Univers* on 26 July: he wanted to show, he wrote, that a priest brought up on the principles of Bossuet and Frayssinous knew how to submit to Rome. 'I hasten to declare that I regard myself as well judged by the Congregation of the Index and that I accept its judgement without hesitation or qualification . . .'. Veuillot added an editorial comment that Bernier should not hide behind the names of Bossuet and Frayssinous, and went on to say that 'everybody knew' that he had already been censured by the Council of Tours. Bernier, who had been promoter of that Council, replied that this was ludicrous; and although condemned by the Index, he said, he was not completely reduced to silence in future. On 2 August *L'Univers* reported that Bernier was being defended by Protestant journals, which approved that gallicanism was indeed '*une secte*'; and this time Bernier had to invoke the law of compulsory insertion to compel Veuillot to print his reply.[29] While he was engaged in this polemic Bernier offered his resignation as vicar-general. Angebault, profoundly distressed for his friend, refused to accept it, wanting to consult some of his colleagues in the episcopate—and for a moment the possibility can be glimpsed of a concerted resistance which at this point, early in the Index campaign, might have changed the entire fortunes of the Gallican Church; but Bernier insisted, and retired to a quiet country parish. Angebault appointed him to a canonry to give him an additional income.

This first exercise having succeeded beyond expectations, *L'Univers* moved on at once to something more ambitious. The *Dictionnaire universel d'histoire et de géographie* by Marie-Nicolas Bouillet was one of the most popular textbooks of the *Université*, reissued seven times since 1842, and widely regarded as the best available guide to classical antiquity and the history of political ideas; the government had placed a copy in every *lycée* and college library, where it was known to students simply as *le Bouillet*. Ultramontane opinion had always found the book suspect for its rather cool treatment of the papacy in European history, but there were two particular reasons why it should have

---

[29] The *Loi de l'obligation d'insérer* of 1822/1849: an editor had to accept a reply to a personal attack if it was written on official stamped paper and countersigned by a magistrate. On the Bernier condemnation, Antonelli to Fornari, 12 Aug. 1850, ASV Parigi vol. 78; *L'Univers* (23 July–8 Aug. 1850).

come under attack by *L'Univers* in 1850. Some years earlier
Bouillet had submitted the *Dictionnaire* to Archbishop Affre in the
hope that it would be approved for use in Catholic colleges and in
the Faculty of Theology at the Sorbonne. Affre had passed it to
the abbé Delacouture, a former professor of dogma at Saint-
Sulpice who was now secretary of the commission which
examined ecclesiastical books for the archdiocese. Delacouture
made a very careful review of the two large volumes and
eventually, in 1848, suggested a number of amendments which
Bouillet incorporated in a new edition at a personal cost of 25,000
francs. This eighth edition was approved by Sibour in a letter of
28 December 1849 in which, on Delacouture's advice, he certified
that it contained nothing contrary to faith or morals and was an
outstandingly good classical and historical textbook.[30] This alone
would have made the *Dictionnaire* an irresistible target; but there
was a second reason. Since early in 1849 Veuillot had been
planning a great publishing project in a hundred volumes, the
Bibliothèque nouvelle, a Catholic reply to the eighteenth-century
encyclopaedists, 'an answer to all difficulties and objections . . .
the Catholic solution to all the problems of the age': du Lac was
to write on doctrine, Théodore Foisset on early Christianity,
Donoso Cortès on Protestantism and socialism, Guéranger on
the Inquisition, Roux-Lavergne on history, and Veuillot himself
on feasts and ceremonies of the church. One of Veuillot's friends
in the clergy volunteered to write two volumes on Satan. The
whole enterprise was meant to shatter the assumptions of
'doctors, notaries, lawyers, judges, rentiers'; the general motto,
to be printed on each title-page, was to be *hors de l'Église point de
salut*.[31] Unfortunately, perhaps fifteen or twenty of the volumes
were certain to find themselves in direct competition with
Bouillet's *Dictionnaire*; it was predictable that Catholic schools
might hesitate to order the *Bibliothèque nouvelle* publications on
history or the classics if they already had *le Bouillet*.

---

[30] AN F. 19. 1947: Account of the Bouillet affair prepared by the directeur général
des Cultes.
[31] Veuillot to Foisset, 25 Aug. 1849 and 22 Mar. 1850; to Mme Dumast, Oct. 1849;
to the abbé Bernier in Rome, 10 May 1850; to Dom Gardereau, 5 Aug. 1850: in
Correspondance, vol. iii, 77–179. Veuillot hoped to make 'almost a fortune'; and it may
be noted that the success of the *Bibliothèque nouvelle* depended on the expansion of the
Catholic secondary school system expected under the Loi Falloux, so that while
Veuillot was attacking the education bill he must have believed that it would succeed.

On 5 July 1850 *L'Univers* announced the first volume in the new series, Roux-Lavergne on the philosophy of history, and on 27 and 30 July Veuillot printed an extended review of the eighth edition of Bouillet. If one had a son just beginning his studies in law or medicine, Veuillot asked, would one place in his hands a dictionary of all the leading prostitutes in Paris? Yet for eight years an even worse book had been carelessly placed in college libraries, spreading its contagion: every one of its fifteen hundred pages was atheistic and corrupt. Bouillet was outrageous, Veuillot said, in his appalling neutrality: the articles on Julian the Apostate, Trajan, Arius, Voltaire, and Hegel described them without any hint of blame. Even the Greek gods escaped without the moral censure they deserved. Christianity was treated simply as 'one of the principal world religions'. The entries on the Church were mischievous: the Popes were discussed as if they were kings or barons; councils were described as being the ultimate ecclesiastical authority; the article on St Peter mentioned primacy of honour but not primacy of jurisdiction; the articles on the Civil Constitution of the Clergy and the Concordat were absurdly even-handed; Saint Martin of Tours was '*said to* have performed miracles'. The response to this attack was everything that Veuillot could have hoped for: Bouillet wrote to *L'Univers* pointing out that the *Dictionnaire* had been approved and commended by the Archbishop of Paris. Veuillot replied that before taking the risk of denouncing a book favoured by Mgr Sibour he had 'asked the opinions of serious and well-considered persons; their unanimous advice was that we should publish our complaints'. There was a strong hint that this advice had come from the Index and that the *Dictionnaire* was being examined at Rome. How had it happened, Veuillot went on, that a book filled with 'impious, obscene, licentious, and filthy material' had been given approval? The kindest explanation was that Sibour had allowed himself to be deceived by a dishonest examiner.

We are reliably informed that the abbé Delacouture's first opinion was that the book was impossible to correct. But, overcome with obsession and importunity, he set to work, and it is known that he obtained notable concessions from M. Bouillet.

The archdiocesan commission did in fact charge a fee for examinations, but Veuillot told the Nuncio that Delacouture had taken a direct bribe of 1500 francs from Bouillet to pass the book. Delacouture wrote a dignified reply denying any 'notable concessions', and showing also that Veuillot had quoted some passages from earlier editions which had actually been removed from the amended eighth edition. Veuillot attacked him again for the 'obscenities' he had failed to remove, and would not print the full text of Delacouture's further reply.[32]

Another shot fired by *L'Univers* also scored a near miss on the *Archevêché*. In two articles on 28 and 31 July 1850 the paper attacked Sibour's appointment of the abbé Maret to a chair in the Faculty of Theology and to a vicar-generalship of the archdiocese. Maret was politically suspect, having been editor of the *Ère nouvelle* in 1848; his gallicanism, *L'Univers* said, was so extreme as to verge on neo-Christianity: 'his politics flow from his philosophy, and his philosophy from his theology'; there had even been something irregular, it was suggested, about the award of his doctoral degree. On 14 August *L'Univers* printed extracts from Maret's *Théodicée chrétienne* and from Lamennais's *Esquisse d'une philosophie* in parallel columns to show that he could not escape the same censure; and the paper pointed out that Sibour, inept as always, had recommended the *Théodicée* for theological students. Maret sent a long and detailed reply to *L'Univers* on 3 September, but there was clearly a possibility that he would receive the same treatment as Bernier.

At this point, exasperated beyond caution, Sibour decided to act. On 24 August 1850 he issued a pastoral letter drawing attention to the recent decree of the Council of Paris on lay writers who dealt with religious subjects. Catholics should be reminded, he wrote, 'that they do not receive the mind, doctrine, and government of the Church from newspapers'; writers who did not respect the authority of the diocesan bishop would be subject in future to canonical penalties. Sibour then added a supplementary letter referring specifically to *L'Univers*, listing its transgressions during the past year and warning the editors that if they continued in this vein they would risk excommunication.[33] Veuillot immediately announced that the editors would appeal to

---

[32] Veuillot's articles in *L'Univers* on 29 and 30 July, 11, 21 and 23 Aug.: Bouillet's reply, 10 Aug.; Delacouture, 16 and 22 Aug. Veuillot's letter to Delacouture, 31 Aug. 1850, in *Correspondance*, vol. iii, 192–3.
[33] V/BN 24239; and *L'Univers* (2–4 Sept. 1850).

the Pope 'as humble toilers for Rome, who want to know plainly if we are dismissed or if we are to continue our daily work'.[34] Through his excellent Roman contacts he knew that he would receive a good hearing. In July and August his Roman correspondent had reported many signs of favour for *L'Univers,* and in August Veuillot's brother Eugène visited Rome and was treated 'like the ambassador of a great power'; the Pope granted him an audience on the day he arrived, decorated him with a papal knighthood, and sent a medal to each member of the editorial staff.[35] The auguries seemed promising. Mgr Fornari encouraged Veuillot to make his appeal in the form of a memorandum for the Nuncio which he undertook to send on to the Pope with his own annotations.

Veuillot's choice of arguments was extremely adroit. Sibour's pastoral, he wrote, was merely another in a long line of attacks on *L'Univers* by those who resented its devotion to the Holy See and to pure Catholic doctrine. The circle of the *archevêché* were, in effect, the allies of the *Journal des débats* and the *Université* and Sibour was now being applauded by the entire anti-Catholic press, as Veuillot demonstrated with a selection of newspaper clippings. With regard to the alleged misdemeanours of *L'Univers* he argued that lay journalists had to fight the daily battles of politics and ideas and could hardly be expected to use the language of cloistered theologians. The journalist had to be free to strike the enemies of the Church, and so long as he was completely Catholic, in the sense of being directly submissive to the papacy, it was better for him not to be controlled by an over-cautious and compromising hierarchy.[36]

This memorandum was not delivered to Fornari for three weeks; and in the meantime Sibour was trying to assess the degree of his own favour or disfavour at Rome. His best source of information was Lacordaire, who had gone to Rome to negotiate his appointment as provincial of the French Dominicans. Lacordaire had been one of the leading ultramontanes in the

[34] *L'Univers* (4 Sept. 1850).

[35] *L'Univers* printed edited versions of Bernier's dispatches; some of the originals are in V/BN 24225.

[36] Veuillot's copy of the memorandum in V/BN 24239; cf. his reflections on the rôle of the Catholic journalist, 'Notes intimes', V/BN 24620, and *L'Univers* (2 Sept. 1850). Veuillot evidently did not think Rome was ready for his view of the Catholic press as an international order of friars.

1830s, but of all Lamennais's original disciples he had been the most affected by the democratic and liberal side of the *Avenir* movement. He was repelled by the aggressiveness of the new ultramontanes: every article on democracy he had written as deputy editor of the *Ère nouvelle* in 1848 had been attacked by *L'Univers*, and Morel's famous Inquisition articles had been cast in the form of a scornful critique of Lacordaire's own lectures on the Dominican Order, in which he had tried to show that the inquisitors had often behaved tolerantly and reasonably; Morel had implied that this apologetic attitude betrayed the feebleness of Lacordaire's Catholic principles. By 1850 Lacordaire was very sympathetic to Sibour, and he was delighted by the action against *L'Univers*. He had not believed the archbishop to be so strong minded, he wrote to Mme Swetchine; the dictatorship of the 'band of mocking spirits' at *L'Univers* 'would have ended by exposing the Church to the distrust and hatred of the majority of people'.[37] He offered his services to Sibour as a correspondent during his visit to Rome; but there was little chance of his finding anything encouraging to report. Sibour's action had only strengthened the impression already created in Rome by Fornari's dispatches and by Corboli Bussi's report of 1849 that the *archevêché* of Paris was a nuisance and an obstacle to unity. Veuillot had spread the alarm amongst the leading ultramontanes that *L'Univers* was in imminent danger of being closed, 'our poor small candle extinguished', and with Fornari's co-operation appeals were now arriving in Rome from Gousset, Pie, Villecourt, Parisis, Gignoux, and other prominent *veuillotistes*, all to similar effect. Catholic journalists full of verve and talent, Pie wrote, could not be sent into battle with their hands tied; 'if the Church really wishes to disband its lay army, let this be proclaimed by the Pope himself'.[38] On the surface, these letters pointed out, Sibour's pastoral was 'a blow against Roman doctrines' such as might have been expected from that quarter, but it had a deeper meaning which Rome should observe: Sibour was trying to

---

[37] Letter of 7 Sept. 1850, in A. de Falloux (ed.), *Correspondance du R. P. Lacordaire et de Mme Swetchine* (1907 edn.), 482–3.

[38] Mgr Pie's letter to Rome via the Nunciature, 17 Sept. 1850, copy sent to Jules Morel, V/BN 24235; Mgr Gignoux of Beauvais to the Pope, 19 Sept., copy sent to Veuillot, V/BN 24225; copies of other correspondence in these files and in Veuillot, *Correspondance*, vol. iii, 193–249.

establish a kind of gallican papacy. An archbishop of Paris who claimed the right to censor the press could control Catholic opinion throughout the entire country; and at the same time he could circulate his own pastorals to every diocese by having them published in the big Parisian daily papers. Fornari told Veuillot that if Sibour had more talent it was certain that he would end as the patriarch of a Gaulish schism;[39] the sarcastic phrase *le patriarche* was picked up and repeated by all the ultramontanes, and, unfortunately for Sibour, also by many gallicans. It was a fundamental weakness of gallicanism that in their insistence on diocesan autonomy the bishops had developed an exaggerated suspicion of primates. 'The Church of France', Clausel de Montals wrote in 1844, 'does not recognize any dictator, or any patriarch, and each of its bishops enjoys absolutely the same doctrinal authority'.[40] Archbishop Affre had been made aware on several occasions of his colleagues' touchiness on this point, and in 1848, for example, he had asked the ministère des Cultes to withdraw a circular tactlessly addressed 'to the Archbishop of Paris, the archbishops and bishops of France'. The reluctance of the bishops to accept a leader or even a spokesman told especially against Sibour because many of them disliked his politics and thought him personally unreliable; so that while the gallican laity generally welcomed his action against *L'Univers* and felt that he had gained in stature by it,[41] his fellow archbishops expressed reservations: if Sibour had consulted them, they told the Nuncio, they would have advised him to treat *L'Univers* very carefully. Mgr Blanquart de Bailleul of Rouen, who hated *L'Univers*, even offered to act as a mediator. Dupanloup was one of the few bishops to give Sibour unequivocal support.[42]

The Curia semed remarkably well informed about all this, Lacordaire reported from Rome. Apart from Fornari's dispatches, Veuillot had been transmitting every nuance of the affair in long letters to his Roman correspondent, and opinion was over-whelmingly against Sibour: everyone Lacordaire met regarded the archbishop as 'the leader of an anti-Roman faction in

[39] Veuillot, *D'après nature, Oeuvres* x, 489.
[40] Sevrin, *Clausel de Montals*, vol. ii, 390.
[41] See the letters of Eugène Rendu to Gino Capponi in September 1850, in A. Carraresi (ed.), *Lettere di Gino Capponi*, 3 vols. (Florence 1882–4), vol. iii.
[42] Fornari kept Veuillot informed of the bishops' opinions: see *Correspondance*, vol. iii, 220–39; and Dupanloup to Antonelli, 4 Sept. 1850, ASV Francia 1850 (III).

France', the man who had advised the Pope to give up the temporal power and was now trying to suppress the most vigorous ultramontane newspaper in Europe.[43] But Lacordaire was not allowing for the Mediterranean subtlety of Curial affairs, or for the pragmatic mood in which paradoxes were easily accepted if they led to a sensible decision. The *archevêché* of Paris might be in disgrace, but ecclesiastical business had to go on. Earlier in the year Sibour had proposed to create several new parishes by splitting off parts of the overpopulated parishes in the centre of Paris. The project was unpopular with those *curés* who were to lose a proportion of their revenue, but was welcomed at Rome because Pius IX was moved by Sibour's eloquent account of the spiritual desolation of the urban masses. The Pope wrote personally to the President of the Republic asking that money be provided for clerical salaries and new buildings, and commended Sibour for his initiative;[44] this was at the height of the imbroglio with *L'Univers*. It was clear that nothing should be done to disturb the archbishop while he was negotiating with the government about funds and parish boundaries. The editors of *L'Univers* were in high favour but it could not be denied, Antonelli told the Nuncio, that they were often provocative and cruel towards respectable opponents, or that they lacked respect for episcopal authority. At the present time 'the threatened appeal by the editors . . . would raise major difficulties and the affair would become very complicated'. Instead of sending Veuillot's appeal to Rome, Fornari was to appoint an intermediary to reconcile the two parties.[45]

Mgr Salinis of Amiens was chosen as a man acceptable to both sides. He found Sibour determined not to give way: 'how could one imagine', he had written to Lacordaire, 'that an Archbishop of Paris should allow himself to be humiliated by a coterie of journalists?'[46] Salinis reminded him that he did not have the full support of the episcopate: many people, he said, felt that *L'Univers* had been harshly treated. Sibour insisted that his pastoral letter had been perfectly justified; but in any case the editors had not published any reply to it: 'my warning might as

[43] Lacordaire to Sibour, 13 Sept. 1850, A. Arch. Paris 1. D. vi (4).
[44] Antonelli to Fornari, 20 Sept. 1850, ASV Parigi vol. 78.
[45] Antonelli to Fornari, 21 Sept. 1850, ASV Francia 1850 (III).
[46] Sibour to Lacordaire, 24 Sept. 1850, A. Arch. Paris 1. D. vi (4).

well have been sent to Peking'. They were diffident, Salinis said,
because they did not think Sibour would treat them paternally.
'Oh, paternally, even maternally, if that is what they want . . .';
and Salinis was sent off to *L'Univers* office. Veuillot was still
striking attitudes of theatrical despair and talking about closing
the paper within a few days, but he was ready to negotiate.[47]
Amongst the many letters of support he had received from clergy
and laity there had been some from experienced observers of
ecclesiastical affairs warning him not to expect a clear judgement
in his favour, because Rome could not censure an archbishop
who had acted strictly within his canonical rights.[48] He let
himself be persuaded to sign a letter drafted at the *archevêché*,
promising 'more prudence, and more balance and maturity', and
agreed to lead a deputation of the editors to present it personally
to Sibour. The interview went badly. Sibour asked them to try to
avoid driving away potential converts. Veuillot replied that one
could not please unbelievers except by remaining silent: did the
archbishop want *L'Univers* to be boring? 'Monseigneur smiled
wearily at everything that was said . . . we avoided asking for his
blessing, and left.'[49] The appeal to Rome was withdrawn, to the
great relief of the Curia, and both sides received letters of
approval from the Pope; Mgr Fioramonti, the papal secretary,
had to draft the letter to Sibour twice to make sure that it did not
seem more encouraging than the letter to Veuillot.[50]

While this affair was still in progress, however, Sibour had
received unpleasant news from another branch of the Curia. In
the first week of September the Nuncio's office informed him that
the Index had condemned Bouillet's *Dictionnaire*, but that the
Pope had ordered the decree to be withheld until the archbishop
and M. Bouillet had been given an opportunity to discuss
amendments. Sibour wrote to R. P. Modena, the secretary of the
Congregation, demanding to know what defects the Index had
found, and received from Modena a list of paragraphs which
coincided very closely with the examples chosen by Veuillot for
his denunciation in *L'Univers*. Bouillet asked Sibour to remind

[47] Veuillot's account of the negotiations in V/BN 24239.
[48] Letters in September from Theodore Foisset, the Spanish philosopher and
diplomat Donoso Cortès, and Emmanuel de Curzon, leader of the legitimist party in
Poitiers, in V/BN 24225.
[49] Veuillot's notes of the meeting, V/BN 24239.
[50] Fornari to Antonelli, 25 Nov. 1850, ASV Parigi vol. 79.

Rome that his *Dictionnaire* was not in any sense a theological statement but simply a compendium of information; if certain facts displeased the Index he would do his best to present them with more finesse.[51] Sibour passed this on, and asked Lacordaire to put a further question to Modena: was the Index also considering a condemnation of Maret's *Théodicée chrétienne*? Lacordaire reported that Modena had spoken of the *Théodicée* 'as a connoisseur and an admirer' and had laughed at the suggestion that it might be under examination. As for Bouillet, if he would agree to make the alterations required, the Index would take no further action and the condemnation would lapse.[52] Bouillet agreed, and worked for almost a year revising his articles on popes, philosophers, and saints. In August 1851 an amended text was sent to Modena, Sibour making it clear at the same time that he would approve this edition as he had approved the previous one; and for the time being *le Bouillet* remained in the seminary and college libraries.

The condemnations of Lequeux and Guettée

The *Manuale compendium juris canonici* was a four-volume work by the abbé Lequeux, director of the seminary of Soissons, first published in 1839/41 and now in its third edition; in 1851 the publishers estimated that about 8000 copies were owned by members of the clergy. Some seminary instructors with Mennaisian leanings had expressed reservations about the book, Lequeux being emphatically gallican on points such as the sharing of authority within the universal Church, the right of bishops to decide whether or not a particular papal decision applied to their own dioceses and the right of the Church of France to decline to receive decisions of the Roman congregations, but the general opinion was that the *Manuale* at least made the study of canon law possible in French seminaries. It had been adopted at once by Saint-Sulpice and Saint-Irenée at Lyons, and gradually came into use in over thirty other seminaries. Lequeux himself, like the abbé Bernier, attracted the particular hostility of the ultramontanes by his performance at one of the provincial councils. When the very ultramontane province of Reims decided to hold its council

---

[51] Correspondence in AN F. 19. 1947: 'Dictionnaire de Bouillet'.
[52] Lacordaire to Sibour, 13 Sept. 1850, A. Arch. Paris 1. D. vi (4); Lacordaire to Maret, 14 Sept. 1850, in Bazin, *Vie de Mgr Maret*, vol. i, 372.

at Soissons in September 1849 Lequeux found himself in a difficult position because as director of the local seminary he was certain to be asked out of courtesy to draft one of the conciliar decrees. His bishop, Cardon de Garsignies, hoping to embarrass Lequeux, suggested that he write the declaration of obedience to the Holy See. As expected, Lequeux's definition of obedience was much too vague for Gousset, Salinis, Gignoux, and the theologians they had brought to the council, and they instructed Gerbet, recently appointed vicar-general of Amiens, to prepare another draft. When Lequeux objected in turn that Gerbet's document contained theological novelties, Gerbet revealed, to great amusement and applause, that the 'novelties' were drawn from conciliar decrees of the Middle Ages.[53] Shortly after this episode Sibour invited Lequeux to Paris to be vicar-general in charge of higher education and lecturer in canon law at the École de Carmes, and thus inadvertently provided the ultramontane zealots with a splendid opportunity. Anything done to discredit Lequeux's book would be a simultaneous blow struck against a well-known gallican theorist, against the École des Carmes enterprise and against the archbishop of Paris. A delation of the *Manuale compendium* to the Index was arranged, this time not by *L'Univers* but by R. P. Gaultier at the Saint-Esprit seminary and Dom Guéranger, with the co-operation of Mgr Gousset of Reims.[54] Lequeux heard a rumour about a delation and made hasty arrangements to go to Rome himself, taking a copy of the *Manuale*; Sibour announced that his new vicar-general was going to study the teaching methods in the Roman universities. At the same time the archbishop circulated to the clergy of Paris a report on the success of the École des Carmes: twenty-four university degrees, including two doctorates, and the first place in a recent university examination. The Nuncio, Mgr Garibaldi, wrote to Rome that Lequeux was coming as a representative of the pernicious school of educators, patronized by the foolish and gullible Sibour, who believed that it was good for priests to be

[53] Garibaldi to Antonelli, 15 May 1851, ASV Francia 1853 (IV); Ladoue, *Mgr Gerbet*, vol. ii, 262–3 adds some details.

[54] Hédouville, 'Romains et gallicans', cites the correspondence of Gaultier, Bouix and Chaillot throughout 1851. Guéranger was an unofficial consultor to the Index and was given official status in November 1851. He had very good relations with the *Correspondance de Rome*, which announced a series of Solesmes publications in its issue of 14 June 1851.

exposed to the scientific and philosophical influences of the Sorbonne. He would try to get some favourable word from the Pope for the École des Carmes, but it was essential that he receive no encouragement. Garibaldi noted that he had given Lequeux a letter of introduction to Cardinal Santucci, who could be trusted to supervise his visit.[55]

The impressions Lequeux gained in Rome were bewilderingly contradictory, as he reported in a series of letters to Sibour in June 1851. He did spend some time looking at higher education. The libraries were excellent, and some of the academics were profound scholars, in rather narrow fields. Everyone he met assured him that Rome admired the intellectual distinction of the French clergy, and it was even implied, with great courtesy and charm, that they recognized a certain backwardness in their own methods and had much to learn from French initiatives like the École des Carmes. This was true enough, Lequeux thought: the teaching at the Gregorian University and the Collegio Romano was 'nothing marvellous'; lectures were uninspiring and remote from reality, the study of canon law was feeble and lifeless, the secular sciences were completely neglected, the parish clergy—so far as he could judge—were far more ignorant than in France. There could be no point in sending French priests to study in Rome.[56]

It is clear from these letters that Sibour had briefed Lequeux to listen for signs of favour not only for the Carmes but for the *archevêché* of Paris. He still hoped that the zealots were wrong, and that to be in good standing with the Holy See it was not necessary, after all, to follow every Roman breeze or to surrender completely to *veuillotisme*. A few weeks earlier he had written to Dupanloup who was visiting Rome: 'Explain to the Holy Father that I am a gallican in the same sense as yourself, that is to say that we are gallicans like Bellarmine. The beloved Pius IX will be content with that, I think, and will be less demanding than Mgr Fornari and his creatures on *L'Univers*.'[57] The news from Lequeux, although conveyed with tact, was hardly reassuring. On all sides he heard praise for the zeal and good intentions of

[55] Garibaldi, 15 May 1851, ASV Francia 1853 (IV).
[56] Letters from Lequeux to Sibour, 3–22 June 1851. A. Arch. Paris 1. D. vi (4). An additional letter to Sibour, apparently not in the archdiocesan archives, is in Séché, *Les Derniers Jansénistes*, vol. iii, 63–4.
[57] Sibour to Dupanloup, 7 Jan. 1851, Dupanloup/BN 24707.

the archbishop of Paris, but not for his judgement: it would have been better, for example, if he had not replied at all to the circular on the Immaculate Conception; but 'well-placed people tell me that you are not to worry'. The Pope received Lequeux with his usual benevolence. He understood, he said, that Lequeux had been a seminary director and that he had written a textbook on canon law; Lequeux listened with painful attention, but the Pope did not pursue the subject. 'Your archbishop has an excellent heart and much zeal for the Church'; then came a barb: 'When Mgr Sibour was at Digne he was an enthusiast for the doctrine of the Immaculate Conception, but now that he has risen in the world he seems to have doubts about it.' The École des Carmes, the Pope went on, was an excellent idea, and no doubt Lequeux would find many useful ideas to copy in the Roman universities, but if it was a matter of an establishment for France 'it would be more advantageously placed somewhere other than Paris, away from the tumult of the political parties and the influence of gallican doctrines.'[58]

When he had been in Rome for about a week Lequeux called on R. P. Modena at the Index and presented him with the four volumes of the *Manuale*. Modena talked amiably about various theological topics but gave no sign that he had heard anything about a delation to the Index. Lequeux called again a week later and tried to bring the conversation around to the merits or defects of his book. He let it be known that he would be glad to discuss anything the Index found objectionable, but Modena was politely vague—'a subtle man', Lequeux reported.[59] An audience he had with the Secretary of State before leaving Rome only added to his bafflement: Cardinal Antonelli urged him to go ahead with the Carmes project as quickly as possible and to disregard the opposition he would encounter; he could be sure of the blessing of God and, more to the point, the goodwill of the Holy See.[60]

[58] Lequeux's account of the audience is in his letters of 3 and 9 June 1851, A. Arch. Paris 1. D. vi (4). The Pope was obviously convinced by Corboli Bussi's report of the previous year.

[59] All the French who had to go to Rome to resolve difficulties in this period were inclined to enjoy playing the rôle of innocents enmeshed in a web of subtle intrigue. Lequeux's suspicions in his own case were probably correct; but sometimes the French saw duplicity and cunning where the real problem was inefficiency.

[60] Lequeux to Sibour, 22 June 1851, A. Arch. Paris 1. D. vi (4).

While Modena was turning Lequeux away with vague reassurances, the Index was in fact well advanced with an examination of the *Manuale Compendium*; the *Correspondance de Rome* hinted at this in a short article on 14 June which Lequeux does not appear to have noticed. By the middle of July a senior Index official had prepared an elaborate report based on a study of all three editions of the book, listing its errors under nine separate headings. Lequeux's interpretations of the rights of the civil power in religious affairs, the powers and autonomy of bishops, the effect of the false decretals of the Middle Ages, the distinction between the ordinary and extraordinary jurisdiction of the Holy See, and the right of national churches not to receive decisions of the Congregations of Rites and the Index were identified with the formal phrases 'false', 'tending towards schism', 'heretical' or 'verging on heresy', and the anonymous Censor added that the *Manuale* contained a number of 'other bold and erroneous opinions which I have omitted for the sake of brevity'.[61] Bouix and Chaillot evidently had access to this document because on 24 July the *Correspondance de Rome* printed a version of it in French under the heading 'Critique littéraire', listing the points in a slightly different order but citing exactly the same quotations and page numbers from Lequeux. It contained two additional points which the *Correspondance* hoped the Index would not fail to notice: Lequeux had fallen into error on the powers of provincial councils, and on frequent occasions throughout his four volumes he had referred students to the authority of older works like Fleury's *Institutions* which were themselves on the Index. The article concluded:

A so-called textbook on canon law, composed for the most part of edicts ... of the civil power, accompanied by a few old canons of councils or decrees of ancient Popes, is a dangerous manual to admit to the seminaries. Such a book, in our view, is not susceptible to correction; it is fundamentally bad. It is not to be tolerated.[62]

Fresh rumours began to circulate and the *archevêché* heard that Veuillot, Guéranger, and others had received letters from Rome

[61] 'Exerptae ex Manuali ... J. F. M. Lequeux propositiones aliquot quae censura dignae videntur': original and a copy in ASV Francia 1853 (IV).
[62] *Correspondance de Rome* (24 July 1851).

to the effect that a condemnation was imminent.[63] Guéranger
told Mgr Pie, whose seminary director wanted to use Lequeux's
Manuale, to have nothing to do with the book because it was
certain to be put on the Index.[64] At this point, however, there
was a hitch. One of the Roman consultors to the Index, Mgr
Giuseppe Cardoni, going through the Censor's draft report point
by point, submitted an absolutely dissenting opinion. Lequeux's
views on the rights of the civil power, he said, were not at all
excessive and were supported by 'much theological and canonistic
opinion'. The doctrine that the Pope had extraordinary but not
ordinary jurisdiction over French dioceses, Cardoni wrote,
deserved to be censured but the Popes had never done so: was
this a prudent moment to begin condemning opinions which had
always been respectable in France? On the disciplinary powers of
the Holy See and the Index Cardoni made a careful distinction
between decrees binding *de jure* and *de facto*: orthodox opinion in
France and Germany was that if a bishop had licensed a book,
for example, the Roman Index in practice could not overrule
him. All these questions, he concluded, required subtlety of mind
and historical discrimination, and although Lequeux was writing
in the gallican tradition he should be given credit for the
seriousness of his approach: 'I cannot agree with the learned
Censor that the book deserves to be condemned by the Index'.[65]

This very good example of the cautious side of Rome was
overruled, and the *Manuale* was placed on the Index on 27
September. Père Gaultier, who had come to Rome to make
himself available as a consultor on the Lequeux case and had
paid several visits to Modena, ran through the streets to see the
decree posted outside the Index office.[66] The *Correspondance de
Rome* printed the condemnation three times in the same issue,
under different headings, drawing attention to the condemnation
at the same time of two books by Professor Nuytz of Turin, a very
militant spokesman of parliamentary ultra-gallicanism.[67] On the

[63] Lequeux complained later to the Nuncio about the rumours following the
Correspondance article: Garibaldi to Antonelli, 26 Oct. 1851, ASV Francia 1852 (III).
[64] Delatte, *Dom Guéranger,* vol. ii, 41–3.
[65] 'Sopra la censura . . . J. F. M. Lequeux': ASV Francia 1853 (IV).
[66] Gaultier's superiors deprecated this display of eagerness. Apart from his own
circle, the Saint-Esprit order was not particularly ultramontane; some of its senior
men were distinguished Jewish converts of moderate opinions, and the prefect of
studies was the abbé Sisson, the editor of the *Ami de la religion.*
[67] *Correspondance de Rome* (4 Oct. 1851).

day that the decree was being issued in Rome Sibour wrote to
Antonelli to express disquiet about the persistent rumours that
Lequeux was to be the victim of 'persons animated by excessive
zeal and personal rancour', and to arrange for him to be heard in
his own defence before anything was done by the Index.
Antonelli replied on 13 October with his 'deepest sympathy . . .
when your letter arrived the affair was already ended'. He would
not comment on 'excessive zeal and personal rancour': how
would he know about such things? 'As a man of rectitude and
wisdom you will surely understand that such passions are foreign
to the Roman Congregations.' The *Manuale* had been denounced
'from several parts of France' and some action had been
necessary. It had been referred to the Index, he added, only after
Lequeux had left Rome.[68] If this last statement was true, Sibour
and Lequeux thought, the examination must have gone ahead at
an almost supernatural speed, unheard of in Rome; but clearly
the atmosphere had changed since the affair of Bouillet's
Dictionnaire: the Index was treating the *Manuale*, in effect, as the
archbishop's second offence, and this time there was to be no
question of prior consultation or of the decree being deferred so
that the author could make corrections. Lequeux called on
Garibaldi at the Nunciature and was not too surprised to hear an
entirely different explanation of why R. P. Modena had been
evasive: Modena *had* known, of course, about an examination in
progress, but officers of the Index were sworn to secrecy. Not a
very well-kept secret, Lequeux retorted: the *Correspondance de
Rome* had detailed knowledge, and letters had been flying about
between the ultramontane circles of Paris, Reims, and Solesmes
for several weeks in advance.[69]

An article by Veuillot on the powers of the Roman Index
appeared in *L'Univers* on 7 October, and on 11 October *L'Univers*
published the Index decree and reprinted the long analysis which
had appeared in the *Correspondance de Rome* in July. It was no
accident, Veuillot wrote, that Lequeux had been condemned in
the same decree with one of the principal theorists of *gallicanisme
parlementaire*: Professor Nuytz, who had great influence in the

[68] Sibour to Antonelli, 27 Sept. 1851, and Antonelli's reply, 13 Oct. 1851, ASV
Francia 1853 (IV).
[69] Garibaldi to Antonelli, 26 Oct. 1851, ASV Francia 1852 (III). By the time
Lequeux spoke to the Nuncio he had seen the article in the *Correspondance de Rome*.

Piedmontese universities, took the extreme regalist position that the Church was merely a corporation within the State and had no rights, spiritual or temporal, beyond those that the State was willing to concede. The point Rome was making, Veuillot said, was that Nuytz was the very image of the professors who would be lecturing to young priests if Lequeux and Sibour had their way: the condemnation of Nuytz was also aimed, obliquely, at the archbishop of Paris and the École des Carmes.[70]

Lequeux wrote to the Nuncio: 'having consecrated my entire life to the service of the Church, and fearing above all to be an object of scandal, I hasten to declare my submission'; but he did not recognize that his book contained errors, as distinct from legitimate opinions, and asked for an opportunity to discuss specific points with the censors of the Index; he rejected any attempt to equate him with Professor Nuytz.[71] Lequeux managed to avoid an abject surrender, but the Index decree was a powerful shock to the senior gallicans and to the entire Sulpician *école* in the clergy. Clausel de Montals wrote to the superior of Saint-Sulpice, Carrière, that 'a violent anti-French cabal at Rome' wanted to condemn books and divide the clergy into hostile factions just at a moment when the position of the Church in French society was at its most delicate (it was six weeks before the *coup d'état*).

They want to dominate, to have a hand in everything, to control everything, to reduce the bishops to being no more than timid servants or valets . . . *Posuit episcopos regere Ecclesiam Dei. Regere,* govern—the word has no suggestion of a servile executor of orders coming from somewhere else.

In condemning Lequeux the Index had condemned a hundred thousand of the old French clergy 'because they thought absolutely as we do'. Lequeux had asked him to intervene, Clausel added, but he was having his own difficulties with the Index over the liturgy question:[72] 'there is nothing to be done for the moment but to pray and keep silent, but we must collect all our forces to prevent true principles from being forgotten altogether'.[73] The ultramontanes had discovered, Dupanloup

[70] *L'Univers*, (7, 11 and 14 Oct. 1851).
[71] *L'Univers* (14 Oct. 1851).   [72] See chapter X.
[73] Two letters from Clausel de Montals to Carrière, Oct. 1851, in Sevrin, *Clausel de Montals*, vol. ii, 629–30.

wrote, that there was no need to try to convince those Catholics who wanted to go on discussing questions which had been freely debated for centuries; it was easier to dishonour and humiliate them and to impose 'the silence of moribundity and death'.[74]

Not everyone was content to pray and keep silent. Remarkably detailed accounts of the affair began to appear in the secular press, Alphonse Peyrat in *La Presse* being so well informed about Lequeux's experience in Rome and about the technicalities of Index procedure that the Nuncio suspected he was being briefed by the *archevêché*. The episcopate, Peyrat wrote, would be spineless if it allowed a learned cleric to be condemned for upholding the maxims that had protected the French Church against the pretensions of Rome since the time of Gregory VII.[75] Mgr Garibaldi was alarmed to find the Parisian laity taking a keen interest, and asked Lequeux himself to do what he could to discourage any polemic, to which Lequeux replied loftily that he could hardly help it if the case aroused widespread comment.[76] When the parliamentarian Jean Wallon prepared a dossier of manuscript correspondence and documents on the case for the Catholic publisher Jouby, the Nuncio persuaded Jouby to suppress it in return for the promise of a papal knighthood.[77] The most substantial protest, however, came in a pamphlet by the abbé Delacouture, who had been collecting arguments on the power of the Index since his experience with the Bouillet affair the previous year and now presented the Lequeux case as a perfect illustration of the gallican position. Was there any need, Delacouture asked, to submit to this particular decree of the Index? He was able to cite distinguished Jesuits and Dominicans arguing that Index decrees were not necessarily binding, and even the ultramontane historian Rohrbacher, in his anxiety to show that the papacy had never made mistakes, had blamed the condemnation of Galileo on the Congregation of the Index which, as he said, was far from infallible. In Lequeux's case the decree was surely invalid because the correct procedure had been flagrantly disregarded. Instead of giving him an opportunity to

---

[74] Dupanloup. 'Rapport au Pape', Dupanloup/AN AB XIX 524: chap. 9.
[75] *La Presse* (15–29 Oct. 1851). The Lequeux case was often the first item in the newspapers even at this time of extreme political tension.
[76] Garibaldi to Antonelli, 26 Oct. 1851, ASV Francia 1852 (III).
[77] Séché, *Les Derniers Jansénistes*, vol. iii, 63 n.

speak in his own defence, as required by the rules of Benedict XIV, the Index had cynically tricked Lequeux by allowing him to return to France not knowing that his book was under scrutiny. The rules stipulated also that Catholic authors in good standing should receive at the worst a decree *donec corrigatur*, allowing for the possibility of corrections, and should be permitted to revise and re-submit the work before any decree was published.[78]

The ultramontane interpretation of the rules of Benedict XIV by *L'Univers* and the *Correspondance de Rome* was rather different: the opportunity to be heard was 'sometimes' given to authors 'where it is appropriate'; and the omission of the phrase *donec corrigatur* in Lequeux's case indicated that the *Manuale* was a work of exceptional depravity, impossible to correct. It was useless for the bishops to hide behind a supposed ancient right not to receive or promulgate Roman decisions: decrees of the Index drew their force from the ordinary jurisdiction of the Holy See over dioceses, and came into effect, Veuillot claimed, as soon as they were published in the Catholic press.[79]

Three months after the decree Lequeux was still waiting for the Index to tell him what defects had been found in his book. 'I presume it is everything that happens to be contrary to the ultramontane movement . . .', he told the abbé Bernier: '. . . I do not know if they understand us at Rome; at least they do not like our usages or our liberties.' It was up to the bishops to organize resistance, but he had no great hope of the episcopate.[80] He paid several visits to the Nunciature to ask for some word from the Index, without success. Eventually, in March 1852, Cardinal de Bonald of Lyons protested to Rome that the Sulpician seminaries, including his own seminary of Saint-Irénée, were in an embarrassing position through not knowing which parts of the Lequeux *Manuale* were heretical. Cardinal Brignole, the Prefect of the Congregation of the Index, sent Bonald a list of the offending passages but told the Nuncio in a covering letter that the entire

---

[78] Abbé A. V. Delacouture, *Observations sur le décret de la Congrégation de l'Index* (1851). Sibour made similar points in a formal protest to the Nuncio on 6 Nov. 1851: ASV Francia 1853 (IV).

[79] *L'Univers* (21 and 23 Oct., 7 Nov. 1851). The *Correspondance de Rome* printed an analysis of the Index rules on 4 Jan. 1852.

[80] Lequeux to the abbé Henri Bernier of Angers, 15 Dec. 1851 and 18 Jan. 1852, in Houtin, *Bernier*, 314–16.

work was objectionable and that the Pope did not think there was any point in making corrections.[81] The Sulpicians withdrew the *Manuale* from their libraries, but instead of replacing it with another textbook they went on lecturing from their own notes, which were strongly influenced by Lequeux. There was one further refinement. When Lequeux's letter of submission reached Rome in October 1851 the abbé Bouix reported that the Index was not pleased with his phrase about submitting simply to avoid scandal, and that he would not receive the approving formula *laudabiliter se subjecit*.[82] The Index decree published on 22 January 1852 said coldly *auctor se subjecit*, a warning to gallicans who knew how to read such nuances.

The *archevêché*, however, might have been excused for not paying much attention to subtleties, because this decree of January 1852 contained another seismic shock for the Gallican Church: together with a collection of works by Proudhon, Eugène Sue, and the Italian philosopher Gioberti it condemned the abbé Guettée's *Histoire de l'Église de France*. Guettée had been theologian to Mgr Fabre des Essarts of Blois and theological adviser to the provincial council of Tours in 1849. His *Histoire* was still in progress, but the first seven volumes had been approved by forty-two diocesan seminaries and by several religious orders; a Jesuit reviewer in the ultramontane *Bibliographie catholique* had praised its scholarship and called it 'a glorious monument'. In 1850 Sibour invited him to a teaching post in Paris to give him access to metropolitan libraries, and the École des Carmes announced that Guettée's *Histoire* would be adopted as a standard text. Its days were clearly numbered. R. P. Gaultier, Mgr Gousset, and *L'Univers* delated it to the Index at more or less the same time in 1851, complaining in particular about Guettée's chapters on councils where he had argued that infallibility belonged to the whole church, that a general council could revoke a papal decision, and that Popes had often been in error. He had also spent rather a lot of time discussing medieval forgeries. The Index agreed, and once again the decree did not add *donec corrigatur*.[83]

---

[81] Cardinal Brignole to Garibaldi, 1 Mar. 1852, ASV Francia 1853 (IV).

[82] Bouix to Gaultier, 30 Oct. 1851, in Hédouville, 'Romains et gallicans', 82.

[83] Guettée, *Souvenirs d'un prêtre romain; Correspondance de Rome* (14 Feb. 1852); correspondance between Rome and the Nunciature in ASV Francia 1853 (III–IV).

Guettée received no direct communication from the Index, and the Nuncio did not reply when he wrote to ask if the decree as published in the *Correspondance de Rome* and *L'Univers* was genuine. He asked for a copy of the consultor's report, again without success. A large number of priests and bishops wrote privately to express sympathy, and he was treated very favourably in the press. The abbé de Cassan-Floyrac wrote in the *Gazette de France* that an Index decree did not mean that Catholics had to shun the book as if it were poisoned; popes and saints in the past had quoted knowingly from works that were on the Index but contained many excellent things: 'The Index, like Homer, sometimes nods . . . Let us take care that we [Catholics] ourselves are not put on the French version of the Index, which is the Index of good sense'.[84] Guettée's *Histoire* presented an unusual problem in that apart from being used in seminaries it was also sold widely to the public. On 14 April 1852 the *Correspondance de Rome* explained under the heading 'What booksellers must do when a book is put on the Index' that condemnation meant suppression, and that the Index had the authority to order a Catholic bookshop to close if it persisted in selling a condemned book. Faced with this highly debatable proposition Guettée's publishers, the Guyot brothers, took fright and withdrew their stock of the *Histoire* from sale; for this 'gesture of religious submission', which cost them a great deal of money, they received a papal letter of congratulation and a gold medal. Guettée went on writing the history for another publisher, with private support from Mgr Cœur of Troyes, Mgr Robiou of Coutances, the *curé* Martin de Noirlieu, and other prominent gallicans, but by the time the twelfth and last volume was completed, later in the 1850s, he had resigned all his appointments and become a priest of the Eastern Orthodox Church.

[84] *Gazette de France* (5 Oct. 1852).

IX

The second phase of the liturgy question

The Gregorian revival

WHILE the campaign for the Roman missal and breviary was succeeding even beyond Guéranger's early expectations, his other initiative, the revival of Gregorian chant, had run into severe difficulties.

To the ultramontanes it followed quite naturally that the adoption of the Roman liturgy required the restoration of Gregorian as the only music which had the solemnity and flexibility to match the Roman texts. The hymns and anthems used in the French Church had mostly been written in the seventeenth century and, according to Guéranger, were tainted with the same classicism and humanism as the gallican breviaries. This point was hotly contested by choirmasters; but Guéranger was on apparently stronger ground when he attacked the use of masses and motets by well-known composers of the modern period. Bach was a Protestant, Mozart was a freemason, and the masses of Rossini, Cherubini, and Ambroise Thomas were secular and operatic to the last degree. The kind of problem the reformers faced is suggested by the composition of the committee in the ministère des Cultes which controlled Church music and the training of ecclesiastical musicians: it included Ambroise Thomas, composer of *Mignon* and director of the Paris Conservatoire, and two of his professors of music, Félix Clément and Georges Bousquet; Paul Scudo, the music critic of the *Revue des deux mondes* and a composer of opera; Adolphe Adam, composer of the ballet *Giselle* and of sixty operas; M. Dietsch, musical director of the *Théâtre de la Nation*; the eminent teacher of elocution and gesture, François Delsarte; an official of the ministry, Auguste Nicolas; one priest, the abbé Leblanc, and two

Catholic MPs, MM. Buchez and Ernouf.[1] The only member of the committee who was favourable to the idea of a Gregorian revival was Félix Clément, who was writing a manual for teachers of plainchant.[2] Paul Scudo's view was expressed in one of his articles for the *deux mondes*: it was hard to believe, he wrote, that the monotonous chanting of half-understood Latin was superior either aesthetically or morally to the performance of a motet by Mozart; one might as well say that the crude pictures of saints sold at church doors were better than Michaelangelo's *Pieta*.[3] The committee as a whole reflected the consensus of opinion amongst choirmasters, organists, and senior clergy that ecclesiastical music, especially in the cities, had to please congregations whose tastes were formed by opera and the theatre.

The ultramontane liturgists, for their part, knew from their own experience with Gregorian chant that if properly performed it was an instrument of great strength, capable of expressing a range of religious emotions which could hardly be encompassed even by the most magnificent climaxes of masses by Mozart or Cherubini. Plainchant, they felt, might be actually the most important element of the liturgical revival; the long line of Gregorian melody echoing in the towering spaces of one of the ancient cathedrals created an almost magical evocation of a medieval age of faith, far more powerful and immediate than the details in a breviary. In many dioceses the choirmaster of the cathedral, his music cabinet stacked with vocal and orchestral parts for masses by composers approved by the ministère des Cultes, had to defend his position against a resolute group of Gregorian enthusiasts amongst the younger clergy. By the late 1840s the movement set going in France by the Mennaisians and given such strong impetus by Guéranger's *Institutions* had produced several schools of Gregorian studies, each one interpreting and collating a different collection of manuscript liturgies. Guéranger and his associates at Solesmes used Benedictine and Cistercian texts, but Solesmes was busy with too many controversies and

[1] AN F. 19. 3947–8 (Musique religieuse 1807–82); F. 19. 3949–52 (École de musique religieuse); *Almanach du clergé* for 1852 and 1856.
[2] Félix Clément, *Méthode complète de plain-chant* (1854); and *Des diverses réformes du chant grégorien* (1860).
[3] *Revue des deux mondes* (15 August 1861).

the liturgical work went slowly. Some individual scholars like the abbé Cloet and R. P. Lambilotte SJ published Gregorian systems of their own.[4] In 1848 a commission set up jointly by the provinces of Reims and Cambrai under the chairmanship of the abbé Tesson, a competent musicologist, was able to take advantage of the discovery of the 'Montpellier Manuscript', a Rosetta Stone of Gregorian music in which a medieval copyist had written both note-symbols and letters; the Reims–Cambrai commission used this as a key to other medieval manuscripts and by 1851 it was confident that it had re-established the original antiphony and gradual of the period of St Gregory the Great.[5]

It was clear, however, that French ecclesiastical music would have to be reformed by French scholarship, because there could be no question here of imitating a Roman model. Rome, the fountainhead of doctrine and discipline, was no help at all when it came to music. The *Correspondance de Rome* complained that the music in Italian churches was horribly secular, as indeed Berlioz and Mendelssohn had described it. One Frenchman reported that in the middle of high mass in a Roman church a priest had stood up and sung an aria by Donizetti. Gluck's overtures were played during requiem masses. The abbé Gay noted that at St John Lateran the Psalms were an excuse for 'solos, duos, and roulades in very bad taste, with accompaniment by organ, cello, and double-bass', and that the church was full of foreign visitors who had come to hear the singers.[6] At the Sistine Chapel they were preoccupied with a reform in a different direction, the revival of Renaissance polyphony, which to the French purists was a surrender to neo-pagan classicism.

The *Civiltà Cattolica* was favourable to the Gregorian revival in France and reported that similar studies were being undertaken in Italy, especially by Mgr Alfieri, 'to re-create the musical

[4] J. d'Ortigue, *Dictionnaire liturgique, historique et théorique du plain-chant* (1853); abbé Cloet, *La Restauration du chant liturgique* (1852); Dom P. Combe, *Histoire de la restauration du chant grégorien* (Solesmes 1969); Leclercq, article 'Lambilotte', *Dict. arch. et liturgie* viii, col. 1076; M. Rambures, 'De la musique religieuse', seven articles in the *Université catholique* (May–July 1852).

[5] Letter of Cardinal Giraud of Cambrai to the Pope, 7 Mar. 1850, and report of the Reims–Cambrai commission, 28 Mar. 1851: ASV Francia 1856 (I). The report is very dismissive of other schools of Gregorian studies at Malines and Turin, and does not mention Solesmes.

[6] B. du Boisrouvray, *Mgr Gay*, 2 vols. (1921), vol. i, 119.

principles of Guido d'Arezzo'.[7] The French were disturbed with the Roman endorsement of Alfieri, and more disturbed when his editions of the antiphony and gradual appeared in print. Alfieri had not felt too constrained by the musical principles of Guido d'Arezzo: his tastes were eclectic and his vocal line full of operatic flourishes. At Solesmes, Reims, and Cambrai they heard with profound distaste that the Congregation of Rites was in favour of imposing 'this coloratura' wherever Gregorian was used; an appeal to Rome succeeded in gaining at least informal approval for the use of French editions of plainchant, but a good deal of confusion remained.[8] Another serious obstacle was the sheer difficulty of Gregorian. A provincial diocese with limited resources could manage to give reasonable performances of masses by Mozart, but plainchant required liturgical specialists trained in Latin prosody and medieval notation. It was hard for congregations brought up on the vocal style of the early nineteenth century to follow trained chanters into the depths of the bass clef or to grasp the nuances of accent in Gregorian melody. An enquiry by the provincial *Sociétés des Savants* in 1853 recognized that parish priests had received practically no musical training in the seminaries and could hardly be expected to teach medieval music to village choirs. A diocesan enquiry at Reims found that too often congregations had to listen to Gregorian badly sung, 'phrases without character, a heap of inert notes that fatigue the ear and say nothing to the heart'.[9] There was stubborn resistance to the Roman pronunciation of Latin, which Guéranger thought was necessary if plainchant was to be sung properly.[10] After a series of disastrous experiences many parishes resigned themselves to doing without music at mass altogether.[11] In city parishes the tastes of choirmasters and the ingrained habits of singers prevailed, and where Gregorian was introduced it had to share the repertoire with traditional

[7] 'La musica religiosa', *Civiltà Cattolica* (1 Oct. 1856). Guido d'Arezzo (990–1050) was one of the pioneers of Western musical notation.

[8] Guillemant, *Parisis*, vol. iii, 70–82.

[9] Ibid. 74.

[10] Rome was still trying to persuade the French clergy on this point in the twentieth century: Letter of Pius X to the Archbishop of Bourges, 10 July 1912, *Actes de Pie X* vii, 168.

[11] Some typical complaints are cited in Ledru, *Dom Guéranger et Mgr Bouvier*, 233–8, 355–7.

anthems and classical masses. The all-Gregorian ceremonies held at Paris later in the century were almost deserted.[12] At Sainte-Clothilde César Franck continued to direct performances of his own highly chromatic choral works. The catalogue of the publisher René Haton in the 1870s included Gregorian chant dressed up with organ accompaniment and additional counterpoint, and modern choral music 'praised and approved by the musical directors of Saint Peter's and Saint John Lateran in Rome'. Félix Clément's admiration for plainchant did not prevent him from composing polyphonic motets 'to accompany the feast-days of the Roman liturgy'. In the most fashionable churches the music remained frankly contemporary: Taine remarked after attending a nuptial mass that 'it was a very fine opera, rather like the fifth act of *Robert le Diable* except that *Robert le Diable* is more religious'.[13] City parishes tried to poach one another's congregations by advertising bigger orchestras and more famous singers.[14] In 1884 the Congregation of Rites, surveying the state of religious music in Europe, felt it necessary to forbid 'operatic and dance music, polkas, waltzes, mazurkas, minuets . . . quadrilles, galops, dances of Scotland, Poland, and Lithuania, erotic popular songs and romances', all of which were currently to be heard in churches to the accompaniment of 'tambourines, bass drums, cymbals, barrel-organs, and pianos';[15] even in the most serious parishes there was a state of confusion in which several competing styles of Gregorian chant existed alongside a deplorable amount of semi-secular music. In 1903 the well-known *Motu proprio* of Pius X inaugurated a determined campaign to replace all other forms of ecclesiastical music by a single approved version of plainchant,[16] but the French preserved an eclectic variety of styles until well after the First World War.

[12] Lanzac de Laborie, 'Dom Guéranger et son œuvre', *Le Correspondant* (10 Mar. 1910).

[13] Quoted by Olivier Rousseau, *Le Mouvement liturgique*, 154 n.

[14] This had been a problem since the 1840s, much deplored by priests who thought that the churches should pay more attention to attracting the simple poor, rather than competing for the fashionable 'first-night' public: see the letters from an anonymous priest to Archbishop Sibour in 1849, edited by Yves Daniel as *La Religion est perdue à Paris* (1978).

[15] Rousseau, *Le Mouvement liturgique*, 155.

[16] *Motu proprio* and additional documents, 22 Nov. 1903, *Actes de Pie X* i, 48–69. A strong impetus was given by the foundation at Rome of the *Rassegna Gregoriana* in 1901.

The liturgies of Troyes, Chartres, and Le Mans

Several times during 1851 *L'Univers* claimed that the gallican liturgies were being swept away by a positive landslide of enthusiasm. Twenty-nine dioceses had adopted the Roman liturgy, and most of the provincial councils had voted for a change, at least in principle. Mgr Wicart of Fréjus wrote in a pastoral that there was no need for tedious 'explanations' to clergy or laity: it was a movement sweeping through the Church as a whole.

Personal preferences, literary tastes, the poetic *éclat* of certain hymns [in the gallican rite]; the instruction that results from bringing together, often in happy juxtaposition, of Old and New Testament texts . . . all these things disappear, or become irrelevant. It is a matter only of returning to the prescriptions, always in force, of the celebrated Bulls of the great and holy Pontiff Pius V—to pray as they do at Rome, in the same words, on the same days, with the same ceremonials, from one extremity of the world to the other.[17]

L'Univers printed scornful articles by Morel and du Lac suggesting that resistance was coming mainly from bishops and vicars-general educated in the pagan classics who preferred Horace and Epicurus to the Christian scriptures, and appealing to the lower clergy to take the initiative to introduce the Roman liturgy in their own dioceses. The *Correspondance de Rome* filled column after column with the activities of the Congregation of Rites and worked hard to create the impression of a central bureaucracy now thoroughly and officiously awake, gathering queries from every part of the Catholic world and issuing judgements, rescripts, and decrees with crushing and final authority. To every problem there was a correct, that is to say Roman, solution. What is the precise wording of prayers to the Virgin Mary on Saturdays? May a protonotary apostolic wear a ring while celebrating mass? May one article of vestments be substituted for another in case of accidental damage? What is the Roman formula for the composition of a Paschal candle? The answer could be a 6000-word article, as it was to a question about the blessing of holy oils, or a brusque 'yes' or 'no'. In fact much of this activity was an illusion; the Congregation was as slow and inefficient as ever, and the *Correspondance* was sometimes

17 *L'Univers* (17 Sept. 1851).

reduced to discussing decrees of twenty years earlier. Throughout 1851 and 1852 the ultramontane bishops still found that Rome was their main obstacle. The Nuncio wrote every few weeks: Soissons wanted to introduce the Roman liturgy before Advent, but had heard nothing; Montauban had sent its breviary to the Congregation two years ago and 'expected to receive it back from one day to the next'.[18] Early in 1851 the *Correspondance* began to publish requests for rulings addressed to the journal itself: would the editors give a judgement on whether to celebrate the feast of Saint Antony with the double-minor or the semi-double rite? Should the Precious Blood be celebrated once in Easter week (double-major) and again in July (double of the second class)? Some of these questions were clearly from priests dissatisfied with decisions by their own bishops: the editors were reassuringly authoritative.

In March 1851 the *Correspondance de Rome* intervened with remarkable effect in the affair of the Troyes liturgy. The diocese of Troyes had consolidated its local liturgies during the Restoration. In 1847 the bishop, Mgr Debelay, became convinced by Guéranger's arguments and adopted the Roman missal and the Roman form of benediction, this latter change causing widespread comment in the diocese because the blessing in the Roman rite was given in silence, where in the gallican rite it was accompanied by a chanted prayer. Debelay was transferred to Avignon in 1849; the new bishop, Mgr Cœur, was a former professor of the Sorbonne and one of the strongest supporters of the old gallican tradition. In his first public address as bishop he let it be understood that he would give permission for any parish to continue using the old diocesan liturgy 'if local circumstances warranted it'. Knowing Cœur's reputation, the Nuncio Fornari had arranged for a Catholic layman, Philippe Guignarez, to report to him any compromising statements from the *évêché*: Guignarez wrote that the new bishop had virtually given a general exemption from the Roman liturgy and had restored the old form of chanted benediction at the cathedral. Fornari passed the correspondence on to Rome in April 1849. Nothing happened, to his great annoyance, until after the Papal restoration; then on 7 September 1850 the Congregation of Rites drafted a formal

---

[18] Garibaldi, 16 July 1851, 13 Mar. 1852: ASV Francia 1856 (I).

letter of censure to Cœur.[19] Six months went by, and Cœur gave no sign that he had been reprimanded. On 14 March 1851 the Latin text of the censure appeared in the *Correspondance de Rome*, and was reprinted in *L'Univers* on 23 March. Cœur wrote immediately to several newspapers to say that he had never received such a letter and that the text in the *Correspondance* must be a forgery. On 14 April the *Correspondance* claimed that the censure was genuine and that it had been posted to Cœur 'more than six months ago'; but on 19 April Cardinal Antonelli wrote to the Paris Nunciature in some embarrassment: it now appeared that through an unfortunate muddle the letter had never left the offices of the Congregation, although a copy had 'accidentally' been given to the editors of the *Correspondance de Rome*. Transmitting Antonelli's apologies to Cœur, Mgr Garibaldi warned him that he would, nevertheless, have to conform to the Roman liturgy; as he told Antonelli, behind the apparently trivial issue of silence or chanting at benediction there was a symbolic confrontation between Rome and the Jansenist tradition. Cœur came to Paris to put his case to the Nuncio. Half of the diocesan clergy and practically all of the laity disliked the Roman rite: why was Rome insisting on it? The gallican usages had been tolerated by the Popes for centuries. Like other bishops, he said, he relied on the famous promise by Cardinal Caprara at the time of the Concordat not to disturb the rules, liberties or privileges of the Church of France.[20] Writing at the same time to Dupanloup, Cœur reported that he had received a letter from the abbé Combalot accusing him of being a schismatic and 'continuing the unworthy work of the eighteenth century', and was having to put up with all kinds of abuse from priests in his diocese: 'are we back in the days of *L'Avenir*?[21]

While Cœur was still negotiating with the Nunciature the *Correspondance de Rome* published two long articles interpreting the judgement of the Congregation of Rites as a humiliating defeat for Cœur, and by implication of the whole gallican resistance,

---

[19] Letters of Philippe Guignarez to Mgr Fornari, and exchange of correspondence between Cœur and the Archbishop of Sens, forwarded to Rome with Fornari's comments in April 1849: ASV Parigi vol. 76.

[20] Garibaldi's dispatches of 2–21 Apr. 1851; Antonelli to Garibaldi, 19 Apr.: ASV Francia 1856 (I). Garibaldi wrote a detailed retrospective account of the affair on 16 Jan. 1852, ASV Francia 1852 (II).

[21] Cœur to Dupanloup, 25 Apr. 1851, Dupanloup/BN 24680.

and hinting that in future Rome would rule in favour of any individual priest who introduced the Roman liturgy against the orders of his bishop.[22] Hearing from Garibaldi that this was probably true, Cœur decided to write directly to the Pope. At this stage of the conflict it was still possible for many of the gallicans to believe that Pius IX was above parties and factions, and that there could be no question of holding the Pope himself responsible for the excesses of the ultramontane movement. Cœur's letter perfectly illustrates this frame of mind. He declared 'from the bottom of my heart the most profound attachment to the person of the Holy Father'. Had he known clearly what the Pope's wishes were he would have hastened to carry them out; now that the Nuncio had made matters clear, he would of course obey. Could the Holy Father understand, however, that Troyes was a diocese full of problems, not easy to resolve by simple fiat? On one side were the people, reluctant to be disturbed in their ancient practices, and on the other the zealots, very undisciplined and unpriestly in their behaviour: 'If the Holy Father, the good and great Pius IX, knew what liberties are taken here, to the serious detriment of ecclesiastical order and the rules of obedience, by a few persons carried away by their own impetuous character . . . If the Pope knew! The Pope, my refuge, my courage, my force . . . the Pastor of all, the immovable foundation of the whole Church.'[23] It was entirely characteristic of Roman proceedings at this time that there was no reply, even after the Nuncio had written twice more to point out that a papal letter would have an excellent effect. Cœur introduced the silent form of benediction in his cathedral, and told Dupanloup that he would have nothing more to do with the liturgy question.

In two dioceses where the ultramontanes thought it particularly important to succeed, Chartres and Le Mans, the liturgy question was resolved by the threat of the Index.

One of Guéranger's most provocative techniques in the first volume of his *Institutions liturgiques* had been to jumble together the gallican liturgies, the Declaration of the Rights of Man and the Civil Constitution of the Clergy to make it appear that all these documents were part of the same movement. Amongst his examples he had cited the diocesan breviary of Chartres which

---

[22] *Correspondance de Rome* (24 Apr. and 24 Aug. 1851).
[23] Cœur to Pius IX, 12 Oct. 1851, ASV Francia 1856 (I).

he said had been compiled after the Revolution by the celebrated abbé Sieyès. The older clergy at Chartres knew that this was not true and denied it, but the damage was done; the story had been repeated in *L'Univers*, and although Guéranger had to delete the passage about Sieyès from subsequent editions, priests all over the country went on discussing this revelation about the pedigree of gallican ritual; the Pope was still telling the story to French visitors twenty years later. In the second volume of the *Institutions* Guéranger attacked the Chartrain liturgy again, this time on aesthetic grounds and with the suggestion that it was a typical product of prelates who had been essentially men of the world. The bishop, Clausel de Montals, was old and frail but still ready for controversy. With the help of R. P. Carrière of Saint-Sulpice he composed a pastoral letter 'on the glory and wisdom of the old Church of France', a panegyric on the gallican tradition from the earliest Gaulish bishops to Bossuet, Emery, and Frayssinous, and an attack on the scholarship and the methods of the *école de Solesmes*.[24] This attracted a good deal of attention. Mgr. Fornari was just leaving for Rome, and Guéranger asked him to refer Clausel's pastoral to the Index. A few months later Clausel received a letter from Fornari, writing, he said, at the Pope's request: the Congregation of the Index had found his praise of the gallican tradition 'reprehensible and excessive', and had it not been for his advanced age and distinguished career he would have been condemned also for what he had said about certain ultramontane clergy who were simply following 'the known will of the Mother and Mistress Church'.[25] Clausel wrote no more about liturgy. He resigned his bishopric in 1852 and the Chartrain rite was Romanized under his successor.

The Le Mans affair had deep roots in the conflicts and rivalries of the Mennaisian period. The director of the Le Mans seminary during the Restoration, Jean-Baptiste Bouvier, was a Sulpician graduate in the tradition of Emery; his *Institutiones theologicae*, known as *La Théologie du Mans*, a textbook with the usual gallican flavour—'by ancient custom the bishops of France do not

---

[24] *Lettre pastorale . . . sur la gloire et les lumières qui ont distingué jusqu'à nos jours l'Église de France, et sur les périls dont elle semble aujourd'hui menacée*, 25 Sept. 1850.

[25] Sevrin, *Clausel de Montals*, vol. ii, chap. 48; Delatte, *Dom Guéranger*, vol. ii, 27–35, 43. Another strong gallican, Mgr Robiou of Coutances, had a similar experience after writing a pastoral letter on the liturgy; the Nuncio denounced it to the Index, and he received a warning: ASV Francia 1856 (I).

recognize the decisions of Roman Congregations as authoritative'—
was used in twenty-six seminaries. In the 1820s the teaching at
Le Mans was challenged by a group of younger instructors and
some of the students who had come under the influence of
Lamennais's *Essai sur l'indifférence*. One of these ultramontane
instructors, the abbé Lottin, also had a long-standing dispute
with his director over the number of students he was expected to
teach. In 1831 Bouvier had Lottin transferred from teaching to
be a canon of the cathedral, a tactical mistake because when
Bouvier became bishop of the diocese Lottin was to be his
lifelong opponent, an ultramontane vote in the cathedral chapter
and a remorseless critic of the bishop's administration.

The most promising pupil at Le Mans had been Prosper
Guéranger, who was appointed to a professorship and made
secretary to the *évêché* while still a student, and it had been a
disappointment for Bouvier when Guéranger attached himself to
the ultramontanes in the seminary and went off soon after his
ordination to join Lamennais at La Chenaie. When Guéranger
reappeared in the diocese, restoring the abbey of Solesmes,
Bouvier was inclined to treat him benevolently and at one point
he intervened at Solesmes to save Guéranger from being deposed
in a minor mutiny amongst the Benedictines: he took the view
that a monastic community deserved his protection so long as it
did not forget that the bishop had a right of supervision and
consultation. When Guéranger announced in 1837 that he was to
be known as 'Abbot of Solesmes', Bouvier made the proviso that
he should not take part in public ceremonies wearing quasi-
episcopal vestments, but it was hopeless to try and confine the
ebullient Guéranger; he appeared in a mitre, wearing a ring, and
carrying a crozier. Solesmes then put forward a number of
candidates for ordination who had been trained entirely by
Guéranger without having passed through a diocesan seminary.
Bouvier declined to ordain them. What would be their situation,
he asked, if they should leave the Benedictines and apply for
postings to parishes? Guéranger did not argue: he ordained them
himself, as if his status was fully episcopal, and went on
conferring orders through the 1840s and 50s; he ordained several
young men who had been expelled from diocesan seminaries.
Bouvier's complaints to the Congregation of Bishops and
Regulars produced no result. In 1845 the Benedictines over-

extended their resources by founding a second community at Paris, and fell into virtual bankruptcy with a debt of over half a million francs. The anticlerical press revealed the existence of large bills for wine and cigars, and Guéranger found himself the object of a great deal of satire. At the height of his embarrassment he heard with chagrin that Bouvier had been appointed by the ministère des Cultes to enquire into the management of Solesmes. He refused to show Bouvier the accounts, claiming that the Benedictines were not subject to diocesan authority and that the Nuncio had encouraged him to send the accounts to Rome. Bouvier appealed again to Bishops and Regulars, and this time he was assured that a reprimand had been sent to Solesmes with an instruction that Guéranger was to obey the lawful requirements of his bishop; but Mgr Fornari would not transmit this reprimand to Guéranger. Instead he set up a 'Committee to Save Solesmes' composed of wealthy laymen, which raised enough money to pay off the debts and make Bouvier's enquiry unnecessary.[26]

It would have been a notable achievement for Guéranger to have won over Bouvier's diocese to the Roman liturgy. After some years of lobbying he had managed to persuade some members of the cathedral chapter, but the diocesan clergy generally agreed with Bouvier's own view that the Le Mans liturgy, codified in 1748, was respectable, dignified, and coherent. Towards the end of 1851, however, Bouvier heard that the monks at Solesmes were saying that the bishop of Le Mans was about to receive a just recompense for the harm he had done the Benedictines during the past fifteen years, in the form of an unpleasant surprise from Rome. He was then told by a friend recently returned from Rome that his *Théologie du Mans* had been delated to the Index because it was supposed to contain the same errors as the works of Professor Nuytz. He wrote in great agitation to the Nuncio: would he be condemned unheard, like Lequeux? Garibaldi told Cardinal Antonelli that he hoped this rumour was not true. The case of Lequeux had been quite different: Sibour and his entourage of ultra-gallican intellectuals deserved any censure the Index cared to apply, but Bouvier was a hard-working and popular diocesan bishop. He was seventy

---

[26] AN F. 19. 2534 (Le Mans: Bouvier); *Corboli Bussi*, articolo v; Delatte, *Dom Guéranger*, vol. i, chaps. 4–9; Ledru, *Dom Guéranger et Mgr Bouvier*, chaps. 1–3.

years old, and his clergy looked upon him as a father. Certainly he was tainted with gallicanism, like all his generation, but he was 'fundamentally attached to the Holy See'; his book was a moderate and reasonable work that had been used for over thirty years and was now in its seventh edition. Antonelli reported that Bouvier could set his mind at rest: there was no examination in progress.[27] Bouvier was then advised by one of his household to write to R. P. Rubillon, the French consultor to the Index. Rubillon replied that he could not imagine where Bouvier had heard rumours of an examination, but he evidently knew the *Théologie du Mans* because he added that 'given the wide diffusion of the work in so many seminaries, Rome would be pleased if certain propositions were amended'.[28]

Bouvier was more alarmed when he heard that Dom Guéranger himself, on a recent visit to Rome, had been appointed a consultor to the Congregation of Rites and the Index. Had the Abbot denounced him? Eventually, in February 1852, he had a letter from Guéranger, who said that he had just heard within the past few days that a rumour was circulating about Bouvier and the Index, and he wanted to assure Bouvier that he personally had nothing to do with any delation; he repeated this several times, adding that it was not in his character to do things in secret: 'if I had thought that for the good of the church a classic work by Your Excellency had to be referred to the Sacred Congregation, I would have acted quite differently'.[29] This was not particularly reassuring, and Bouvier thought it odd also that Guéranger asked that his denial be kept as a strict secret, but for the time being he heard no more about problems at Rome. Then at the beginning of May he found himself and his diocese suddenly notorious.

At a diocesan synod in the middle of the previous year Canon Lottin and two of his supporters had formally moved that the diocese adopt the Roman liturgy; Bouvier had ruled them out of order. Guéranger had then persuaded Lottin to write directly to

---

[27] Bouvier to Garibaldi, 17 Oct. 1851; Garibaldi's dispatch, 26 Oct.; Antonelli to Garibaldi, 11 Nov.: ASV Francia 1852 (III). There are signs in Garibaldi's correspondance at this time that various works by Maret, Bautain, and Lacordaire were being considered by the Index.

[28] R. P. Rubillon to Bouvier, Jan. 1852, in Ledru, *Dom Guéranger et Mgr Bouvier*, 217.

[29] Ibid., Guéranger to Bouvier, 2 Feb. 1852, 218.

Rome asking a number of questions on liturgy, and in January 1852 these questions had come back to Lottin with the delphic replies of the Congregations of Rites:

Q. Were the changes in the breviary of Le Mans in the year 1748 lawful?
A. Negative.
Q. Is this liturgy, however, now sanctified by age and custom, and can the priests of the diocese continue to use it with a clear conscience?
A. Negative.[30]

Lottin had held this document in reserve; but on 4 May 1852 the *Correspondance de Rome* published it, without naming the diocese but with a commentary implying that after this judgement there could surely not be any further resistance to the Roman liturgy in any French diocese. Gossip soon established that the questions had originated at Le Mans, and there was a great stir amongst the lower clergy. At the same time Bouvier received two letters from members of religious orders with excellent contacts at Rome: one warned him that the Index was currently examining the *Théologie du Mans,* and the other claimed to know that the book had been denounced by 'the same people who obtained the recent reply from the Congregation of Rites'. He had evidently been wrong to rely on official answers from Rome, he told the Nuncio; the threat of the Index was clearly related to his obduracy on the liturgy question. As it happened, he said, he had been examining the diocesan breviary and could see a way in which the Roman rite could be introduced, provided the zealots could be persuaded to wait until circumstances allowed it to be done without undue fuss. In the meantime he would continue his usual practice of allowing individual priests to recite the Roman breviary if they asked special permission; and he would write to the Pope asking for an authoritative direction. Mgr Garibaldi still could not believe that Bouvier was in any danger from the Index, and thought that the rumours must have been started by malicious gallicans to discredit the methods of the Holy See. It was embarrassing, he told Antonelli, because only a few days

---

[30] Text in *L'Univers* (17 July 1852); the case is discussed in the Sulpician *Mémoire* of October 1852 (see chapter X below.)

earlier he had assured the French Foreign Minister that the Index was certainly not examining Bouvier.[31]

On 24 May Bouvier had another letter from Guéranger, this time admitting that the *Théologie du Mans* had been delated to the Index; he had heard about this in Rome as long ago as 'at the end of last November', he said, forgetting that he had already claimed to have heard it for the first time in February. But he expressed surprise: the *Théologie* was a classic and not at all a work of extreme gallicanism; who could have denounced it? The whole business was a mystery. Bouvier should write to Rome offering to bring out a revised edition; and he happened to know, he wrote, that 'if Your Excellency would consent to issue an ordinance for the re-establishment of the Roman liturgy, it would produce a very good effect'.[32] Bouvier now understood the situation perfectly. He wrote to the Pope on 30 May and sent a copy of his *Théologie* as a token of his willingness to consider amendments. Its arrival at the Index offices coincided with another enquiry from Cardinal Antonelli, and enabled R. P. Modena at last to give a direct answer: the Index was indeed examining the *Théologie du Mans,* he told Antonelli on 16 June, because the bishop of Le Mans himself had sent a copy and asked for an examination.[33]

On 17 July *L'Univers* published the integral text of the Lottin document, this time naming the diocese. Half of the Church already knew about the replies from the Congregation of Rites; now everybody knew, and there were editorials in the secular press. Mgr Sibour wrote to commiserate with Bouvier about the untenable position of bishops if priests were encouraged to correspond directly with the Roman Curia and obey its instructions. It was particularly absurd that this should be happening with regard to the liturgy, a matter on which the Popes had always been so tolerant. Sibour was surprised to hear that Bouvier was ready to abandon his diocesan liturgy:

In fact, Monseigneur, it is not a Pontifical ruling, it is not a Brief, it is

[31] Bouvier to Garibaldi, 18 May 1852, and Garibaldi's dispatch of 22 May: ASV Francia 1852 (III).

[32] Guéranger to Bouvier, 24 May 1852, in Ledru, *Dom Guéranger et Mgr Bouvier,* 220–2.

[33] Modena to Antonelli, 16 June 1852: ASV Francia 1852 (III). Cf. the French ambassador's audience with Pius IX on 14 June 1852, discussed in chapter X below.

not an act of the Sovereign Pontiff himself which has been conveyed to you; and even if such a thing had been sent, even in the most imperative form, you would still have had the right in both the letter and the spirit of canon law to suspend the execution of the measures prescribed while you appealed to the Head of the Church. But how far from having the force of a Pontifical act is a simple decision emanating from a congregation, of which you have not even been notified officially . . . You know better than I do that the jurisdiction of the Roman Congregations has never been recognized in France. That of Rites had even less right to interfere in your diocese, where the Roman liturgy was never in force . . . Where are we going, Monseigneur, and what will be the end of these enterprises?[34]

Even Mgr Garibaldi, convinced as he was of the essential rightness of the ultramontane cause, was beginning to worry about clerical indiscipline. When he contemplated the results at Le Mans, where priests who had been Bouvier's pupils in the seminary were now writing letters to the press gloating over their bishop's embarrassment and predicting the condemnation of his textbook, he had some doubts about the tactics the Nunciature had encouraged for the past four years. He asked Antonelli again to use his influence to see that the Index did not add to Bouvier's difficulties.[35]

When the Pope wrote to Bouvier on 2 September, after a delay of three months, he promised that Bouvier's dignity and honour would be respected and that he would be notified of any corrections required in his books so that he could prepare a revised edition; but Bouvier heard nothing from the Index. On 28 October he issued a rather double-edged pastoral: 'although the liturgy of this diocese was perhaps one of the most irreproachable of the liturgies of the last century . . . in spite of its genuine beauty and the remarkable balance of its component parts, we have taken the decision to replace it with the Roman liturgy'; and a month later, still not having heard from the Index, he announced that he would go to Rome. On hearing this Guéranger sent one of his monks to Rome ahead of the bishop to brief the Congregation of the Index on the defence Bouvier would probably use. When Bouvier arrived he was received very aimiably by Pius IX, and felt bold enough to ask if he could be

[34] Sibour to Bouvier, 21 July 1852, copy in AN F. 19. 1947.
[35] Garibaldi, 26 Sept. 1852: ASV Francia 1852 (III).

given the opportunity to discuss the *Théologie du Mans* with 'wise and moderate men'. 'We are all moderate in Rome', said the Pope, smiling; but the corrections required turned out to be endless. The entire six-volume work had to be reconstructed before a new edition was permitted.[36]

The Le Mans affair accelerated 'the veritable carnage which devastated the gallican liturgy',[37] as one faint-hearted bishop after another hurried to establish his credentials with the Holy See. Mgr Morlot of Tours told the Nuncio that after hearing the news from Le Mans he was ready to obey the wishes of His Holiness on the liturgy question, or on any other question, and that in spite of the grave difficulty and inconvenience he would take steps to introduce the Roman rite as soon as possible 'by the inclination and the movement of a heart filled with the most profound respect and the most filial submission';[38] in private he told one of his friends that 'they want to make us more and more like Italy, under the pretext of drawing us closer to the centre of unity'.[39] Letters flowed in to the Nunciature from bishops who had been 'moved by the recent decision of the Congregation of Rites . . . to express our feelings of filial piety towards the Sacred Person': their diocesan liturgies were ancient and distinguished, they said, they were understood and cherished by the laity in the parishes, but nevertheless they would be changed at the first opportune moment. Some dioceses asked plaintively if they could keep one small devotion to a popular local saint, adding that of course they would not insist.[40] Sulpician-educated priests watched this undignified scramble with amusement. Canon Follet wrote to one of his old professors at Saint-Sulpice from the diocese of Amiens, where the bishop was trying to convince the clergy of the need for haste and had called in the abbé Combalot to preach on the cultural primacy of Rome; but there had been a delay in

[36] Garibaldi's dispatches for Nov.–Dec. 1852, in ASV Francia 1852 (II–III); Bouvier's pastoral and other documents in Ledru, *Dom Guéranger et Mgr Bouvier*, 224–31.
[37] E. Amann, article 'Veuillot' in *DTC*.
[38] ASV Francia 1856 (I).
[39] Quoted by L. Baunard, *Un siècle de l'Église de France* (1919), 160.
[40] Letters to the Nuncio from Bourges, ASV Francia 1852 (II); from Angers, Saint-Dié and Versailles, ASV Francia 1856 (I). Thirteen other dioceses went over to the Roman rite in 1852.

printing copies of the Roman ceremonial, 'at which we do not complain'.[41]

Within two years the Romanization of the liturgy was almost complete; any stragglers were harassed by the Papal Legate, Cardinal Patrizi, when he came to France in 1856 to baptize the Prince Imperial.[42] The Congregation of Rites made it clear that it would tolerate no exceptions. Guéranger himself received a surprise. He had drawn up a special liturgy for Solesmes, based on ancient Cluniac and Benedictine texts, and submitted it for the papal blessing; in 1856 it was rejected by the Congregation of Rites. Guéranger vowed never to return to Rome in the lifetime of Pius IX, and refused a personal invitation to attend the Vatican Council in 1869.[43] The last bishops to go over to the Roman rite were Bonald at Lyon, Ginoulhiac at Grenoble, Mathieu at Besançon, and Dupanloup at Orleans who held out until 1875 by a series of legalistic manœuvres. In 1863 Cardinal de Bonald and a group of his senior clergy went to Rome to ask the Pope if the ancient and picturesque Lyonnais liturgy, parts of which could be traced back to the fifth century, could somehow be exempted. 'Very well', said Pius IX, 'you may keep your liturgy.' The Lyonnais delegation were astonished and delighted and for a moment thought that they had won an unexpected victory. But the Pope continued: they could keep the liturgy in so far as it was a matter of the colour of vestments and some other minor details. 'Your breviary and missal, on the other hand, do not really belong to the ancient liturgy'; it was common knowledge that the French liturgies had been compiled in the eighteenth century—and Cardinal de Bonald and his colleagues listened with deepening gloom as the Pope went on to speak of gallican parlements, sceptical bishops, Jansenism, humanism, the breviary of Chartres, and the abbé Sieyès.[44]

[41] Canon Follet of Montdidier to M. Boiteux, 26 May and 10 Oct. 1852: S. Sulp/AN AB XIX 518.

[42] Note by M. Tardif, 13 Nov. 1856, AN F. 19. 5434.

[43] H. Leclercq, 'Liturgies néo-gallicanes', *Dict. d'archéologie chrétienne et de liturgie* ix, col. 1729.

[44] AN F. 19. 5435 (Affaire de la liturgie lyonnaise); Cardinal de Bonald, 'Lettre au clergé de son diocèse touchant la question liturgique', 4 Feb. 1864, AN F. 19. 2531.

X

Gallican resistance in 1852

The supression of the Correspondance de Rome

IN his private memoir of the rise of ultramontanism, written
twenty years afterwards, Mgr Dupanloup, still reluctant to
recognize the broader motives which had led the lower clergy
and some of the laity to be so receptive to ultramontane ideas,
blamed the Romanizing movement entirely on the 'thoughtless
and heartless fanatics' of the *Correspondance de Rome* and *L'Univers*
who had succeeded in pushing the Church towards a centralized
autocracy modelled on the absolute monarchies of the seventeenth
and eighteenth centuries. As if centralized absolutism was not in
reality a very fragile system, always eventually overthrown by
revolution, Dupanloup reflected; he and his fellow Catholic
liberals had believed since the 1830s that the Church should
observe the success of stable and peaceful societies like England
where the central power was tempered by local liberties and
constitutional forms. Unity without uniformity was too subtle a
concept for the coarse minds of these 'journalists . . . without
mission or mandate': 'they crushed down to the level of a
mechanical and deathly sameness everything that had contributed
to the life, the force, and the greatness of the diverse Churches'.
By 1852, he wrote, the ultramontane press had become more
influential than the Nuncio, the Roman Secretariat of State, or
the College of Cardinals, and far more powerful than the
demoralized French episcopate; the bishops, persuaded to make
one concession after another by their very respect for the papacy,
which the *école de l'Univers* exploited shamelessly, now saw their
dioceses slipping out of control, their decisions overturned by the
Roman congregations and the lower clergy taking their instructions
directly from newspapers which claimed to be expressing the
wishes of the Pope.[1]

In April 1852 Dupanloup supervised the drafting of a protest
in the form of an open letter, *Le journalisme dans l'Église*, which

[1] 'Rapport au Pape', Dupanloup/AN AB XIX 524, dossier 3.

suggested that a French faction at Rome was deliberately
dividing the bishops and encouraging insubordination amongst
the clergy in order to give the papacy an excuse to intervene in
the French Church. He circulated this in manuscript to several of
the leading gallicans; only one of them, Mgr de Marguerye, was
brave enough actually to sign it, but all agreed that it should be
sent to the Pope, in the belief that Pius IX would be disturbed if
he knew the full extent of ultramontane intrigue. *Le journalisme
dans l'Église* was received at Rome with chilly disapproval.
Cardinal Fornari wrote an analysis of it and the Nuncio was
instructed to convey the message that the complaint was
rejected.[2] But shortly after this, at the end of June 1852, both
gallicans and ultramontanes heard with great surprise that the
Correspondance de Rome had been suppressed, as the result of
diplomatic pressure from the French government.

The new government of Louis Napoleon, as part of its
campaign to win over conservative opinion, had shown very
marked favour for the Catholic Church in the first six months
after the *coup d'état* of December 1851: the Prince-President made
a number of speeches which seemed to show his wish for a
religious revival in France, the *budget des Cultes* was augmented
with extra funds for church building and clerical salaries, the
Pantheon was restored to religious worship as the church of St
Genevieve, some university courses by prominent rationalists
were suspended, and local authorities were instructed to interpret
the Loi Falloux of 1850 very loosely so as to give the greatest
freedom to the religious orders in the schools. At Rome, after a
momentary hesitation while the papal court considered the
prospect of another Napoleon, the response was very favourable,
and the Pope congratulated both the ambassador and the
commander of the French military garrison; characteristically,
the Secretariat of State sent no clear instructions to the Nuncio at
Paris, and Garibaldi had to read the Roman correspondence in
L'Univers to see that the papacy welcomed the *coup d'état*.[3]

[2] *Le Journalisme dans l'Église, ou la Correspondance de Rome soumise à l'examen* . . .:
manuscript and printed copies, covering letters, e.g. from Guibert, Marguerye, and
Blanquart de Bailleul, report by a panel of cardinals chaired by Fornari, and
dispatches between the Nunciature and the Secretariat of State: ASV Francia 1854
(IV) and 1856 (I).
[3] *Bettoni*, 255. On the relations of the new government with Rome in 1852,
Maurain, *Saint-Siège*, 1–30.

In this early phase the government imagined that it could patronize religion without having to take sides in the gallican–ultramontane conflict. Louis Napoleon himself was inclined at first to favour the ultramontane party. He was on good terms personally with some of the leading ultras like Gousset and Salinis, and he could not help noticing that while the gallicans in general had held back, the *école de l'Univers* had supported him with unrestrained enthusiasm. The ultramontane bishops had greeted 'the Christian Prince' with fulsome pastoral letters which they were to find unbearably embarrassing a few years later, and *L'Univers*, seeing the *coup d'état* as the final defeat of liberal parliamentarism—'Rome can hardly do anything but applaud on seeing this great volcano, the one which set the others on fire, now extinct'—did everything possible to encourage a *ralliement* of clergy and laity.[4] Veuillot told the diplomat Henri d'Ideville later that Louis Napoleon 'could have become the temporal head of all the Catholics in Europe. I dreamed of a greater role for him than that of Alexander or Charlemagne; he could have conquered the world by reuniting all the Catholic nationalities, and Rome and Paris would have been its two poles . . . But alas!', Veuillot added, 'the man did not understand his part'.[5] Veuillot's influence persuaded even the royalist clergy of Brittany and the Vendée to support the Prince-President, and indeed moved almost the entire body of Catholic legitimists, with the exception of a few *réfractaires* like Pie and Dreux-Brézé, to accept the new régime at least as a step in the right direction; there was some speculation in the press that Veuillot would be offered the editorship of the official *Moniteur*, or a seat in the Senate. The leading gallicans were much more cautious. Bonnechose, Marguerye, Cœur, and Morlot agreed to support the régime with reservations, although their reservations soon disappeared. Dupanloup protested, and was never entirely reconciled with Louis Napoleon. Sibour and the circle of the *archevêché* thought of themselves as republicans and after the *coup* Sibour considered joining Victor Hugo at the head of a mass protest in the streets.

---

[4] Jules Morel in *L'Univers* (8 Feb. 1852).
[5] H. d'Ideville, *Journal d'un diplomate en Italie*, 2 vols. (1872–3), vol. ii, 273, 278. Veuillot's ideas about secular politics during the Second Republic are discussed by H. Arnold, *Schreibweise und Funktion der Ultramontanen Tradition in Frankreich 1848–1851* (Bern/Frankfurt 1975).

He was won over by his friendship with Fortoul, the ministre des Cultes, who convinced Sibour that the new régime was the only safe road to genuine reform in both State and Church; and after observing the events of the first half of 1852 the archbishop was struck by the possibility that a Bonapartist government might be more capable than any other of protecting the Church of France against the encroachments of Rome.[6]

As 1852 went on, the habitual outlook of the ministère des Cultes was able gradually to reassert itself. After the elections in April it was clear that under a veneer of Bonapartism the men of the new régime belonged fundamentally to the old Orleanist political class, and that *gallicanisme parlementaire* was still the prevailing attitude towards religious affairs. Although the new government stifled political comment it left the press relatively free to discuss intellectual topics, including religion, and the metropolitan newspapers made it obvious that the educated public was extremely irritated by the triumphalist tone of the Church since the *coup d'état*, by editorials in *L'Univers* about the reign of Christ on earth, sermons against the *Université* as insulting as those of the forties, and the spectacle of *curés* bullying schoolmasters in the provinces;[7] at the same time the *procureurs généraux* were reporting that Catholic zealotry was creating amongst the masses a disrespect for religion in general which could easily have political consequences. The ministère des Cultes had an even weightier case to argue which was bound to appeal to Louis Napoleon's cabinet: the activities of the Roman congregations as interpreted by the *Correspondance de Rome* and *L'Univers* represented a threat to the Concordat, the most distinguished and lasting example of Napoleonic statecraft. The concordatory system which guaranteed that the Church would continue to be moderate, acceptable, and essentially French depended on the expectation that bishops would be obeyed by their clergy and respected by the laity, but letters were arriving at the ministry almost every day from bishops complaining that the episcopate was in severe difficulties and that the government

---

[6] Victor Hugo is said to have had Sibour in mind when he wrote the fierce passage in *Les Châtiments* about the archbishops rallying to Louis Napoleon: *Oeuvres complètes de Victor Hugo* (1910), vol. iv, 37.

[7] See the letters from Poitiers in 1852 in Hippolyte Taine's *Correspondance de jeunesse 1847–1853* (1914) for good detail on this period after the *coup d'état*.

was doing nothing to protect it. The *Correspondance de Rome* was flatly contradicting everything that the French clergy had been taught in their seminaries, claiming that the Gallican Church was a new creation of the nineteenth century and had no special claim to respect, that the Pope had immediate and ordinary jurisdiction over all dioceses and that the bishops were merely papal clerks. From March 1852 the *Correspondance* began to publish commentaries on new episcopal appointments, selectively quoting the text of each nomination in such a way as to suggest that the bishop had been chosen in the first instance by the Holy See instead of by the ministère des Cultes. When the successful candidate was an ultramontane there was an admiring paragraph about his piety, learning, and dedication, but the *Correspondance* was very brief with gallicans, giving not much beyond the candidate's date of birth; when Mgr de Marguerye was translated to Autun it said acidly that 'he has the same qualities as he had when the Holy See approved his first appointment to Saint-Flour'.[8] In February 1852 *L'Univers* published a series of articles advising the clergy to subscribe to the *Correspondance de Rome* and pay close attention to it, because it represented the learned and experienced Congregations 'who govern the Church; every one of their decrees . . . has the same authority as if it emanated directly from the Roman Pontiff'. Only people who lived in the past, *L'Univers* went on, could object to the *Correspondance* and its mission; the frail spiders-webs of gallican theory could not hold back the mighty movement towards complete unity.[9] The discussions in the *Correspondance* of matters relating to the Index were also becoming more and more provocative, referring pointedly to 'decrees of the Cardinal Inquisitors' and 'the congregation of the Universal Inquisition'.

The ministère des Cultes was more worried, however, by the reality behind this verbal warfare. There was the case of the abbé Domergue, for example. In 1847 the bishop of Nantes, without holding a formal inquiry, had dismissed Domergue as *curé* of Vertou for drunkenness, dishonesty, and flagrant immorality. In

---

[8] *Correspondance de Rome* (24 Mar. 1852).

[9] *L'Univers* (23 Feb. 1852). The abbé Bouix wrote to Gaultier that Rome had 'seen heresies rise and fall, and the Pope needs only to touch one of these presumptuous structures with his little finger for it to fall in ruins': letter of 4 Mar. 1852 in Hédouville, 'Romains et gallicans', 86.

1851 Domergue appealed to Rome, and the Curia ruled that although the original allegations appeared to be well founded it would have to rule against the bishop and reinstate Domergue, since the Holy See did not recognize dismissals by bishops *ex informata conscientia*.[10] For several months at the end of 1851 and the beginning of 1852 the *Correspondance de Rome* and *L'Univers* kept the Domergue case alive and encouraged priests with grievances to appeal to Rome, pointing out that in canon law a bishop was powerless to act while an appeal was in progress. In the middle of June Fortoul, whose desk at the ministry was covered with memoranda by senior officials in his department analysing the threat to the Concordat, and with angry letters from Mgr Jacquemet, Domergue's bishop, and from Marguerye, Angebault, Blanquart de Bailleul, Guibert, and several others, decided to ask the Ministry of Foreign affairs to act; he prepared a formal protest against the Domergue decision, the activities of the congregations of Rites and the Index, and the excesses of the *Correspondance de Rome*, and the ambassador in Rome was instructed to convey the gist of it directly to the Pope.[11]

On 14 June 1852 the ambassador, the comte de Rayneval, had an audience of two hours with Pius IX. Reyneval would not have been Fortoul's first choice for a mission of this kind. Unlike most French ambassadors to Rome in the nineteenth century he was an optimist, always ready to put the best possible construction on whatever he heard. The Pope listened, he reported, with close attention to each of the main points and 'his replies showed, as we might have expected, the elevation and moderation of his mind'. On the liturgy campaign:

I did not provoke the movement . . . It has arisen spontaneously, exclusively in France. I could not fight against it. It is clear that everything which tends to make the unity of the Church more complete, more total, is a good thing. And so I accepted this tendency, I encouraged those bishops who expressed favourable intentions, but I allowed the others the most complete liberty. It is their affair and they are perfectly free to resolve the matter according to the promptings of

[10] Correspondence in ASV Francia 1853 (V); and Maurain, *Saint-Siège*, 83–6.
[11] Fortoul's minute to the Foreign Minister, Turgot, 12 June 1852, and other relevant correspondence, in Maurain, *Saint-Siège*, 50–73. The Nunciature received two long and cogent arguments from Blanquart de Bailleul and Guibert which convinced Garibaldi that the *Correspondance de Rome* was doing more harm than good to the ultramontane cause: ASV Francia 1854 (IV) and 1856 (I).

their own consciences and their assessment of local circumstances . . . Some have judged it difficult or impracticable, and have declined; I do not blame them.

On the Index:

I cannot understand what foundation there can be for this rumour, a hundred times repeated, that the condemnation of M. Lequeux was only the prelude to a series of similar actions against your principal authors and even your bishops. I have never said anything of the kind, I have never dreamed of it . . . My duty, my desire, is to calm and not to provoke.

The French were excitable, the Pope said, and debate in France often went beyond the limits of good manners, but in reality there was nothing to be feared from Rome—the Holy See deprecated all excessive and unbalanced zeal and wished only for peace.

With regard to 'a certain newspaper in French printed at Rome' (whose issue of 14 June had appeared on the morning of Rayneval's audience, although he had not seen it, containing an article indicating that large numbers of rubbishy and erroneous works of theology were under examination, and that French authors should take the affair of Lequeux's *Manuale* as a warning) the Pope claimed that in order to preserve his independent judgement he had deliberately refrained from ever reading it. It had the imprimatur? But that merely certified that the *Correspondance de Rome* contained nothing contrary to faith or morals, and did not guarantee positive approval of its contents. The editors of the *Correspondance* had been told long ago to avoid citing material that referred specifically to France, and to confine themselves to commenting on decrees that had universal application in the church; he was sorry to hear, the Pope said, that they might have departed occasionally from this rule.[12]

But to general surprise, diplomatic pressure succeeded where the gallican protests had failed. On 20 June the Pope told Rayneval that after examination he had decided to close the *Correspondance de Rome*. The whole matter had been blown up out of proportion, he said: 'at least people will be convinced now that it was neither supported nor inspired by the Holy See . . .'. Rayneval told his ministry that he had congratulated the Pope warmly on this decision. It had all been an affair of a handful of

[12] Rayneval to Turgot, 14 June 1852, in Maurain, *Saint-Siège*, 74–9.

extremists, he said, and once exposed to the light of day their intrigues had been rendered harmless. The Curia had even re-examined the case of the abbé Domergue and ruled that Domergue should be offered compensation but not reinstated. What more could the French government ask? Rayneval thought that the ministère des Cultes could be responsible for many of the difficulties because of the professional tendency of ministry officials to distrust everything said or done at Rome; at Foreign Affairs they knew better: 'it is the great art of the Court of Rome to know how to conciliate the most opposed interests'.[13]

He wrote this on 30 June. On the following day the Congregation of the Index condemned the ninth edition of Bouillet's *Dictionnaire universel* which had been revised and amended to take account of the criticisms made by the Index itself two years earlier. 'After all the declarations, corrections, and pecuniary sacrifices made by the author', Mgr Maret wrote, 'I would have thought that this affair was completely finished, and I find it hard to explain this new and gratuitous insult offered to the archbishop of Paris.' 'What!' wrote another of Sibour's friends, 'our works judged in the shadows by a few monks or Italian prelates, judged without being heard'; surely churchmen 'cannot help blushing to see an ecclesiastical tribunal so out of touch with the rules of justice followed by lay tribunals in all civilized countries'. Sibour collected a set of documents for the ministère des Cultes 'to reveal the full infamy of this hateful intrigue', in the hope that the government, having succeeded in closing the *Correspondance de Rome*, might now do something for Bouillet; for the moment, however, the government decided that no action was likely to be effective.[14]

The Sulpician Mémoire

By the middle of 1852 some of the leading gallicans were almost ready to consider an alliance with *gallicanisme parlementaire*.

---

[13] Ibid., Rayneval, 30 June 1852, and cf. his dispatches from 20 June to 4 Aug. 80–101.

[14] Sibour's memorandum, copies of nine documents on the Bouillet affair, and extracts from letters received by Sibour, in AN F. 19. 1947; Maret's letter in Bazin, *Vie de Mgr Maret*, vol. i, 385. The government did support a further approach to the Index by Bouillet in January 1853, and eventually he prepared a tenth edition rather than see his book banned from all Catholic libraries.

Sibour, now wholly in favour of Louis Napoleon and very impressed with the grasp of ecclesiastical affairs displayed by Fortoul and his directeur général des Cultes, Baron Contencin, could feel the temptation to throw in his lot with the government and to rely on the Organic Articles to protect the Church of France.[15] There was a risk, of course, that in their anxiety to seek official protection from the Romanizing movement the gallicans might find themselves yoked in partnership with something equally dangerous, because during 1852 *gallicanisme parlementaire* was showing a distinct tendency to harden into scepticism and anticlericalism. Opinion at the ministry, in the *Corps législatif,* and in the press was now very strongly against Rome and against *veuillotisme.* There was a great deal of hostile comment amongst the educated public over the episode of the *Correspondance de Rome,* and renewed annoyance when *L'Univers,* having disposed of Bouillet, began threatening to use the Roman Index against other prominent *universitaires* like the philosopher Auguste Nicolas and the impeccably Catholic Frédéric Ozanam, and resumed its satirical *Galerie des professeurs de la Sorbonne.* The bishops could see clear signs of an Orleanist–Voltairean revival which might eventually bring religion under even tighter official control than during the July Monarchy. The Nuncio noted that he no longer seemed to meet anyone in official circles or in society who was friendly towards the Church.[16]

At about the time of the Bouillet judgement the possibility of a reaction of this kind led to the idea of a declaration or manifesto which would define *gallicanisme ecclésiastique* by distinguishing it both from ultramontanism and from the gallicanism of the jurists. It was becoming urgent to establish a core of gallican doctrine that could be defended, because a mood of discouragement was spreading in the episcopate. *L'Univers,* one churchman said, had constituted itself a faculty of theology which was examining each bishop and announcing 'pass' or 'fail'; the Church was falling under the control of 'an irregular power which cannot be disciplined, like the praetorians or the janissa-

---

[15] Maurain, *Saint-Siège,* 93–113.

[16] Garibaldi, 25 July 1852; Bonnechose to Donnet, 10 Aug.; Dupanloup to Garibaldi 11 Aug.; Donnet to Antonelli (on the case of Auguste Nicolas and *L'Univers*) 28 Aug. 1852: all in *Bettoni,* 300–4, 408–17. Cf. the book by H. Gaultier de Claubry, *L'Univers en présence de lui-même* (1856).

ries'.[17] Some bishops considered premature retirement. Robiou of Coutances, hounded by ultramontane clergy in his diocese and with his pastoral letter on the liturgy question denounced to the Index, resigned, was persuaded by Fortoul to stay, and finally retired to a canonry in November.[18] Something had to be done to break the pattern of a conflict in which the ultramontane party was always active, endlessly pressing forward, challenging, thrusting, while the gallicans were forced into the weaker position of parrying and giving ground, never knowing where their opponents would strike. In August 1852 Sibour asked the abbé Lequeux to draft a memorandum analysing and defending the fundamental gallican doctrine on the rights of national churches, and circulated manuscript copies to a dozen of the senior bishops for comment. Lequeux's draft was felt to be too aggressive and another version was prepared by three Sulpicians, Carrière, Galais, and Icard, with Galais apparently responsible for the final draft;[19] and at the beginning of October five hundred copies with the title *Sur la situation présente de l'Église gallicane relativement au droit coutumier: Mémoire adressé à l'Épiscopat* were sent to all bishops, vicars-general, directors of seminaries, and heads of religious orders. No author was named. Only a few years earlier it had been the ultramontane spokesman who had felt it necessary to publish anonymously. In this case, however, apart from reasons of prudence, the *archevêché* evidently believed that leadership would be more acceptable to the bishops if it was anonymous.

The *Mémoire* reiterated all the gallican arguments, from the broader questions of the apostolic origins of bishops and the fundamental structure of the Church to the more immediate matter of the rights of the French Church *vis-à-vis* Rome, but it was easily the most cogent and best-documented of all gallican statements so far in the nineteenth century; every point was

---

[17] R. P. Valroger of the Oratory to Dupanloup, 6 July 1852, Dupanloup/BN 24712.

[18] Robiou to Fortoul, letters of Mar., Apr., and Nov. 1852, AN F. 19. 6179; Garibaldi's dispatch of 15 Aug. 1851: ASV Francia 1856 (I). Cœur, Marguerye, and some others also considered retirement.

[19] This is the most likely conclusion about the authorship: Sevrin, *Clausel de Montals*, vol. ii, 670–2; A. Mater, *L'Église catholique* (1906), 56; Montclos, *Lavigerie*, 46 ff.; P. Mabile, *Vie de Mgr Mabile*, 2 vols. (1926), vol. ii, 173. (My own copy of the *Mémoire* was originally bound for the Franciscan order in Paris with the name 'Gallais' stamped on the spine. A. G.)

supported by deductive argument and authority in the best
manner of Sulpician teaching on ecclesiology. Its general theme
was that gallican doctrines did not concern faith or dogma but
were respectable and permissible opinions about the best way to
advance the interest of the Church in the world: they had been
held by some of the most distinguished saints and prelates of past
centuries and could not now be censured by the papacy as if they
were heresies or offences against discipline. Gallicanism was not
an extreme decentralist movement which might loosen the bonds
of Christendom, and it did not attempt to cut French Catholics
off from Rome. The *Mémoire* did come close to decentralism in
claiming that in the early Middle Ages the different provinces of
the Church existed alongside one another essentially as equals,
citing Saint Gregory encouraging Augustine to introduce into his
infant Church of England 'whatever you have found most proper
to please God, whether you found it in the Roman Church, the
Gallican Church or any other'. It stopped well short of the
position that sterner gallicans might have preferred, however, by
admitting that the Pope had primacy of jurisdiction as well as of
honour. What, then, stopped the papacy from governing national
Churches directly? The existence of customary law, hallowed by
centuries of harmonious and agreeable practice, under which
bishops admitted the right of the Pope to act in matters of wide
importance, and Rome agreed that the local bishop was the best
judge of ordinary affairs and should not be overridden without
exceptional cause. This balance was what made a centralized
religion acceptable to local people anywhere in the world: unity
of fundamentals must be flexible enough to contain local variants
in customs, ceremonial, and administration, and French bishops
in particular must have the right not to receive rules made at
Rome, made perhaps to solve Italian problems, which would
cause severe difficulties if put into force in France. Authorities
from Saint Basil to Suarez and decretals of Gregory IX and
Boniface VII were marshalled to show that local usage had the
force of law in the Church if it was not manifestly immoral, was
followed by a majority of the faithful, and was of reasonable
antiquity, some canonists having considered that a hundred
years, a period beyond a single lifespan, ought to be sufficient.

Perhaps there were too many authorities. The *Mémoire* might
have been more compelling if it had stuck to the pragmatic point

that religion survives and flourishes where it has deep organic roots and some degree of local autonomy, and argued that a policy of centralized authoritarianism was simply ill-advised and inopportune in the nineteenth century. But professional pride and the challenge of their opponents' tactics forced the Sulpician authors into a competitive brandishing of documents and citations. Their constant appeal to authority slightly took away the force of their own vehement objection to 'the canonical revolution' in which ultramontane experts were digging amongst the hundreds of volumes of Roman decrees and producing obscure canons to confound the French bishops. The abbé Bouix in his *Tractatus de principiis juris canonici* was citing papal documents 'hitherto unknown in France', the *Mémoire* said, to prove that the Popes could annul civil legislation, abrogate concordats, make dogmatic decisions without consultation, abolish any part of canon law, and condemn even the most ancient customs, and that the national churches had freely given up their supposed rights in the seventeenth century, or in the tenth century or the sixth.

The *Mémoire* dealt effectively with the other Roman revolution, the recent awakening of the Congregation of Rites and the Index. It analysed the case of Mgr Bouvier and the Le Mans liturgy and concluded that Rome had departed outrageously from a sensible code of practice. At the time of the Concordat the Papal Legate had explicitly recognized the right of the French Church to keep its liturgies; but in any case, it pointed out, many seminary libraries had copies of the *Res liturgicae* by Cardinal Bona, published in the seventeenth century with papal approval, which laid down that Missals conformed to the Roman usage so long as they contained the essential elements of the Mass, and that it was of no consequence 'that they omit a Psalm . . . or that they do not read the same Epistles and Gospels as at Rome, or do not celebrate the same saints' days . . . Assuredly, none of this amounts to introducing a diversity of rite'. The Index was an even greater intrusion. The condemnations of Lequeux, Guettée, and Bouillet were not only wrong in substance but showed appallingly bad judgement; fortunately there could be no doubt that the French church could decline to receive them. The true role of the Roman congregations was to make themselves useful to the bishops of the world by offering technical guidance, and by serving as a channel for correspondence with the Holy See: their rescripts had the force of knowledge and skill, but nothing more. The *Mémoire* urged the bishops to apply a critical and historical approach to Roman decrees, comparing them with other decisions in the past and with canon law, and gave examples of how this might be applied to the Roman amendments to the acts of the Councils of Paris, Lyons and Rouen: 'let us not, at least, take them as the solemn oracles of the Holy See . . . or infallible judgements proffered ex cathedra'. The *Mémoire* ended with a warning: the claim by ultramontane zealots, apparently well founded, that they had privileged access to Rome and could predict the outcome of disputes, and the new phenomenon of priests appealing directly to Rome instead of to their metropolitan archbishop—these two things by themselves, it was suggested, could provoke a revival of the harshest kind of nationalistic *gallicanisme parlementaire*. It was essential for the French Church to earn public respect by addressing itself with confidence to the question of its own authority and discipline.

Predictably, the *Mémoire* had a mixed reception, and some ultramontane bishops sent their copies straight to the Nunciature for transmission to the Index. Reading the copy submitted from Amiens Mgr Garibaldi detected Sibour's influence in its wording. He could only hope, he told Antonelli, that distribution would stop with the original five hundred copies and that the *Mémoire* would not spread to sow doubt amongst the mass of the clergy on whom the progress of the ultramontane movement depended. A great deal of damage was already done. Since the Le Mans decision it had seemed likely, he thought, that Rome might have been able 'to persuade the bishops politely, with prudence and discernment, not pushing or jostling them, that they themselves should carry out the destruction of the gallican customs . . . without inopportune discussions and debates'; but now the controversy had been stirred up again.[20] The *Mémoire* had indeed lifted the spirits of the gallican bishops. After reading only half-way through it Clausel de Montals wrote to Carrière at Saint-Sulpice that he could not wait to express 'my admiration, my joy, my consolation at this very critical moment; the *Mémoire* will save the Church of France, and will give very useful and I believe very

[20] Garibaldi, 17 and 20 Oct. 1852, ASV Francia 1852 (III); *Bettoni*, 318–23.

efficacious advice to the Holy See': Clausel thought that the 'consummate ability and admirable clarity' of the book indicated that his old friend Carrière himself was the main author.[21] Mazenod of Marseilles wrote to Mgr Robiou that the *Mémoire* showed 'that one can be Catholic and Roman without being obliged to curse all our holy predecessors'.[22] In the opposing camp the reaction was summed up by Mgr Salinis: 'What could be more indeterminate, more flexible, than this so-called customary law that they claim to oppose to the decisions of Rome? If these principles . . . come to prevail we will escape from the authority of the Holy See and fall into confusion and anarchy.'[23] The *Mémoire* was very timely, the abbé Bouix told R. P. Gaultier, because some people at Rome had believed that gallicanism was really defunct, and that the bishops were protesting about liturgies and other matters only out of injured dignity and had no coherent body of French doctrine behind them: now there could be no more doubt about 'a vast system of opposition to the authority of the Holy See'.[24] Mgr Gousset, expecting that the *Mémoire* would in fact be seen by large numbers of clergy, wrote an extended reply to it as a pamphlet and sent a shorter version to be published in *L'Univers*. He chose to treat the *Mémoire* with scorn rather than waste time refuting its individual arguments, because, he wrote, the anonymous authors stood condemned by their own words; it was quite easy to demonstrate by extended quotation that they wanted to limit the universal jurisdiction of the Pope, a self-evidently absurd and dangerous position for Catholics. Gousset also convoked the Council of Reims to meet again at Amiens to condemn the tendencies of the *Mémoire*, which it duly did in February 1853.[25] But it is hard to estimate the full effect or influence of the Sulpician initiative because shortly after its publication another event occurred which pushed it to some extent into the background: the Index condemned Bailly.

[21] Sevrin, *Clausel de Montals*, vol. ii, 671.

[22] Ibid., vol. ii, 672.

[23] Salinis, quoted by Garibaldi in his dispatch of 20 Oct. 1852, *Bettoni*, 322.

[24] Bouix to Gaultier, 25 Dec. 1852, Hédouville, 'Romains et gallicans', 102.

[25] Mgr Gousset, *Observations sur un mémoire adressé à l'épiscopat* (Dec. 1852). On Gousset's action against the *Mémoire*, Garibaldi, 13 Jan. 1853, ASV Francia 1853 (III).

Bailly's Theologia

The *Theologia dogmatica et moralis* by Louis Bailly was an eight-volume work first published in 1789, with a second edition by the author in 1804 to take account of the French Concordat. Amongst textbooks of theology it had the rare distinction of being actually readable and popular with seminarians, or at least those capable of appreciating the clarity of its style and the richness and subtlety of its illustrations; even ultramontanes like Pie and Gousset had loved Bailly as students and had been willing to overlook the fact that it was a monument of eighteenth-century gallicanism.[26] By 1830 it had been adopted in more than three-quarters of the French seminaries. To meet some of the criticisms by ultramontane seminary instructors during the Mennaisian period an amended edition was prepared in 1829 which relegated the strongest gallican statements, for example on the power of a general council to overrule a Pope, to an appendix under a heading which suggested that they were purely hypothetical. In 1842 the abbé Receveur published a further edition which softened Bailly's arguments with explanatory comments: where Bailly recognized 'the body of bishops united with the Pope' as the supreme and infallible authority, capable of defining dogma, Receveur commented that a simple majority of the episcopate was enough to validate a papal declaration on dogma, and that the bishops' consent needed only to be tacit; but ultramontane critics complained that the text was still too gallican.[27]

In August 1852 Pius IX discovered from an unguarded remark by an Irish seminary director during a private audience that Bailly was in use in seminaries all over Europe; enquiring further, he found that the Spanish bishops were just about to adopt it, on the recommendation of the Sulpicians in Paris. The Pope remembered Bailly very well, having removed it from his diocesan seminary when he was bishop of Spoleto. He ordered the Index to find a copy and examine it without delay, and in the meantime the Paris Nuncio was asked to find out to what extent seminaries in France founded their teaching on Bailly.[28] Mgr

[26] The *Theologia* incorporated material from Bailly's *Tractatus de Ecclesia* of 1771: AN F. 19. 1933 (dossier 'Théologie de Bailly'); *Correspondance Pie/Cousseau*, 143.

[27] On the successive editions of Bailly: Garibaldi, 20 Oct. 1852, ASV Francia 1853 (V); and abbé E. Michaud, *De la falsification des catéchismes français et des manuels de théologie . . . de 1670 à 1868* (1872).

[28] Antonelli to Garibaldi, 31 Aug. 1852, ASV Francia 1853 (V).

Garibaldi made extremely discreet enquiries to avoid creating alarm at a critical time so soon after the condemnation of Bouillet's *Dictionnaire,* and reported that there was no call for any urgent action. Bailly was certainly used almost everywhere but it was taught through lectures which buried its gallican propositions under masses of commentary and qualification. At Saint-Sulpice they studied Bailly more intensively, but alongside several other books which allowed students to see it in perspective. 'We will probably never get a perfect textbook', and this one did have considerable merit; was he mistaken, in any case, Garibaldi asked, in remembering that in 1820 the Index had declared that even the earliest editions of Bailly contained nothing reprehensible? The proper course was to leave the matter to the good instincts of seminary instructors who knew how to prepare commentaries based on sound doctrine.[29]

This advice went for nothing. On 7 December 1852 the *Theologia* was condemned by the Index *donec corrigatur,* creating a shock in France which far surpassed the effect of the condemnations of Lequeux and Bouillet. Nobody, Dupanloup wrote, could fail to see the result of telling priests in this sudden and callous manner that ever since the Concordat their respected instructors had been working from a heretical textbook, and that the older generation of clerics had been raised on errors; it would give the younger men a contempt for the whole edifice of ecclesiastical learning and an unhealthy fear of the capricious power of Rome.[30] Mgr Guibert thought that if the Pope's real aim had been to remove Bailly from the seminaries a private letter to each bishop would have accomplished this quietly and without publicity, but clearly the intention had been to deliver a public insult.[31] 'With what severity they now forbid opinions which used to be free, and which have not prevented our dear and beautiful Church of France from distinguishing itself in the eyes of God and of men', wrote Mgr Chalandon of Belley.[32] All those preachers and writers, and especially those missionaries whom

---

[29] Garibaldi, 20 Oct. 1852, ASV Francia 1853 (V). Garibaldi noted that some seminaries had replaced Bailly with Bouvier's *Théologie du Mans,* which left them in an equally embarrassing position.

[30] 'Rapport au Pape', Dupanloup/AN AB XIX 524.

[31] Follenay, *Guibert,* vol. ii, 150.

[32] Letter to R. P. Carrière, 9 Jan. 1853, Hédouville, 'Romains et gallicans', 145.

France had sent out in such numbers to America and Asia, all
brought up in heresy—even bishops like Bonnechose and
Angebault who had been inclined to agree that Bouillet's
Dictionnaire had deserved its fate, and that Lequeux might have
been a little over-confident, found the Bailly decision impossible
to accept; but in practice it had to be obeyed. Ultramontane
students had already taken the *Theologia* from the shelves of some
seminary libraries; at the Saint-Esprit seminary in Paris R. P.
Gaultier and his pupils burned the eight-volume set in the
courtyard. Some bishops stalled for time by asking what was
coming to be the usual question: was the Index decree genuine?
Of course it was genuine, Melchior du Lac retorted: it had
appeared in *L'Univers*, transmitted by unimpeachable sources.
Du Lac noted that some dioceses hoped to keep using copies of
Bailly 'with corrections'; he happened to know, he wrote, that
they had no idea what corrections to make.[33]

On 19 January 1853 the Pope announced what he seems to
have considered a concession of almost quixotic generosity: in
view of the difficulty of replacing textbooks at short notice in the
middle of the academic year the French seminaries could go on
using Bailly until the next summer vacation.[34] This did not solve
the problem of a substitute book. *L'Univers* recommended the
works of R. P. Gury SJ, although the abbé Delacouture pointed
out in the *Journal des débats* that Gury himself was ambiguous
about the right of French bishops to ignore the Roman Index;
Mgr Gousset recommended his own revised edition of Bergier's
Dictionnaire de théologie which by chance had appeared just at that
moment. But would any book be safe? The Catholic publisher
Poussielgue complained to the Nuncio that his business could
easily fall into a chronic state of uncertainty. R. P. Carrière told
Garibaldi that Saint-Sulpice would continue to use Bailly on
neutral topics like the theology of the sacraments and rely on
lecture notes in more sensitive areas, but he was worried that
several texts used by the Sulpicians were liable to the same
censure as Bailly, including his own treatise on marriage which

[33] *L'Univers* (1 Jan. 1853). The publisher of Bailly claimed later in the year that he
could supply a list of errata which would make the *Theologia* safe to use again, but this
was stopped by the Nuncio's office: *Ami de la religion* (8 Sept. 1853), and ASV Francia
1853 (V).
[34] Antonelli to Garibaldi, 19 Jan. 1853, ASV Francia 1853 (V).

had already survived an examination by the Index in 1839.[35] Comment on the Bailly case managed to make itself heard in the secular press even in competition with the great preoccupation of the hour, the inauguration of the Second Empire, and in January, after the ministère des Cultes had dealt with another mass of angry correspondence from the gallican bishops, Fortoul arranged for the ambassador in Rome to raise the subject with Pius IX. This time Rayneval found the Pope immovable. He had found out about the use of Bailly by accident, he insisted: 'I would never have imagined that the French clergy, who profess to be attached to the Holy See . . . should draw their doctrine from such a source. So far as discipline is concerned, Bailly is the enemy of the Holy See.' He repeated the same words to Rayneval in another audience a month later, and expressed surprise that the French bishops should have taken a very reasonable decision so badly.[36]

---

[35] Garibaldi reports conversations with Carrière and Poussielgue in a long letter to Cardinal Brignole, Prefect of the Index, 23 Jan. 1853, ASV Parigi, vol. 44.

[36] Rayneval, 24 Jan. and 24 Feb. 1853, in Maurain, *Saint-Siège*, 145, 178.

XI

The encyclical *Inter multiplices*

Sibour and Veuillot in 1853

IT seemed inevitable to everyone who had followed the conflict
since 1848 that the tactical moves and counter-moves, the
advances, retreats, and provocations would culminate eventually
in a hand-to-hand encounter between the self-appointed champions
of the two parties, the archbishop of Paris and the editor of
L'Univers—two very unevenly matched opponents.

By 1853 Sibour was not in a strong position within his own
archdiocese. Every gallican bishop had to deal with some degree
of opposition from ultramontane priests but Sibour was exceptional
in having provoked unrest even amongst the predominantly
gallican clergy of Paris. When he was first made archbishop, with
a reputation for having been the only provincial bishop to have
supported the Allignol brothers' agitation in the 1840s, he had
begun a series of reforms to improve the conditions of the junior
clergy and had revived a scheme with Affre had been considering
at the time of his death. In city parishes the assistant priests did
most of the household visiting, said the requiem masses and
performed the marriages while the *curés* appropriated the lion's
share of the *casuel*; Sibour proposed that each parish should have
a treasurer who would distribute the revenue more equitably. He
had to withdraw this plan because of legal objections by the
ministère des Cultes, but the very suggestion made Sibour
unpopular with the senior *curés*, who may have admired him as a
defender of the Church of France but came to detest him as an
administrator. He irritated them still more seriously when in his
anxiety to strengthen Paris as a centre of gallicanism he began
calling learned and talented priests from other dioceses to fill
parishes in the capital. The Parisian *curés* welcomed the
appointment of gallicans, but not gallicans from the provinces,
and they became even more turbulent when they found that in
some cases Sibour was redrawing their boundaries to create new
parishes for his protégés. The arrival of gifted new men like the

abbé Meignan, who had studied for several years in Germany before Sibour gave him the parish of Saint-Louis-d'Antin, the abbé Gabriel of Montpellier whom Sibour invited to Saint-Merry so that he could help to edit the *Moniteur catholique,* and the brilliant abbé Christophe, former chaplain of the French Embassy in Rome who was given the newly created parish of Saint-Marcel, caused extreme irritation amongst the Parisian clergy; they were not impressed with the explanation that it was all part of the archbishop's campaign to provide more pastoral care for the urban poor.[1]

Sibour's politics also had made him unpopular with a significant part of the clergy. In 1851, when the newspapers were full of talk about 'the Red Spectre' and the possibility of a presidential *coup d'état,* he had issued a pastoral letter forbidding the priests of the archdiocese to take any active part in politics and especially in electoral campaigns. Conservative Catholics, including men like Clausel de Montals who had been his strongest supporters in the gallican resistance, were furious and said openly that Sibour's real motive was to stop the clergy from speaking or writing for conservative causes, and that he had no objection at all to priests electioneering for the Republican left. The abbé Combalot, with private encouragement from Cardinal Fornari in Rome, wrote in a pamphlet that priests ought to be twice as active politically as ordinary citizens, and accused Sibour of being a creature of the Republicans who had appointed him in 1848;[2] several bishops protested to the Nunciature that the archbishop of Paris was trying to lay down a quietist political line for the French clergy as a whole. Sibour extricated himself from this mess as well as he could, but in the next twelve months he gave ammunition to his critics by supporting various Republican initiatives and making speeches that could be construed as being political. At one point Cardinal Antonelli asked the Nuncio if it could possibly be true, as reported in the left-wing press, that Sibour had spoken at a co-operative

---

[1] Letter of M. Ferrier, a member of one of the *conseils de fabrique,* to Louis Veuillot, in 'Notes intimes', V/BN 24620; abbé Félix Coquereau, Chaplain-general of the Navy and chaplain to Princess Mathilde, mentions the archbishop's problems in a letter to Cardinal Donnet, 9 Aug. 1854, Donnet/AN 160 AP. ii.

[2] Combalot, *Lettre . . . sur l'intervention du clergé dans les affaires séculières et politiques,* and *Deuxième lettre . . .* (June 1851); cf. Combalot's earlier *Lettre sur le scrutin électorale* (1849); letter of Mgr Fornari to Combalot, in Ricard, *L'Abbé Combalot,* 409 n.

workshop employing ninety cabinet-makers and had said how delighted he was to see before him not a crowd of workers and one master, 'but ninety masters'. It was true, Garibaldi replied; there was no end to the archbishop's extravagances.[3]

In October 1852 Sibour was invited to Vienna for a religious ceremony and used the visit to try to assess the feelings of the German and Austrian bishops towards the new ultramontanism. Mgr Garibaldi arranged with his colleague the Nuncio at Vienna to inform Rome of any indiscretions Sibour might commit. The Nuncio, Viale-Prelà, reported a long discussion between Sibour and the archbishop of Speyer, Mgr Weiss, in which Sibour expressed concern that ill-informed Congregations at Rome were interfering in the affairs of European dioceses and setting them in a turmoil, and asked Weiss how they saw this problem in Germany; Weiss, a staunch ultramontane, painted a picture of a submissive German episcopate united in joyful obedience to the Holy See, which was not altogether true. Viale-Prelà found Sibour 'equally mediocre in talent and in character', but thought that his innate piety made it unlikely that he would cause any real harm.[4] Garibaldi did not agree: he could see disasters in the future which no amount of piety would prevent. The possibility of schism had always been part of ultramontane rhetoric but the Nuncio and some of the bishops were now taking more seriously the idea of Paris as 'the Rome of the gallicans and heretics, of all those who dream of a national religion';[5] with a gallican archbishop and a strong French sovereign working together in harmony the conditions could exist for the creation of an autonomous patriarchate. On 8 December 1852 Garibaldi reported a small, but, he said, highly significant example of Sibour claiming independent jurisdiction. He was 'saddened and stupefied' to read in *L'Univers* that the archbishop had given the entire *Corps législatif* a dispensation from the laws of abstinence in order to attend a banquet celebrating the inauguration of the Empire. Sibour must have known perfectly well that in canon law only the Pope could grant a mass dispensation, but he

[3] Correspondence in ASV Francia 1851 (II); complaints of senior clergy against Sibour's politics in ASV Francia 1851 (I).
[4] Mgr Viale-Prelà to Antonelli, 5 Oct. 1852, and enclosed leter from Mgr Weiss, ASV Francia 1852 (III).
[5] Mgr Parisis, quoted by Limouzin-Lamothe and Leflon, *Affre*, 252.

appeared to be basing his decision on a paragraph in the recent Sulpician *Mémoire* 'asserting that French bishops had full apostolic authority to make decisions on local disciplinary matters such as fasting. The archdiocese was beginning to put the mischievous and insubordinate *Mémoire* into practice; but at the same time, Garibaldi noted, Sibour seemed pathetically anxious to be reassured that he was still in good standing at Rome. The Nuncio described with bleak amusement how whenever he had to pass on some communication from the Holy See the archbishop would insist on opening it immediately and reading it in the Nuncio's presence, and would try to interpret the honorific salutations at the beginning of a papal letter as signs of genuine esteem. His face—never exactly inscrutable, Garibaldi observed—lit up when he came to some purely formal compliment to himself or to 'the specially beloved archdiocese of Paris'; but Cardinal Antonelli's dispatches in December 1852 and January 1853 left no doubt that Sibour's reputation at Rome was at its nadir.[6]

By contrast Veuillot was in the highest favour. Diplomats complained that the papal court took more notice of *L'Univers* than of all the ecclesiastical and diplomatic correspondence. Papal chamberlains said that it was the only newspaper that Pius IX read every day. The abbé Louis-Gaston de Ségur, a convinced ultramontane who had recently been appointed Auditor of the Rota for France and saw the Pope regularly,[7] reassured Veuillot that attacks like Dupanloup's *Le journalisme dans l'Église* could not possibly do him harm. 'The Pope knows from top to bottom what is happening in France. He finds our bishops extremely mean-spirited and very imprudent'; there were 'at least thirty of them who can hardly be regarded with pride—*protestants en herbe*, in the Pope's own phrase. It was fortunate, Pius IX had told Ségur, that he could rely on the loyalty of the lower clergy and the vigilance of *L'Univers*.[8] Veuillot knew that not everybody at Rome shared the Pope's

---

[6] Garibaldi, 8, 18, 19 Dec.; Antonelli, 24 and 31 Dec. 1852: ASV Francia 1852 (III).

[7] The government had many occasions to regret having nominated Louis-Gaston de Ségur to Rome—he had been chosen because of his family's Napoleonic connections—and there was some relief in the ministère des Cultes when he had to resign the post in 1855 because of failing eyesight. He was later to be one of the leading writers on theocratic royalism and an adviser to the pretender Henry V.

[8] L.-G. de Ségur to Veuillot, 14 July and 10 Aug. 1852, V/BN 24225.

admiration for him. The Secretariat of State was known to believe that *L'Univers* habitually went too far and would one day provoke reprisals by the French government. Veuillot had heard from Ségur and other well-placed friends that alongside resounding successes like the denunciation of Bouillet there had been some small failures. There were complaints in 1852, for example, that the column by his Roman correspondent, the abbé Bernier, was gossipy and trivial and sometimes artlessly gave away delicate diplomatic manœuvres. Bouix and Chaillot, resentful that they should have been suppressed while *L'Univers* was still flourishing, said tartly that Veuillot and most of his fellow editors, were after all, amateurs, and that France needed a newspaper written by men who really understood canon law and theology.[9] Veuillot, however, was receiving quite sufficient proofs that he was taken seriously at Rome. The editors of the *Civiltà Cattolica* had asked for his help in explaining the proposed dogma of the Immaculate Conception,[10] and in May 1852 Cardinal Fornari appointed him officially to prepare draft proposals for the list of errors of modern thought which at that stage was intended to form part of the dogmatic declaration; he was one of only two laymen in Europe to be approached, all the other members of the drafting panel being well-known ultramontane theologians.[11]

At the beginning of 1853 Veuillot was in a peculiarly exalted and crusading mood. While everyone had been waiting expectantly for his reactions to the Sulpician *Mémoire* and the Bailly affair he had been distracted by a double bereavement in his household. In July 1852 his youngest daughter Thérèse had died of one of the fevers infesting Paris. Since his conversion in 1839, Veuillot reflected, he had felt the hand of God in every aspect of his life, guiding him through triumphs and crises, but this time he could sense a warning against pride. Perhaps a few transitory successes had turned his head: 'I was becoming too familiar with God's favour'; to convey this message, God had taken one of his children. Veuillot found the thought consoling, even exhilarating—

---

[9] Letters of Bouix to Gaultier, July–August 1852, in Hédouville, 'Romains et gallicans', 93 ff. Chaillot founded the *Analecta juris pontificii* and Bouix later edited a *Revue des sciences religieuses*, but neither of these journals had the notoriety of the *Correspondance de Rome* or the success of *L'Univers*.

[10] R. P. Carlo Curci to Veuillot, 23 Feb. 1852, V/BN 24633.

[11] Fornari to Veuillot, 20 May 1852, V/BN 24633; the other layman approached was Count Avogadro della Motta of Piedmont.

but it was only the first of a series of personal tragedies. On 24 November 1852 Mathilde Veuillot died of septicaemia after giving birth to another daughter. This time it was harder to find any consolation in the workings of Providence, and he experienced something of the black resentment that was to seize him again in 1855 when three of his young daughters were to die within a few weeks, leaving their father with the fear that he might be 'forever the object of the implacable anger of God'.[12] For a long time after Mathilde's death he could think and write about nothing but his grief. Tormented by regret for many missed opportunities for happiness when he had been absorbed in the daily work of *L'Univers* and had neglected Mathilde, never imagining that he would lose her so soon, he searched amongst her few letters and papers for a sign that she had really loved him in spite of his imperfections as a husband. Years later the sight of her handwriting could reduce him to tears. Then, abruptly, as the new year began, he pulled himself together and set to work with a harsh vigour, more than ever convinced that he was the instrument of a supernatural plan.

In 1849 Veuillot had met the Spanish philosopher Donoso Cortès, Marquis de Valdegamas, who was passing through Paris on his way to a diplomatic posting. Cortès's work represented an extreme development of the ideas of Maistre and Barruel regarding the intellectual origins of social discord, the existence of *la Révolution* as an international committee of conspirators, the fatal role played by the voltairean bourgeoisie in undermining the foundations of order, and the absolute necessity for European politics to be supervised by a centralized Roman papacy. Veuillot was deeply impressed—'bewitched', according to one of his friends[13]—and arranged to have two of Cortès's books published in French, introducing him to readers of *L'Univers* as 'the last of the great opponents of the eighteenth century', and at the end of 1851 his major work, the *Essai sur le catholicisme, le*

---

[12] 'Notes intimes', V/BN 24620, entry of 22 July 1852 on the death of Thérèse; entry of August 1855 on the deaths of the other children.

[13] Albéric de Blanche, a contributor to *L'Univers* on Spanish questions, quoted in P. Dudon, *Albéric de Blanche 1818–1854* (1912), 215. Donoso Cortès himself was a recent convert to Catholicism: see Veuillot's obituary of him in *L'Univers* of 22 May 1853, and his introduction to the *Oeuvres de Donoso Cortès*, 3 vols. (1862), Cortès was godfather to Veuillot's daughter Thérèse.

libéralisme et le socialisme, appeared as one of the volumes in Veuillot's *Bibliothèque nouvelle*.

The book had been out for over a year when in January 1853 the *Ami de la religion* printed a series of five articles attacking its overheated and apocalyptic treatment of Catholic theology.[14] To Veuillot this represented a challenge from a quarter which had given him a great deal of trouble in the past few years, the *évêché* of Orleans, because the articles were signed by the abbé Gaduel, a former Sulpician who was vicar-general of Orleans and an intimate friend and adviser of Mgr Dupanloup. For all his problems with Paris and with Sibour, Veuillot could not help feeling a certain contemptuous fondness for the archbishop, but where Sibour was merely impulsive and wrong-headed Dupanloup was a dangerous opponent, clever and unscrupulous in argument and truly sinister, Veuillot thought, in his illegitimate birth—'a son of Agar, a son of the left hand'—and the wide influence he exercised through being confessor to so many upper-class families.[15] At Orleans he had made the *évêché* and the seminary into gallican enclaves, surrounding himself with Sulpician-educated intellectuals like Gaduel and the abbé Charles Place; ultramontane opinion agreed that if he were ever to succeed Sibour at Paris the patriarchate would be in sight.[16] On two particular recent issues, the controversy over whether the Church should welcome or reject the Loi Falloux, and the attempt by the *école de l'Univers* in 1852 to have the pagan classics eliminated from secondary education, Dupanloup had been Veuillot's main adversary, travelling all over the country organizing support from fellow bishops and writing hundreds of letters, and in both cases he had in effect defeated *L'Univers*, at least in the eyes of public opinion. So when the new challenge from Orleans was presented in 1853 Veuillot reacted with more than characteristic mordancy: the abbé Gaduel and, he wrote, 'those more substantial figures' who stood behind him were not only incompetent in theology, less skilled in fact than laymen like Donoso Cortès and himself, but could hardly be counted as real Catholics.[17] Gaduel claimed to be deeply shocked by this

---

[14] *Ami de la religion* (4 Jan.–1 Feb. 1853).

[15] 'Notes diverses', undated, V/BN 24620.

[16] Mgr Rendu of Annecy discussed this prospect with Veuillot in a letter of 15 Aug. 1856, V/BN 24226.   [17] *L'Univers* (25–31 Jan. 1853).

counter-attack, although he must have expected something of the kind, and with Dupanloup's strong encouragement he appealed to Sibour to exercise some discipline over a newspaper published in his archdiocese.

Sibour's ordinance and Veuillot's appeal to Rome

Gaduel's complaint reached the *archevêché* at the same time as another document, a cogently written attack on the *école de l'Univers* which was being circulated not by one of the more combative gallicans but by a bishop noted for his habitual caution, Guibert of Viviers. The cause of Christianity itself would inevitably suffer, Guibert wrote, if the reckless ultramontane attacks on the traditions of the French Church convinced the political class, with its strongly gallican bias and its touchiness about national identity, that the Catholic religion was essentially foreign and unpatriotic. This would be even more ruinous in the 1850s than it had been in 1791. Guibert went on to make a point which he evidently hoped would appeal to moderate opinion in Rome: what would happen to the virtue of obedience in the Church if the clergy allowed themselves to be led by self-appointed laymen into what was openly being described as a crusade against their own bishops? It was no use pretending that 'obedience to Rome' was a practical way of running the Church:

> As they practice it, Christian obedience becomes very convenient. It is easy to make eloquent protestations of submission to an authority four hundred leagues distant, and to proclaim each day that all one's writings, one's words and one's most intimate thoughts are submitted to the Church of Rome, if by this formula one dispenses oneself from all control of the authority closer at hand.

It was a licence for anarchy; the structure of the Church would dissolve if each individual claimed to be directly in touch with the papacy and was ready to denounce anyone who disagreed with him as 'an enemy of Rome'.[18]

This had been said before, but it was doubly effective coming from the circumspect Guibert. In the first two weeks of February it became known that Mazenod, Dupanloup, Mathieu, and

---

[18] *Lettre circulaire de Mgr l'Évêque de Viviers* (Viviers 1853). Guibert had submitted the text to his former superior and mentor, Mazenod of Marseilles, who strongly approved it.

Morlot were organizing protests to the Pope along the lines of the Viviers pastoral and that as many as forty bishops were ready to endorse Guibert's main points. In spite of objections from the Nuncio who pointed out that a collective *démarche* of bishops would be contrary to canon law,[19] a number of letters were written and Mgr Gros of Versailles, who was leaving for an *ad limina* visit, offered to take them to Rome. The mirage of resistance could be seen glimmering on the horizon. Sibour felt that Gaduel's appeal could not have come at a better moment and that the time was surely right for a frontal attack on the ultramontane party; and without consulting any of his circle of advisers he issued an ordinance on 17 February 1853 which was to have an extraordinary effect on the future of the French Church. The *école de l'Univers*, he wrote, was leading an ecclesiastical revolution: it had already 'brought serious disorder into the ranks of the lower clergy, who are now mistaking intemperate passion for pious zeal and interpreting contempt for episcopal authority as a sign of devotion to the Holy See'. In particular, Veuillot's treatment of a theologian like the abbé Gaduel was a disgrace to Catholicism. In future no member of the diocesan clergy or of the religious orders in Paris was to read *L'Univers* or to write for it; no more copies were to be bought for religious establishments; and Sibour concluded with a splendidly Canute-like paragraph ordering the Catholic press in Paris never again to mention the words 'ultramontane' or 'gallican'.[20]

The reply in *L'Univers* was ominous: their editor-in-chief happened to be in Rome, and would appeal. Immediately after writing his last article on the Gaduel controversy Veuillot had asked Mgr Salinis, who was taking the decrees of the ultramontane Council of Amiens to be approved by the Pope, if he could go with him to Rome; he wanted to assess the degree of his favour and admitted frankly that he was coming in the hope of a papal

[19] Seven years later the Curia was to make repeated efforts to organize a collective *démarche* of French bishops in favour of the temporal power of the papacy. On the gallican protests of February 1853, letters of 'N. D.', a priest in the household of Mgr Morlot of Tours, to Léon Aubineau at the *Univers* office, 5 and 22 Feb. 1853, V/BN 24235; letter of the abbé Roux, professor of dogma at Saint-Sulpice, to the abbé Boiteux, 26 Feb. 1853, S. Sulp/AN AB XIX 519; and Garibaldi's dispatches of 1–16 Feb. 1853. ASV Francia 1853 (III).
[20] *Ordonnance de Mgr l'Archevêque de Paris . . .*, 17 Feb. 1853; copy in ASV Francia 1853 (III).

decoration which would put him in a stronger position *vis-à-vis* the French bishops.[21] He had spent a fortnight in Rome visiting cardinals and Jesuits and attending masses, and had been granted a long private audience with Pius IX who covered him with compliments but also told him, very gently and benevolently, that he might have handled the affair of Bouillet's *Dictionnaire* better by delating the book discreetly to the Index instead of creating a public uproar; and he heard nothing of events in Paris until in the last days of February packets of letters and press clippings began arriving with the news of the Viviers pastoral and of Sibour's condemnation of *L'Univers*.

The letters from his supporters were full of enthusiasm for Veuillot to 'fight and win'. Mgr Pie was organizing a campaign of support from ultramontane bishops. Gerbet had written to his friends at Rome. Gousset had sent a memorandum to Cardinal Fornari outlining a technical case against Sibour's action, strongly supported by the Nuncio; but Veuillot's fellow editors at *L'Univers* advised him to keep away from technicalities and base his appeal simply on the broader interests of the Holy See in France. Unless Rome seized this opportunity to strike firmly, French Catholicism would fall under the control of Sibour and Dupanloup, 'the enemies of the Church'. *L'Univers* was not only the organ of Rome but above all 'the priests' newspaper', and in claiming to bridle and control it Sibour was trying to dictate the opinions of the entire clergy, as a step towards establishing a patriarchate; Veuillot must make it clear at Rome that Sibour wanted eventually to have all French ecclesiastical writing and journalism submitted to the *archevêché* for approval, which would mean in effect approval by those arch-gallicans Lequeux, Delacouture, and Maret. Melchior du Lac and Gustave de la Tour passed on this advice in almost daily letters, and also two suggestions for the substance of an appeal. Firstly, Veuillot should ask the Pope to declare the writers of *L'Univers* 'diocesans of all France': nine-tenths of their readers were outside Paris, and this declaration would emancipate the paper from local control in any diocese so that no individual bishop would be able to discipline or silence it. Secondly, as Gerbet and La Tour pointed out, he should emphasize that Rome's excellent relations with

---

[21] Veuillot to Eugène Veuillot, 14 Mar. 1853, reporting a conversation with Mgr Fioramonti, *Correspondance* iv, 82–3.

the government of Napoleon III would be upset by the suppression of *L'Univers*. Veuillot's own *ralliement* had influenced the majority of the lower clergy to accept the Bonapartist Empire, and Napoleon III would no doubt be annoyed if Rome acquiesced in a defeat for 'the only religious newspaper that is favourable to the new government': privately, La Tour had doubts about this latter argument since he knew from his parliamentary colleagues that the Emperor's entourage, gallicans to a man, had long ago recovered from any feelings of gratitude to *L'Univers* which they had felt in the months following the *coup d'état*, but he thought that Rome might not be aware of this and urged Veuillot to stress the point.[22] Du Lac also forwarded two marvellously characteristic letters from Dom Guéranger. 'Hold high your banner!', he wrote on 21 February: 'it is a matter of saving orthodoxy in France . . . I am completely yours, in war as in peace'; but Guéranger went on to recommend that the banner be held high with 'absolute discretion . . . let nothing transpire of your projects'. Four days later he wrote again: 'be discreet, and for the love of God do not let *my* name be mentioned'.[23]

Veuillot redoubled his visits to Curial officials and heard two very encouraging assessments of the situation. The abbé Bouix, consulted about the rights of the laity in canon law, told him that under a bull of Eugenius IV, luckily not well known to gallican canonists, any judgement against a layman was automatically suspended as soon as the appellant arrived in Rome and laid his case before the Pope; and what he heard from the Pope's correspondence secretary, Mgr Fioramonti, made him still more confident: Pius IX was irritated by the Viviers pastoral because it had provoked the gallican grandees into writing insubordinate letters to Rome, and he was showing anger and impatience at the news of Sibour's ordinance. If Veuillot cared to submit a formal appeal, he was told, there would be an immediate reply. On 3 March he sent Fioramonti a letter in his best vein of mock

[22] Garibaldi to Antonelli, 20 Feb. 1853, ASV Francia 1853 (III); letters from du Lac to Veuillot, 24 Feb. and 5 Apr.; La Tour to Veuillot, 21, 23, 24 Feb., 1 and 7 Mar.; abbé des Garets to du Lac, 22 Feb.: all in V/BN 24226; *Correspondance Pie/Cousseau*, 151–2. Du Lac also passed on a message from one of his friends who held a minor post at the *archevêché* that Sibour was more than usually isolated and friendless since his ordinance, and that Maret and others in his circle thought he had plunged to certain disaster.

[23] Guéranger to du Lac, 21 Feb. 1853, V/BN 24633; 25 Feb., V/BN 24226.

modesty: others had made the technical and political points; he was only a humble servant of religion whose crime in some people's eyes was that for twelve years he had borne the heat of the battle in defence of the Holy See; his enemies were the Pope's enemies; Pius IX had only to say the word and he would gladly change his methods, or lay down his burden altogether. On 9 March he was handed a letter signed by Fioramonti but redrafted three times, Fioramonti said, by the Pope himself.[24] Its balance between mild criticism and fulsome praise was perfect: in explaining and defending the excellence of the Holy See and the irresistible force of its authority the editor of *L'Univers* should take care to be moderate in style and to avoid personal attacks;

but although the resentments and divisions which have come to light recently appear to be of a certain degree of gravity and may be seen as an obstacle to your newspaper, I am persuaded that this state of affairs will not last long; indeed, I am confident that those who, for the moment, are against you will soon be unanimous in praising the talent and zeal with which you never cease to uphold religion and the Apostolic See.[25]

The Fioramonti letter was in all the French newspapers by 16 March. Rome was full of illusions, Guibert commented; they knew nothing about the use and abuse of a free press, since they had no proper press of their own: 'it seems that men of sense are rare in Rome at the moment'.[26] On 10 March Fioramonti had written also to Sibour, a serpentine letter weaving its way through eleven pages of subordinate clauses, euphemisms, and reservations, sympathizing ironically with the moral anguish Sibour must surely have felt in deciding to take an action which was certain to be a triumph for the sceptical and irreligious classes in French society who had always seen *L'Univers* as their principal opponent—how he must have suffered at being applauded by the anticlerical press!— from which there emerged at the end a clear and unpalatable message: he had given offence at Rome by banning a worthy newspaper which was guilty only of 'irregularities of form'; he was to lift his prohibition and make

---

[24] Veuillot's letters from Rome, 18 Feb.–14 Mar. 1853, in *Correspondance* iv, 49–77.
[25] Full text in Veuillot's 'De la presse religieuse laïque', *Mélanges* v, *Oeuvres complètes* xxxi. 344–82.
[26] Follenay, *Guibert*, vol. ii, 144.

his peace with the editor-in-chief.[27] Sibour sat down at once to write an elaborate justification of his ordinance, explaining in particular that he had not meant to kill *L'Univers*, as Veuillot was claiming. Most of its subscribers, he agreed, were outside Paris and could continue to read the paper if they wished. He must, however, control his own diocese; and he told Fioramonti that he refused to believe that the Holy See would entertain an appeal by a group of ambitious lay zealots against the perfectly legitimate authority of a metropolitan archbishop: 'it would turn upside down the entire economy of ecclesiastical government'. The Holy See, he wrote, seemed disturbed by the problem of disunity, but did anyone at Rome imagine that the only way to avoid disunity was to leave Catholic journalists free to write whatever they liked? If the Pope had more confidence and trust in the episcopate the Church could accomplish great things in France: 'what is impossible today would become possible tomorrow'.[28] For the moment he received no reply.

At Rome Veuillot was now a celebrity. He continued his round of visits and kept foreign prelates and diplomats waiting in anterooms for hours while he chatted with the cardinal prefects of Congregations; influential members of the papal household like Mérode and Talbot called on him, secretaries and chamberlains, protonotaries apostolic, 'one whole day full of Jesuits'. The euphoria faded a little when he discovered that the Fioramonti letters were not by any means the end of the affair, and that the Curia had yet to give a formal ruling on the rights of Catholic journalists. He had spent some time cultivating the officials of the Congregation of the Council and was now disconcerted to find that his appeal against Sibour had been referred to the Congregation of Bishops and Regulars. Who did he know at Bishops and Regulars? Fornari and Marini, two strong supporters, sat on its committee, but the prefect and the secretary of the Congregation were said to be professionally inclined to take the side of archbishops against their critics and were quite likely to treat the Viviers pastoral seriously, or even to see some merit in Sibour's case. The notorious long view of Rome might work against him. As the days went by his letters revealed a gradual

[27] Letter drafted by Fioramonti and corrected by Pius IX, sent over the signature of Cardinal Antonelli, 10 Mar. 1853, ASV Francia 1853 (III).
[28] Sibour to Antonelli, 19 Mar. 1853, ASV Francia 1853 (III).

change of mood. Rome was everything he had remembered it to
be from his first visit in 1839: everywhere he encountered smiling
benevolence, Christian kindness, a truly medieval detachment;
the conversations were incomparable for their elevation and
unworldly charm, an immense refreshment for the spirit; he was
devastatingly, horribly bored. He missed the cut and thrust of
Parisian debate and the excitement of each day's issue of
L'Univers, he missed his colleagues and his children, and he was
beginning to notice the drawbacks of living in a city which he had
praised so often for its proud defiance of modernity. Behind the
smiles the faces were often grubby; at the Carmelite monastery
where he stayed briefly the cook was also the stableboy and did
not believe in washing his hands: 'Brother Luigi is the dirtiest
good fellow in Rome and the *banlieue*, which is saying a great
deal.' It rained incessantly, he had a bad cold, transport was
inefficient and expensive, there were vast armies of fleas. Every
additional day in Rome, he felt, would surely count in his
heavenly ledger as penance.[29] At this low point he found that the
Pope expected him to write a conciliatory letter to Sibour. He
was annoyed by the even-handedness which required him to
humiliate himself although everyone he met in Rome agreed that
he was in the right, and he had great difficulty in composing the
letter. 'When the Pope says that I am to be kind to opponents,
what does he mean?' Eventually he wrote promising moderation,
'that kind of moderation which does not preclude the free, frank,
and energetic defence of the truth'; not even for the Pope, he told
his brother, would he say more than that. He hoped Sibour
would be maladroit enough to reject the letter.[30] In this
depressed and angry frame of mind he found it hard to take any
pleasure in the encouraging news arriving every day from Paris,
where his opponents seemed to be anxious to present him with a
strategic victory. More provocative letters were arriving every
day from gallican bishops—'indiscretions' at the Secretariat of
State allowed him to read a lot of this correspondence—and Mgr
Garibaldi wrote to point out that the Sulpician *Mémoire*,

---

[29] Veuillot's letters from Rome, 25 Feb.–18 Mar. 1853, *Correspondance* iv, 54–95. In
central and northern Italy it happened to be the wettest spring in living memory, as
many travellers reported.
[30] V/BN 24620; Veuillot to Eugène, 22 Mar. 1853, *Correspondance* iv, 90; and *Louis
Veuillot*, vol. ii, chap. 20.

originally supposed to be confidential, had now been put on sale to the public;[31] and in the middle of March Sibour made another blunder. One of his suffragans, the ultramontane Dreux-Brézé of Moulins, had issued a pastoral letter defending *L'Univers* and suggesting that anyone who tried to hinder the work of such a notable defender of the papacy must be in league with secularists and agnostics. 'What a bomb on the *archevêché!*' wrote Jules Morel: 'the Nuncio is delighted'.[32] Without calculating the effect he was likely to produce, Sibour reported Dreux-Brézé to Rome for slandering a fellow bishop, and asked for an immediate judgement.[33]

The Roman machinery had been stalled, and 'the poor archbishop has come to our rescue' by setting it in motion again, Veuillot reported. For several weeks there had been rumours than an encyclical condemning gallicanism had been drafted but held in reserve, and now Veuillot heard from the editors of the *Civiltà Cattolica,* and from Fioramonti 'who knows everything', that the decision had been made to publish it. He heard also that Mgr Blanquart de Bailleul of Rouen was coming to Rome to argue for the rights of the gallican episcopate—'but he will arrive, I hope, too late'.[34] Blanquart came in the last week of March, bringing a *cahier de doléances* written largely by Dupanloup and endorsed by several of the senior bishops, defending 'the customs and usages of a great church of thirty-six million Catholics' and protesting vehemently against each of the advances made by the ultramontane party since the 1840s. Dupanloup and Blanquart reiterated the fundamental argument that the Church in France owed whatever success it had enjoyed since the Revolution precisely to the fact that it had been able to reconstitute the old religion with its local roots and its age-old autonomy. Now a group of *enragés* were stirring up a falsely democratic agitation which would very quickly destroy the special character of French Catholicism. When the document came to the delicate matter of how far Rome itself was responsible for encouraging clerical indiscipline in France it adopted the tactful line that Rome's

[31] Garibaldi, 8 Mar. 1853, ASV Francia 1853 (III).
[32] Morel to Cousseau, 23 Feb. 1853, *Correspondance Pie/Cousseau,* 146–7.
[33] *Lettre . . . déférant au Saint-Siège la Lettre-circulaire de Mgr l'Évêque de Moulins:* copy in ASV Francia 1853 (III).
[34] Veuillot to Eugène, 4 Mar. 1853, *Correspondance* iv, 72.

actions so far had been entirely innocent. How could the Sacred Congregation of Rites possibly have known, when it gave a ruling in favour of a priest against his bishop in a matter of liturgy, that the *Correspondance de Rome* and *L'Univers* would give the maximum publicity to this 'victory' and claim it as further proof that the French bishops were the enemies of the Holy See? But where the Congregation of Rites had simply made innocent mistakes, the Index, urged on by zealots and delators in France, had behaved with active malevolence. First Bouillet and Lequeux and then, worst of 'all the humiliations heaped upon us', the case of Bailly: without any prior warning or consultation from Rome the bishops and seminary directors had opened their newspapers and found that they, and generations of devoted churchmen in the past, had been exposed to derision, 'that the Index had condemned, alongside a list of works by heretics, enemies of religion, and obscene authors, a work of theology . . . which we and our predecessors had placed confidently in the hands of our priests and seminarists'. The memorandum repeated the warning of the Sulpician *Mémoire* of November 1852 that if the *école de L'Univers* continued to provoke internecine strife in the French Church, 'bringing theology and canon law down into the streets to fight battles before the public', eventually the civil power would intervene and impose strict control over religious life; and it added an even more potent argument: 'religious journalism can pass easily from one excess to another . . . its nature is to be capricious and changeable'; the people who wanted to create sweeping changes in ecclesiastical government would end by turning their disruptive zeal on the papacy itself. 'The Third Estate in 1789 abolished the nobility while claiming to be full of respect for the royal power; in 1793 it erected the scaffold for the king on the ruins of an annihilated nobility'. Suppose that the new Mennaisians, like Lamennais himself, began to take ecclesiastical democracy seriously?[35]

The Blanquart–Dupanloup appeal was directed to the Pope personally and worded to give the impression that the French bishops still believed Pius IX to be above the ultramontane manœuvres, and perhaps unaware of them. After a few days in Rome Blanquart realized that this line would no longer do.

---

[35] The original draft is in Dupanloup/AN AB XIX 522; Maurain, *Saint-Siège*, 191–206 quotes the most important passages.

Everyone knew, for example, that it had been the Pope who had ordered the Index to condemn Bailly; after a brief hesitation Blanquart struck out the entire passage dealing with the Bailly case before submitting the memorandum to the Pope's secretary. He wrote to Dupanloup:

I find the general feeling here not at all favourable to the cause of the Archbishop of Paris . . . I should say that at every point there is more goodwill towards *L'Univers* than towards anyone who attacks it. They say always that it has not sinned against faith or morals. For my part I reply that it has sinned against moderation, respect, the authority of the bishops, their mutual solidarity, their relations with their priests, etc., but all that is little understood.[36]

A few days before the encyclical was to be published the ambassador, Rayneval, always an optimist, predicted that the French government need have no fear of an insult to the Church of France or a crushing defeat for the Archbishop of Paris: the encyclical would be a product of Rome's timeless wisdom and foresight; all opinions would be conciliated and reconciled; it would satisfy everybody.[37] This was exactly what Veuillot feared. Presented with this exceptional opportunity to bring down the gallican *archevêché* of Paris at a vulnerable moment, he thought, Rome would inevitably bungle it; as usual, lethargy and timidity would prevail.[38] He was vastly reassured when he saw the text of the encyclical on 1 April. *Inter multiplices* intentionally began with the same phrase as the encyclical of 1690 which had condemned the Four Gallican Articles.[39] Its language, a long way from the infuriated bellowing of *Mirari vos* and *Singulari nos*, was patient and gently paternal but not even Rayneval could have mistaken the message which rang out like the strokes of an iron bell. The doctrines of the Sulpician *Mémoire* of 1852 on the plural and conciliar nature of the Church, the autonomy of dioceses, the 'gallican liberties', and the purely advisory nature of decisions by the Roman Congregations were declared absolutely unacceptable, and the *Mémoire* itself was placed on the Index. The bishops were told that their seminaries could use only books

---

[36] Blanquart de Bailleul to Dupanloup, 28 Mar. 1853, Dupanloup/AN AB XIX 526.
[37] Two dispatches from Rayneval on 24 Mar. 1853, in Maurain, *Saint-Siège*, 187–9.
[38] *Correspondance* iv, 91.
[39] Latin text and French translation in *L'Univers* (11 Apr. 1853).

specifically approved at Rome. There was no direct order to adopt the Roman liturgy, but the terms of praise for those bishops who had adopted it left the others in no doubt that their orthodoxy was suspect. In the middle of the encyclical was a passage which the Pope told Mgr Salinis he had included 'especially for Veuillot': the bishops were instructed to 'give their most paternal solicitude and encouragement to those men who, animated by a Catholic spirit and skilled in letters and sciences, devote their days to writing and publishing books and newspapers which propagate and defend Catholic doctrine, so that all opinions contrary to the authority of this Holy See may disappear . . .'.

Blanquart de Bailleul, who had intended to spend at least a month visiting the churches in Rome, packed his bags immediately after reading *Inter multiplices* and took the first boat home; he told Salinis that 'it will crush the life out of the episcopate' and that Veuillot would return as a conqueror.[40] In Paris the editors of *L'Univers* attended a special communion to celebrate;[41] letters of congratulation began to come in to the editorial offices from the leading ultramontanes, who were anxious to have Veuillot himself return to consolidate the victory: 'what a marvel this encyclical is!'; 'we are hungry and thirsty to see you'.[43] But Veuillot was still enmeshed in a series of appointments with Roman notables. He had long talks with Antonelli and Fornari, invitations from Fioramonti and Modena, a standing invitation at the *Civiltà Cattolica* office—in the midst of his triumph he discovered that he was being kept in Rome until the Curia knew what Sibour was going to do. Veuillot hoped that the archbishop would do something foolish or provocative and be censured by the Congregation of Bishops and Regulars. But Sibour was stunned by *Inter multiplices*, which was much worse than anything he had expected. He wrote to the Nuncio: 'I had the right to wait until I had been given some proper satisfaction before withdrawing my ordinance of 17 February, but after the encyclical . . . the archbishop of Paris does not wish to wait for anything more';[43] and he sent a letter to the press announcing a virtual surrender.

[40] Veuillot to Eugène, 3 Apr. 1853, *Correspondance* iv, 104.
[41] Du Lac to Veuillot, 5 Apr. 1853, V/BN 24226.
[42] V/BN 24226: the phrase quoted is from Mgr de Salinis.
[43] Sibour to Garibaldi, 8 Apr. 1853, ASV Francia 1853 (III).

He recognized the encyclical as a direct rebuke, he wrote, and in the face of the obvious disapproval of the Holy Father he 'spontaneously' lifted his prohibition against the *L'Univers*.[44] For this gesture he received an insufferably roundabout letter from the Secretariat of State expressing the Pope's pleasure and congratulating him—in so far as he could untangle the syntax—for having hastened to display 'the spirit of unity and peace which has now been restored to the worthy episcopate of France by the action of the August Pontiff'.[45] A few days later another letter arrived, this time from Veuillot. It had been conveyed to Veuillot that the Pope expected him to write personally to Sibour thanking him for lifting his prohibition. Veuillot, who felt that Sibour would always remain 'the thorn in the flowers of my triumph', was reluctant, but he knew that the letter would be as much for the Pope's eyes as for Sibour's. He composed a rhapsody of exaggerated conciliation: 'Everyone admires you, and I bless you . . . We [at *L'Univers*] are your children, Monseigneur, your devoted children. We want to deserve your goodwill; all our efforts will be directed to that end. I wish, ardently, that our work might become one of the joys of your episcopate'. He would call on Sibour when he returned, and 'you will be able to read my soul . . . you will see how your person and your authority are dear to me . . .' and so on.[46] The Pope read this with the highest approval, and arranged for it to be handed to Sibour by the Nuncio.

Veuillot's last week in Rome was full of satisfactions. The Pope had asked the Index to examine Donoso Cortès's book on Protestantism and socialism which had been the original occasion for the dispute, and Veuillot heard at the Index office that it had been found absolutely blameless in doctrine and that the Index had recommended that it should be translated into Italian; on the other hand 'four gross heresies' had come to light in the abbé Gaduel's review.[47] Various cardinals assured him that he was now a power in the Church. At his final private audience the Pope overwhelmed him with fatherly approval, with only the lightest suggestion that *L'Univers* in future might

[44] *L'Univers* (9 Apr. 1853).
[45] Antonelli to Sibour, 20 Apr. 1853, ASV Francia 1853 (III).
[46] Veuillot to Sibour, 16 Apr. 1853, *Correspondance* iv, 120.
[47] Letter of 8 Apr. 1853, *Correspondance* iv, 111.

keep in mind the virtue of charity. The papal decoration was
ready to be presented, but Pius IX was persuaded at the last
moment that it would be interpreted as a provocative gesture;
four months later the problem was solved by giving the medal to
Taconet, the nominal proprietor of *L'Univers*.[48] Veuillot arrived
back in Paris on 26 April, and went to see the archbishop after a
few days. Sibour had not been sure how to take Veuillot's
conciliatory letter but he knew that every detail of an interview
would be reported to Rome, directly or indirectly, and so he
suppressed his feelings. He embraced Veuillot, and the two men
sat down to a long and slightly uneasy conversation, victor and
vanquished assuring one another that the past was forgotten and
that a new era of concord was beginning.[49] Both of them knew
that this was unlikely; but for the moment Veuillot was genuinely
moved by Sibour's apparent magnanimity. Several weeks elapsed
before he could bring himself to criticize the *archevêché* again in
print.

Whatever concessions were made, Veuillot reflected, and
whatever interpretations were placed on particular phrases in the
encyclical, nobody could escape the fact that *Inter multiplices* was
an ecclesiastical event of the first order, demonstrating, inciden-
tally, the great superiority of Catholicism over Protestantism: the
Holy See had intervened with an authoritative judgement to
settle an ancient and profound division of opinion in the Church.
The ultramontane party in France should be happy to have
rendered a supreme service to the papacy in this post-Revolutionary period. At Rome 'they did not know their real strength;
they will know it better now, and will not forget it'.[50]

[48] Garibaldi, 26 Mar. 1853, ASV Francia 1853 (III); Fioramonti to Veuillot, 28
Aug. 1853, V/BN 24633.
[49] Veuillot to Salinis, 27 Apr. 1853, *Correspondance* iv, 125. Veuillot's account of the
meeting is in his usual vein of sarcasm and contempt, but it is quite obvious that he is
touched by this brief interlude of friendliness. He asks Salinis to imagine him in future
dining at the *archevêché*, asking prominent gallicans to pass the salt and 'offering wine
to M. Gaduel'.
[50] Veuillot to Eugène, 17 Apr. 1853, *Correspondance* iv, 121 ff.

XII

The low point of gallican fortunes

The Immaculate Conception and the surrender of the archevêché

THE encyclical had been received in France with universal joy and satisfaction, Mgr Garibaldi reported. It would have a soothing effect; the gallicans, he said, had wanted to avoid giving the impression that they were being bullied into line by *L'Univers*, but now that the Pope had spoken they would be 'happy to move spontaneously and sincerely towards Rome'.[1] Garibaldi knew perfectly well that the gallicans had in fact reacted to *Inter multiplices* with anger and resentment. Very bitter remarks were being relayed from the *évêchés* and Dupanloup in particular made no secret of his opinion that it was the *coup de grâce* of the old French Church.[2] His own copy of the encyclical had arrived with a covering letter expressing the Pope's extreme annoyance with the memorandum drafted by Dupanloup and presented at Rome by Blanquart de Bailleul; he could restore himself to some degree of favour, Garibaldi hinted, by making a public gesture of submission which might convince the many bishops who looked to him for a lead.[3] Dupanloup wrote what was expected of him, a letter expressing 'veneration, love and submission to the Holy Father' and dissociating himself from the more extreme forms of parliamentary gallicanism, but he did not specifically renounce any of the ecclesiological arguments put forward in his memorandum or in the Sulpician *Mémoire*;[4] from this time onwards his gallican opinions hardened.

Sibour had written assuring the Pope that he would have no difficulty in following the advice given in the encyclical and that 'nowhere in the world could there be an episcopate more devoted to the Holy See';[5] but behind these civilities he was angry and

[1] Garibaldi, two dispatches on 16 Apr. 1853, ASV Francia 1853 (III).
[2] 'Rapport au Pape', Dupanloup/AN AB XIX 524: chap 10.
[3] Garibaldi to Dupanloup, 7 Apr. 1853, copy in ASV Francia 1853 (III).
[4] Ibid., Dupanloup to Garibaldi, 9 Apr. 1853; Dupanloup's letter to the Pope in Lagrange, *Vie de Mgr Dupanloup*, vol. ii, 136.
[5] Sibour to Antonelli, 5 May 1853, ASV Francia 1853 (III).

discontented, and hoped to be able to keep some kind of resistance alive. As a sardonic member of his household noted, in the threatening atmosphere created by the encyclical the archbishop, previously so reckless, now preferred to act by urging others forward while remaining in the background himself.[6] He told Lequeux to make a fresh approach to the Index regarding corrections to his book, and he encouraged Guettée, Delacouture, and Prompsault to publish technical criticisms of *Inter multiplices*. Prompsault's *Observations sur l'Encyclique*, written with Sibour's approval, began bluntly: 'It would be a great pity if so high an authority should fall into error, but an even greater pity if Christian society should be allowed to suffer the disastrous consequences'; and Prompsault went on to emphasize what many gallicans took to be a crucial point, the well-documented promise by the papacy at the time of the Concordat that 'the ancient liberties of the Church of France' would not be disturbed. The Pope read this and made some irritated comments about Prompsault to the French ambassador.[7] Sibour's circle, however, was to be disrupted in the following year. Towards the end of 1854 it was announced from Rome that the commission preparing the dogma of the Immaculate Conception had finished its work and that the solemn definition would take place on 8 December. Historians of the First Vatican Council have generally looked back to the definition in 1854 as a constitutional precedent and a decisive step towards the dogma of separate papal infallibility, since in this case the Pope proclaimed a dogma on his own authority without calling a Council. The bishops had already been consulted, in a sense, by the encyclical *Ubi primum* in 1849, but they had been asked for opinions, not for votes, and they had never been told the result of the world-wide enquiry. In October 1854 a limited number of bishops from each country received invitations to attend the proclamation.[8] The deliberate choice of well-known ultramontanes and the passing over of gallicans—Cardinal Gousset was invited but Cardinal de Bonald, his senior in the episcopate by thirteen years, was

[6] Guettée, *Souvenirs d'un prêtre romain*, 87–8.
[7] Abbé J.-H. Prompsault, *Observations sur l'Encyclique du 21 mars* (1853), 1; Rayneval dispatch of 20 June 1853, in Maurain, *Saint-Siège*, 225.
[8] Correspondence in Dupanloup/BN 24681; Victor Pelletier, *Mgr Dupanloup: épisode de l'histoire contemporaine* (1876), 38; U. Maynard, *Mgr Dupanloup et Mgr Lagrange son historien* (1884), 326.

not—was apparently designed to avoid any resemblance to a General Council. Bishops who wanted to attend without an invitation were told that they would not be admitted to whatever deliberations took place; but it was made clear, in any case, that there was not to be much talk: the bishops were not to discuss either the dogma itself or the wisdom of proclaiming it. Even some of the French who favoured the new dogma were disturbed, and the few gallicans who went to Rome hoped that an opportunity would arise to register a protest. In the event the best that the opposition could do was to ask, through two bold spokesmen, that the Bull proclaiming the dogma should include some mention of 'the consent of the episcopate'; but this was rejected. At the preliminary ceremonies and at the solemn definition on 8 December all attention was focused on the person of Pius IX, and the bishops, as the ultramontane abbé Combalot described them, 'counted for nothing—they were equivalent to choirboys'.

Remembering that amongst his many other offences he had covered himself with opprobrium by opposing the Immaculate Conception in 1849, Sibour had not expected to be invited to Rome at all; but the Pope now believed that the *archevêché* of Paris could be conquered by gentle persuasion, and gave instructions that Sibour was to be treated as an honoured guest. Instead of having to search for lodgings like most of the visiting bishops he was given a splendid apartment in the Vatican, and had three private audiences in which Pius IX was astonishingly affectionate and kept turning the conversation away from the problems of the past few years. Dinners were arranged with Antonelli and the prefects of Congregations, and great efforts were made to convince Sibour that the malign wizards and ogres he had imagined at the Curia were actually reasonable and conciliatory men, always ready to act in the best interests of the archdiocese of Paris. As a sign, however, of the concessions he was expected to make, the Pope asked him to serve the special mass to celebrate the new dogma, giving the ultramontanes the enjoyable spectacle of the greatest opponent of the Immaculate Conception humbly holding a candle beside the high altar of Saint Peter's. When he returned to Paris Sibour put on a brave face. If only he had gone to Rome sooner, he told the ministre des Cultes, and seen for himself the high regard they had for the French episcopate he could have established a close working relationship with the Curia and completely outmanœuvred *L'Univers*;[9] but it soon became evident that he had conceded almost everything. Copies of the Sulpician *Mémoire* were collected and suppressed. The priests whose books were on the Index were purged from the circle of the *archevêché*: Lequeux was moved from his vicar-generalship in charge of education to an honorific post without any duties; Prompsault, whose latest pamphlet, *Du siège du pouvoir ecclésiastique dans l'Église*, had been delated to the Index while Sibour was in Rome, was abruptly dismissed from the chaplaincy he had held for thirty years—he died shortly afterwards; Guettée was asked to resign and to leave Paris altogether. A formal announcement was made that Paris would adopt the Roman liturgy. Even the archdiocesan catechism was rewritten and emerged full of Roman nuances like the additional phrase in the answer to the question: 'What is the Church?'

The Church is the society of the faithful established by Our Lord Jesus Christ, spread over the whole earth, and submitted to the authority of its legitimate pastors, *principally of Our Holy Father the Pope.*[10]

The ultramontane victory

'How could the affair have been handled better?', the Pope asked Louis Doubet, president of the *Cercles catholiques*, in July 1853. The gallican bishops who were trying to limit the power of the Holy See, he said, had been publicly and definitively reproved, and at the same time the editors of *L'Univers* had been told privately to behave with moderation and charity.[11] Doubet could see that to have achieved the soothing effect which the Pope thought he had created, the public rebuke and the private advice should have been arranged in reverse; but Rome, having mentioned moderation so often, did nothing to encourage it or to ensure that the gallicans who had lost the substantive argument were not harassed and humiliated. Throughout the 1850s the Holy See looked on approvingly while Veuillot and his friends

[9] On Sibour's visit to Rome, Fortoul, *Journal*, vol. i, 92; abbé Léon Sibour to Fortoul, 3 Dec. 1854, AN F. 19. 6179; Sevrin, *Clausel de Montals*, vol. ii, 714; Delatte, *Dom Guéranger*, vol. ii, 110 f.
[10] Cited in *L'Observateur catholique* (1 June 1856).
[11] Doubet's account of the audience on 15 July 1853, in J. Gay, *Les Deux Romes et l'opinion française* (1931), 232–42.

whipped the Church of France into a Roman shape. Secure in its unique position after *Inter multiplices L'Univers* was dominant and untouchable, defining the limits of orthodoxy, pressing forward, satirizing, threatening, changing the topic for discussion every few days—civil marriage, science, Protestantism, the liturgy—'so that we all have to follow willy-nilly', one bishop wrote, 'into whatever regions it chooses'.[12] The phrase *depuis l'Encyclique* ran through all Veuillot's editorials, and the defeated gallicans repeated *depuis l'Encyclique* in varying tones of dismay and chagrin.

Veuillot was now the virtual commander of the lower clergy. He travelled through the dioceses 'like a visiting Pope', generally avoiding the *évêchés* but being entertained at enthusiastic meetings of priests. Young *desservants* and seminarians wrote him collective letters of allegiance; they were to be the middle-aged priests of the Third Republic who would plunge into the wrong side of every major public debate from the *affaire du 16 mai* to the *affaire Dreyfus*. The circulation of *L'Univers* rose to 8000, with 11,000 copies being printed of some issues.[13] Although Veuillot declined a Roman offer to supply news and documentation directly from the Secretariat of State, which would have given *L'Univers* semi-official status, he and his fellow editors were linked to Rome during the fifties by a dozen excellent channels of communication.[14] The paper's well-advertised influence with the Congregation of the Index meant that its review columns were scrutinized with painful attention; to reach a clerical readership a book had to be reviewed in *L'Univers*, and authors knew that what Veuillot, or Morel, or du Lac said about their work today, the Index might say tomorrow.

[12] Cœur to Dupanloup, 3 Oct. 1853, Dupanloup/BN 24680.

[13] Melchior du Lac gives these figures in family correspondence in the 'Dossier du Lac', V/BN 24635. Like other newspapers *L'Univers* sometimes understated its print runs in returns to the Ministry of the Interior. The official circulation varied between 5000 and 8000.

[14] Besides the contacts Veuillot had already established with Fioramonti, Modena, and the *Civiltà* editors, he now corresponded with Mgr Berardi, head of the papal secretariat, and with three well-informed Curial officials, Nardi, Estrade, and Lasagni, and with Cardinal de Villecourt who had become one of the Pope's advisers on French affairs after the death of Fornari in 1854: V/BN 24225-8, 24633. Villecourt's secretary commented about a French delegation which came to Rome in 1858 especially to complain about *L'Univers*: 'Poor fellows, they little know where they are treading': abbé Baseredon to abbé A. Dust, 20 Nov. 1858, V/BN 24227.

The universal fear of the Index in the Church after 1853 was well illustrated by the disarray of the Sulpicians. Their humiliation could hardly have been more public, since the *Mémoire* of 1852 had been read by every bishop and seminary director in the country and by many thousands of former pupils of the order, and reviewed by the secular press, and its condemnation by the Index had sent a shock wave through the Sulpician seminaries. There were rumours that all the textbooks used at Saint-Sulpice were under examination at Rome, that Saint-Sulpice was to be taken out of the jurisdiction of the archdiocese of Paris and put under the direct control of the Pope, and even that the order was to be disbanded. None of these things happened, but there was a continuous pressure, exercised crudely in *L'Univers* and in anti-Sulpician speeches at provincial councils, and more subtly through the Nunciature, to persuade the order to institute its own programme of change. Saint-Sulpice adopted the Roman liturgy. Lecture notes were revised so that there could be no possible risk from the Index: was it permissible, for example, lecturers wondered, to tell seminarians that in normal circumstances priests should obey their bishops, and that a direct order from the Pope to an individual priest would be rare and exceptional? When the Sulpicians published a new edition of Icard's *Praelectiones juris canonici* in 1859, rewritten to eliminate references to the liberties of national Churches, *L'Univers* complained that it was still not explicit and positive enough about papal supremacy and Icard had to prepare a further edition in 1862. Icard himself was known to belong to the school of the authors of the *Mémoire*, and was not allowed to succeed as director of Saint-Sulpice when R. P. Carrière died in 1864; the Curia appointed one of the few ultramontanes in the Order, R. P. Caval, and gave the Sulpicians a 'Cardinal Protector' in Rome—Clement de Villecourt, a passionate supporter of *L'Univers*. The Sulpician intellectuals were never fully reconciled to defeat: 'We carry in ourselves the future of the Church', Baudry told his pupil Hyacinthe Loyson; 'nothing must be destroyed, but everything must be transformed';[15] but the order was compelled to play down the 'legend' of its earlier gallicanism; certainly a later generation of students, like the abbé Frémont in the 1870s,

---

[15] Quoted by A. Houtin, *Le Père Hyacinthe dans l'Eglise romaine* (1920), 68.

could see little to suggest that Saint-Sulpice had once been the centre of an independent national tradition.[16]

Throughout all the seminaries there was a general 'renovation' of textbooks after 1853 in which Icard, Bailly, and Lequeux were replaced by the manuals of Gousset, Bouix, and the Roman theologian Perrone, and Fleury and Guettée by the ultra-papalist histories of Rohrbacher, Blanc, and Darras. In some cases a familiar author's name and a familiar title still appeared on the library shelf but the text inside the covers had been revised beyond recognition by an ultramontane editor. Seminarians who saw only the new edition of Bouvier's treatise on the Church, issued after Bouvier's death, might not have realized that it bore no resemblance to the original: every mention of Roman decisions not being accepted in France had been deleted; the 'harmless belief in the Immaculate Conception' had become 'a dogma resting on a foundation of divine truth, always held by the Church'; the 'open question' of whether or not a General Council is superior to a Pope was 'now resolved: the Pope's authority is absolute'; even Bouvier's metaphor about the Church being a body 'with the soul ruling the head and the limbs' had been changed to make the head rule both soul and limbs.[17]

The effect of all this was that the young priests trained after 1853 were cut off from the past of their own Church. They had no opportunity to compare their textbooks with the teaching received by an earlier generation, and their lecturers no longer felt that it was safe to recommend the literature of the most distinguished periods in French Catholic history: the ultramontane historians recommended to priests and seminarians by *L'Univers* treated Pascal, Bossuet, Fénélon, and the Benedictines of Saint-Maur as part of the same movement as Luther and Calvin, and wrote about the early nineteenth-century gallicanism of Frays-sinous and Emery as if it was an anachronistic minor heresy, long ago discredited. There was a persistent rumour throughout the

[16] There is considerable material on the Sulpician retreat from gallicanism in the papers relating to the nunciature of Mgr Sacconi, ASV Francia 1854–6; S. Sulp/AN AB XIX 517–9; Montclos, *Lavigerie*, 50 ff.; Agnès Siegfried, *L'Abbé Frémont 1852–1912*, 2 vols. (1932), vol. i; Hédouville, *Mgr de Ségur*, 174–227.

[17] In his preface the editor says that he is grateful for suggestions about defects in the earlier editions of Bouvier by Mgr Gousset, Dom Guéranger, the abbés Bouix and Rohrbacher, and *L'Univers*: J. B. Bouvier, *Institutiones theologicae* . . . (edn. of 1856): vol. i: *De vera religione; de Ecclesia.*

fifties that the Index was preparing a condemnation of Bossuet. This was unlikely, in reality, since Rome knew from the Paris Nunciature that it would have been taken by the government as an insult to French literature; and, in any case, every one of the main gallican propositions associated with Bossuet's name was already on the Index. At the provincial council of La Rochelle in July 1853 the ultramontane majority introduced a motion to censure the entire works of Bossuet, so that a formal request for action by the Index would have followed automatically. As chairman of the council Cardinal Donnet refused to receive the motion, and then found himself the subject of a campaign of anonymous attacks and rumours that his own sermons would be delated to the Index. Letters passed around the *école de L'Univers* exploring the possibility of some action against Donnet; eventually he had to write a crawling apology to the Roman Secretariat of State for any favourable remarks he might have made about Bossuet in the past, and for having defended the Sulpician Order during one of the council debates.[18] The 'fear of attracting the lightning', in Dupanloup's phrase, affected even clerics whose work had nothing to do with ecclesiology or dogma. *L'Univers* insisted that Rome had, in effect, condemned the École des Carmes and with it the ideal of a scholarly and scientific clergy. 'Nobody is left in peace', wrote the abbé Vollot, one of those priests who had been sent by the *archevêché* of Paris to study in Germany: 'unless one declares, apropos of a treatise on leeches, that one "submits to the judgement of the Church, Mother and Mistress", and that the proofs have been corrected by Roman theologians, all is lost.'[19]

There were occasional attempts during the fifties to challenge the monopoly of *L'Univers* in Catholic debate, and one of them provides a glimpse of a defeated and bitter Sibour in the last year of his life.[20] In October 1856 Sibour's friend the abbé Gabriel, *curé* of Saint-Merry—one of the few friends he had left, as most of

---

[18] Donnet to Cardinal Antonelli, 10 Oct. 1853, ASV Francia 1853 (IV); Mgr Doney of Montauban to Jules Morel, 30 Aug. 1853, Donnet/AN 160 AP. ii.

[19] Quoted by G. Weill, *Histoire du catholicisme libéral en France 1828–1908* (1909), 157–8.

[20] He was assassinated by a deranged priest, the abbé Verger, in January 1857. Ironically, Verger was a fanatical opponent of the dogma of the Immaculate Conception and believed Sibour to be one of its leading supporters: he shouted 'Down with goddesses!' as he stabbed the archbishop.

the gallican party thought that he had behaved badly in 1854 in dismissing men like Lequeux and Prompsault who had risked their careers for him—drew up a prospectus for a new journal to appeal to educated Catholic opinion, and for a series of books on historical and philosophical questions. Sibour wrote immediately urging him to abandon the project. Gabriel had recently been to Rome and had been given to understand that he was in reasonable favour; Sibour warned him not to read too much into displays of cordiality. 'At Rome they are as changeable as the waves'; intellectuals especially should remember Rosmini, condemned by the Index a week after the Pope had told him that he was a cardinal *in petto*. It was hopeless to publish anything,

at least until the freedom of the evangelical word, destroyed by the Index, is restored to us . . . The Grand Lama Veuillot has under his orders a crowd of inquisitors, frocked and unfrocked, crossed and mitred, who will find you a hundred heresies in the most orthodox page . . .[21]

Gabriel appears to have taken his advice.

As they relapsed into silence or contemplated early retirement the gallican bishops were mocked by the chorus of invocations to 'the infallible Pope-King' which burst out from the ultramontane party. For the *école de L'Univers* the double victory of *Inter multiplices* and the Immaculate Conception had swept aside all the frustrating reservations and qualifications which gallicanism had put in the way of papalist doctrine since the time of Lamennais. The usual rhetoric of 'Saint Peter always living in his successor'— some of Veuillot's friends used to write *le Saint Pierre* instead of *le Saint Père*—was transcended: the Pope was now virtually a member of the Trinity, 'the Word Incarnate which continues in history'. He was preserved from sin as well as from error, *innocens, impollutus, segregatus a peccatoribus*;[22] the abbé Darras in his *Histoire de l'Église* transformed the degenerate Popes of the ninth and tenth centuries into models of sanctity to make the point that a man elected to the office is divinely changed into an image of Christ. The language became peculiarly feverish after the proclamation of the Immaculate Conception. The more cautious view, which satisfied moderate ultramontanes like Gerbet, that

---

[21] Sibour to the abbé Gabriel, 10 Oct. 1856, A. Arch. Paris 1. D. vi (4).
[22] Roger Aubert gives some good examples in *Le Pontificat de Pie IX* (1963), 301–3.

defining a dogma meant simply the Church's recognition of a truth which had always existed,[23] was not enough for the more forward theorists who made the Pope a necessary part of the divine mechanism: a dogma may exist in the mind of God but it has no real meaning, it is not in any sense 'true', until it has been validated by a papal definition. In 1854

> the Pope-King opened his infallible mouth and spoke. He defined the dogma. Oh unique moment! The heavens, the angels, the Church, the hierarchy, the faithful . . . the whole universe hung upon his word.[24]

The gallican-ultramontane conflict in France had stimulated the always latent tendency of the Holy See to become obsessed with the question of its own authority. In papal documents of the fifties there was less and less theological argument, in particular less quotation from scripture or the Fathers than in the time of Gregory XVI, and more repetition of formulae about total supremacy and absolute obedience; the correspondence passing through the Secretariat of State gives the impression that the whole management of the Church, or even the whole of Catholic doctrine, has been reduced to the calculation of who could or could not 'be relied on in all circumstances to act enthusiastically to defend the rights and privileges of the Holy See'. Bishops wrote expressing 'unlimited adhesion and subordination to the centre of Catholic unity', and Fioramonti and Antonelli replied conveying 'the profound satisfaction with which the Holy Father has read of your complete surrender to his will and your sincere devotion to his Sacred Person'. *Inter multiplices* itself is a masterpiece of narcissism—'It fills Us with inexpressible joy to see with what filial piety, what love, what ardour you glory in your devotion to Us and to this Chair of Peter'—but far surpassed later by the deification of Pius IX during the temporal power crisis and by the rhetoric of the *Civiltà Cattolica* group towards 1870: 'From his throne', Matteo Liberatore wrote, 'there springs forth a light which illuminates and kindles the universe'.[25]

[23] *Lettre pastoral* . . . *Ineffabilis Deus*, *Oeuvres de Mgr Gerbet*, 2 vols. (1876), vol. i, 142–4.
[24] From the abbé Combalot's introduction to his published sermons: quoted by Ricard, *L'Abbé Combalot*, 501.
[25] Matteo Liberatore SJ, *La Chiesa e lo Stato*, quoted in Anon., *Ce qu'on a fait de l'Église* (1912), 74. The other quotations above are from a mass of similar correspondence in ASV Francia 1852–4.

Gallican authors, noting sourly that one of the crimes for which they could be put on the Index was to have accused the papacy of a greed for domination, circulated spoof papal letters in *samizdat* copies: 'With what delicious emotion, venerable brethren, we perceive you prostrate at our feet . . .'; one of these which survives in Dupanloup's papers purported to be an encyclical from 'His Holiness Mgr Veuillot, most illustrious Patriarch and Coadjutor to the Holy Father, and Vicar of Jesus Christ'.[26]

[26] Dupanloup/AN AB XIX 524.

XIII

The revival of gallicanism and the Vatican Council

A gallican revival

THE survival and partial recovery of gallicanism in the French Church, to the extent that it was able to mount a strong resistance against unlimited papal supremacy at the Vatican Council in 1870, was made possible by the movement of public opinion on religious affairs during the Second Empire. The ultramontane victories in the early fifties had irritated and disturbed the political class, and after *Inter multiplices* and the Immaculate Conception, Mgr Cœur observed, the triumphalism of the *école de L'Univers* could easily have raised 'hatreds against Catholicism that not even a hundred apologists working for a hundred years will be able to dissipate'.[1] *Veuillotisme* drove away one potential convert, Émile Ollivier, who wrote in his journal in May 1853 that the aspect of modern Catholicism he found most unappealing was its refusal to admit any diversity of opinion: 'It seems to me that I have now emerged from my Catholic temptation. It was a sickness, a lapse of intelligence . . .'.[2] The educated public was able to follow the nuances and subtleties of ecclesiastical debate through the excellent coverage of religion in the serious press: the *Moniteur* and some other papers had sources in the ministère des Cultes, and the abbé Delacouture was now established as the ecclesiastical correspondent for the *Journal des débats*—it had been a mistake of Rome not to have removed Delacouture from the *archevêché* along with Lequeux and Prompsault, because his very effective articles on gallican–liberal themes were widely reprinted in other papers. Readers of the daily press, and students at the Sorbonne who could hear some of the leading gallicans lecturing every day in the Faculty of

[1] Cœur to Dupanloup, 3 Oct. 1853, Dupanloup/BN 24680.
[2] Ollivier, *Journal 1846–1869*, ed. T. Zeldin and Anne Troisier de Diaz, 2 vols. (1961), vol. i, 158, entry for 12 May 1853.

Theology, had no trouble in understanding the shades of opinion in the clergy and the minor dramas of obstinacy or surrender; and the overwhelming reaction was of anger with Rome and sympathy with the gallicans, mingled with impatience at the way the bishops had allowed themselves to be intimidated individually instead of presenting a united front. Prominent Catholic laymen themselves shared the general resentment at the way an 'anti-French' movement had been stimulated by Frenchmen. 'The French clergy are accused of being ultramontane', Adolphe de Circourt told Nassau Senior in 1854, 'but it would be more true if the Pope were called cismontane . . . Our bishops and our clergy are his advisers; they are the public whose advice he courts.'[3] Lamennais and Montalembert had exalted the papacy beyond reason or good sense, Louis de Kergorlay wrote, and twenty years later it had grown into a monstrous semi-deity before which all consciences had to bow down; gallicans like Sibour and Delacouture were right to resist, but they should look further into the future, he thought, towards the revival of a completely decentralized, pre-Constantinian Church based on discussion and consensus.[4] Louis Doubet thought that if Pius IX were to die it would create the opportunity for the French government to exert pressure on Rome for a change of direction.[5] The election of Dupanloup to the Académie française in May 1854 was generally understood as a calculated compliment by the intellectual community, almost a consolation prize, to 'a bishop in the line of succession from Bossuet, Frayssinous, and Quélen'.[6]

From the beginning of Louis Napoleon's regime the government itself had the strong inclination towards *gallicanisme parlementaire* which might have been expected from the Orleanist background of most of the ministers. According to Circourt, when they turned their attention to religion 'the cabinet bitterly regret that their predecessors, ever since 1830, have allowed the rights of the State

---

[3] Senior, *Conversations with M. Thiers, M. Guizot . . .*, vol. i, 357.

[4] There are many comments to this effect in Kergorlay's voluminous papers on ecclesiastical affairs written in the fifties: Kergorlay/Arsenal 14094: 170–84; 14108: 20.

[5] Gay, *Les deux Romes*, 242.

[6] Cœur to Dupanloup, 20 May 1854, Dupanloup/BN 24680. The electors had also noted that Dupanloup was one of those bishops who had not made any show of support for Louis Napoleon after the *coup d'état*. Towards the end of the Empire he became much more favourable to the régime.

in ecclesiastical affairs to erode away almost completely; they will exert themselves to restore the courage and confidence of those gallicans who still exist in the Church';[7] but for the first few months after the inauguration of the Second Empire in November 1852 the government had to act cautiously because of the affair of *le Sacre*. Louis Napoleon was anxious to convince the more conservative European powers about the legitimacy of the Bonaparte dynasty and knew that it would create an excellent effect if the Pope could be induced to come to Paris to crown him as the Emperor Napoleon III. The negotiations dragged on until in April 1853 the ministère des Cultes succeeded in persuading the Emperor that French public opinion would never swallow the concessions Rome was asking in return, the abolition of the Organic Articles and the restoration of the religious ceremony for all marriages, and the idea was abandoned; but during this time the government had deliberately held back from giving any encouragement to the gallican party in the crises over the condemnation of Bailly, the Fioramonti letters, and the encyclical, for fear of antagonizing Pius IX. After the middle of 1853 this constraint was removed.

Fortoul and his senior officials at the ministère des Cultes had analysed each step in the ultramontane campaign since 1848 as containing an implied threat to the concordatory system. The legitimate influence the State should exercise in ecclesiastical affairs would disappear, Fortoul told his cabinet colleagues, if the French bishops came to be governed directly by the Index and the Congregation of Rites, and by papal encyclicals;[8] and Rome was continuing every day to upset the delicate structure of clerical discipline in France. Instead of acting to restrain the ebullience of the ultramontanes in the parishes the Holy See was encouraging priests to appeal to Rome on all kinds of questions; the Ministry noted also that since *Inter multiplices* Pius IX himself had developed the habit when giving audiences to visiting French priests of making disparaging remarks to them about their own bishops, telling a deputation from Marseilles, for

[7] Circourt to Cavour, 7 Feb. 1853, *Carteggio Cavour-Circourt*, supplement to *Cavour e l'Inghilterra: II: I conflitti diplomatici del 1856–61*, vol. ii, 247.

[8] Memorandum drafted by the directeur général des Cultes, Contencin, and sent by Fortoul to the Foreign Minister, Drouyn de Lhuys, Apr. 1853, AN F. 19. 1934; Fortoul to Cœur, 1 Sept. 1853, AN F. 19. 2590; Maurain, *Saint-Siège*, 219–24.

example, that Mgr de Mazenod was a misguided old fool for
having put his name to the Dupanloup–Blanquart memorandum
in March 1853. Rome had also begun using a tactic which was
obviously against the spirit of all European concordats. While
the government carefully guarded its right to nominate bishops,
there was nothing to stop the Holy See from appointing French
priests to be protonotaries apostolic, prelates of the household or
assistants at the Pontifical throne; these ranks had doubtful
status in canon law but they conferred the privilege of wearing
varieties of episcopal costume, and of having some kind of direct
access to the Curia. Hitherto they had been given out rather
sparingly but from 1852 onwards the bishops were irritated to
find 'these violet creatures' appearing in every diocese, always,
by a remarkable coincidence, priests like Victor Pelletier at
Orleans who had distinguished themselves as opponents of their
évêchés, claiming special places beside the bishop in public
ceremonies and the right to have their polemical writings printed
by the diocesan publishers; armed with a Roman title which
some of them interpreted as being more or less equivalent to
'Papal Legate' they assumed the leadership of the ultramontane
opposition in the dioceses of gallican bishops. The ministère des
Cultes was not sure whether or not it should take this seriously as
an attempt to set up a parallel or shadow hierarchy.[9]

A further stiffening of public opinion occurred through the
French involvement in Italy during the middle years of the
Second Empire. The temporal power crisis of 1858 to 1861,
although it appeared to have no direct bearing on the debate
about the internal structure of the Church, in fact greatly
strengthened the gallican cause in France by emphasizing the
Pope's status as a foreign sovereign. The Mortara case in 1858,
when a six-year-old Jewish boy was taken away from his family
in Bologna by papal gendarmes and placed in a Roman seminary
on the pretext that he had been baptized secretly by a servant girl
and was therefore technically a Catholic, threw a very unfavourable
light on the clerical administration of the Papal States; and in
1859 and 1860, while behaving in every respect like a small but
refractory European power, the Holy See weakened its claims to
supreme spiritual authority by asserting that the temporal power

[9] Memorandum by Adolphe Tardif, 3 Mar. 1856, AN F. 19. 2450; unsigned report,
'Honorific titles accorded by the Holy See 1840–1880', AN F. 19. 2451.

was a spiritual question. Flat declarations from Rome that the Pope's right to rule central Italy was to be accepted by Catholics on pain of mortal sin, the excommunication of the Piedmontese government and even of businessmen who invested in Piedmontese bonds, and the floating of papal loans on European stock exchanges to buy rifles and artillery for what the Pope insisted was a religious conflict—the operatic adventures of the papal army and the papal navy kept French newspaper readers amused throughout 1860, although they did not amuse the Italians—made it harder for the public to accept the idea of Roman supremacy over the national churches: if Italian dynastic politics were *de la foi*, what could be the limits of papal jurisdiction? At the same time the Italian question provoked the ultramontane party to withdraw its support from the French government. The *école de l'Univers* had already become disillusioned with the Empire in the late fifties as the image of Napoleon III as the new Charlemagne faded away. Orleanism had appeared again; Salinis complained to the government about the tendency of episcopal nominations; Veuillot complained about the appointment of unreconstructed gallican jurists like Dupin and Bonjean to senior posts in the law and to the Senate; Pie, Morel, and Combalot attacked the rage for scientific progress, the growth of the Paris stock exchange, the multiplication of licentious theatres, 'the pernicious seduction of the waltz', the luxury of the Imperial court, 'the hundred thousand roués' and 'the fornicating monarchs who gather in Paris, the modern Babylon'.[10] The Italian War of 1859, with its obvious threat to the Pope's kingdom, was a final disenchantment. Priests were arrested for holding rallies in favour of an Austrian victory; when the prosecutor in one such case remarked that 'a priest is a citizen before he is a priest' a group of young clergy in the public gallery shouted 'no! no!'[11] In January 1860 *L'Univers*, then at its peak with 12,000 subscribers, was suppressed for printing a papal document which could have been interpreted as an excommunication of Napoleon III, and later in 1860, as the Papal States were absorbed into the new Italian kingdom with the apparent acquiescence of the French government, the ultramontane party rejected the Empire

[10] Baunard, *Histoire du cardinal Pie*, vol. i, 640; Morel to Cousseau, 20 Mar. 1857, *Correspondance Pie/Cousseau*, 625; Ricard, *L'Abbé Combalot*, 472.

[11] Report to the Minister of the Interior, 11 June 1860, AN F. 18. 297.

altogether and went over in a body to legitimism and the cause of the exiled Bourbon claimant Henry V. The parish clergy made a tremendous effort to marshal Catholics into a concerted opposition, presenting the events in Italy as an apocalyptic confrontation between the papacy and the forces of *la Révolution*; sermons—often, as the *police des cultes* noted, the same sermon in every parish on the same Sunday—called on congregations to take up arms against Garibaldians, Liberals, Jews, Protestants, and Bonapartists, and to fight for the restoration of the Bourbons. Chaplains in military barracks urged the troops to desert. Fleurs-de-lys appeared on the vestments of ultramontane bishops; Mgr Pie compared Napoleon III to Judas and Pontius Pilate and was prosecuted for sedition.

To the government's relief the campaign was a total failure. The parishioners turned out to be surprisingly well informed and cynical about the Pope's problems. Apart from the detailed reporting of Italian affairs in the press, even in remote villages people knew a good deal about the Papal States through sons and brothers who had served as conscripts in the French occupation force in Rome. Congregations complained that *le curé nous ennuie avec son pape* and stopped priests in the middle of sermons. Everybody noticed that the most violently outspoken clergy continued to draw their official salaries. Collections for the papal defence fund called the *Denier de Saint Pierre* sometimes produced only a few centimes and the *curé* had to add a donation himself 'to preserve the honour of my parish'. Most of the support for the *Denier,* and practically all of the French volunteers for the corps of papal Zouaves formed in 1860 for the reconquest of the temporal power, came from two groups: the minor provincial aristocracy, especially in Brittany and the Vendée where the cause of Rome was linked, by convoluted logic, with the tradition of the Vendéean wars, and the influence of *L'Univers* was particularly strong; and a minority of *dévot* families of the middle class, often members of the Saint Vincent de Paul Society and with relatives in the priesthood.[12]

The government was able to draw several conclusions from the temporal power episode. Firstly, close observation of Roman diplomacy by the ambassador and the commander of the

[12] The extensive documentation on the temporal power episode is surveyed in A. G. Gough, 'French legitimism and Catholicism' (Oxford D.Phil. 1966).

occupation force confirmed that relations with the Holy See had been damaged irretrievably by the French support for Italian unification, and that Pius IX would remain suspicious of France no matter what ecclesiastical policy the government chose to pursue in the future. Secondly, the ultramontane party had made an error of judgement by throwing in its lot with the lost cause of legitimism, and the leading *ultras* in both clergy and laity had squandered their credit in politics by their exaggerated language and behaviour in 1860. Thirdly, the Catholic laity in rural parishes had shown themselves to be not overwhelmingly devoted to the Pope. There had been some ambiguity about the effect of the ultramontane movement on the mass of Catholics. Congregations had found the ultramontane style of piety congenial with its special encouragement of the cults of the Virgin Mary and the Sacred Heart and its renewed emphasis on novenas and indulgences, but they had been very troublesome in wanting to preserve their local liturgies and were certainly 'gallican' in their opinion of Gregorian chant. In some circumstances, laymen as well as clergy could feel the attraction of appealing to Rome over the head of their bishop. But when asked to rally to the defence of the Pope they had displayed no enthusiasm at all. The Italian question thus confirmed the already strong tendency of the government, and after 1860 there was increasingly open and tangible official support for a gallican revival in the Church.

A revival of *gallicanisme ecclésiastique* had begun in Paris even before the death of Sibour, centred around the Faculty of Theology under the deanship of Mgr Maret. The Faculty had an equivocal position in the system of clerical education because the Holy See, in its intense suspicion of anything to do with the Sorbonne, had refused several requests by the government to grant canonical recognition to the Faculty's degrees in theology,[13] but it provided academic appointments and a public forum for a group of talented liberal clergy. It was imprinted with Maret's own independent style of scholarship; the staff included the abbé

---

[13] Fifteen or twenty priests graduated from the Faculty each year but their degrees were not recognized at Rome. The Holy See gave ostentatious patronage to the new *Séminaire française* founded at Rome in 1854 by an ultramontane group led by Gaultier and de Ségur in order to attract students away from Paris. It was moderately successful, but until after the eighties it had a distinctly aristocratic and legitimist tone and took very few students with middle-class backgrounds.

Meignan, who had studied at four German universities, Lavigerie, the first doctoral graduate of the École des Carmes, Gratry, Perreyve, Perraud, and several others who contributed occasional lectures. The École des Carmes also, subdued but not broken by the condemnations of its textbooks, went quietly on with its work of introducing priests to university studies. Its director in the fifties was the remarkable abbé Cruice who had published monographs on the Greek Fathers and on Jewish history, and an abridged French translation of Gibbon; in 1861 he was succeeded by Hugonin who had links with the University of Louvain and was the author of a treatise on matter and form in Aquinas which caused the Roman Index to accuse him of Platonism and ontologism.

Maret struck up a working relationship with the ministère des Cultes in the mid-fifties and came to be the government's principal adviser on currents of ideas in the Church. Fortoul, who was Minister until 1856, was privately sympathetic to the gallicans and urged them in confidential letters to show 'good sense, patriotism, and if necessary courage' in resisting initiatives like the ultramontane attempt to censure Bossuet,[14] but in the practical matter of increasing the gallican representation in the episcopate he could do very little, since he had to contend with lobbying by the Nuncio and by *ultras* like Gousset and Parisis who still retained some prestige as early supporters of the Empire. Fortoul's nominations were divided about equally between the two parties. His successor, however, was the former *procureur général* of Paris, Gustave Rouland, who referred to the Church of France in his memoranda as *le culte national* and had strong views on ecclesiastical affairs; he said in his first official appraisal of the religious situation that he believed ultramontanism to be essentially a political movement which was trying to break the spirit of national episcopates as a first step towards imposing a theocratic form of government on all Catholic countries. He was quickly on excellent terms with Maret and on very bad terms with the Nunciature. The partnership of Maret and Rouland achieved a notable success when the opportunity arose with the death of Sibour in January 1857 to find a gallican candidate who might be capable of revitalizing the *archevêché*. Maret recommended

---

[14] Fortoul to Cardinal Donnet, 20 July 1853: Donnet/AN 160 AP. ii.

Cœur of Troyes, who declined—'I would be impotent . . . The poor prelate invested with this title would be no more than the executor of the exalted decrees of the cardinals at the *Univers* office'[15]—but in turn recommended Morlot, the archbishop of Tours, a man who had been extremely careful in public statements since 1853 but was known by his friends, and also by his enemies since his dinner-table conversation was secretly reported to *L'Univers*, to be an unrepentant gallican who was looking forward to 'something being done to repair the shame and ignominy the episcopate had received from Rome'.[16] He was reluctant at first to be thrust into the firing line in Paris but accepted after some personal persuasion by the Emperor. Under Morlot the *archevêché* became at least as gallican as it had been before 1848. Lequeux's old post was now occupied by the abbé Darboy, the former editor of the *Moniteur catholique*, whose views on the autonomy of national churches went even further than those of Lequeux and Prompsault. The abbé Delacouture was still a canon in residence. The archpriest of Notre-Dame, Le Courtier, the vicar-general for finance, Ravinet, and the principal secretary, Cuttoli, were strong liberal–gallicans; and Morlot continued the practice of bringing gallicans in from the provinces, like the abbé Bécel of Vannes whom he appointed to La Trinité. After 1860 the conditions for a revival were greatly improved by the suppression of *L'Univers*, which did not reappear until 1867.

Once a nucleus had been re-established at Paris the obvious field for action by the gallican party was in episcopal appointments, not so much for the sake of any immediate influence, because in reality not much could be accomplished in dioceses which had already gone over to the Roman liturgy and where the clergy were mostly ultramontanes, but in order to create a substantial gallican vote in future councils and synods. Maret told Rouland and the Emperor, in a long memorandum of 1862 which represented the thinking of the Parisian gallicans, that the present problems of the Church had arisen because there had been no General Council since Trent. Instead of calling the

[15] Cœur to Rouland, 18 Jan. 1857, AN F. 19. 6178 (dossier 'Maret'; and a letter to Maret quoted by Bazin, *Maret*, vol. i, 427.

[16] Morlot's conversation reported by the abbé 'N. D.' to Léon Aubineau at *L'Univers*, 4 Aug. 1853, V/BN 24235.

episcopate together the papacy was using a technique of consulting bishops individually, in complete secrecy, as had been done with the dogma of the Immaculate Conception, then making a final and binding decision without announcing the results of the consultation. In these conditions the Roman bureaucracy increasingly dominated the ecclesiastical apparatus, the episcopate had been reduced to nullity and the national identity of churches was disappearing. Maret recommended that the French government should support any initiative to persuade Rome to call a Council to resolve the questions of papal jurisdiction and the role of the Curia, and if possible to settle the matter of the temporal power;[17] and in the meantime it was important to create a gallican majority in the French hierarchy.

Under Rouland (Minister from 1856 to 1863) and Jules Baroche (1863–9) the ministère des Cultes became extremely receptive to advice on episcopal nominations from Maret and his circle, and they, for their part, came to rely increasingly on an alliance with the government. After the temporal power crisis and the Syllabus of Errors in 1864 Maret, Darboy, and the rest of the gallican party knew that there was no point in looking to Rome for a change towards 'the wise middle course and the conciliatory policies which will allow the Church to keep its excellent and peaceful relations with lay society';[18] they found it much easier to negotiate with a French government which was clearly, if hesitantly, moving in the direction of constitutional liberalism than with a Roman bureaucracy which was becoming year by year more authoritarian and eccentric—and on a personal level it was certainly more pleasant dealing with Baroche and the senior officials at the ministère des Cultes than with Antonelli and Modena. The relationship was so close by 1865 that ultramontane critics revived the accusation formerly levelled at Sibour, that 'governmental' bishops were on the road to a French schism. It was true that since 1860 there had been speculation in political circles about the possible advantages of an *Église nationale*; not another Cult of the Supreme Being with artificial doctrines and liturgy but 'a Christianity and a Church

---

[17] The memorandum is printed in Bazin, *Maret*, vol. ii, 244 ff.

[18] Maret, *Du Concile général* (see n. 32 below), vol. i, xv; and cf. the work published by Cruice before his promotion to the episcopate, *De l'accord de la religion et de la liberté* (1863), chap. 1.

of our own', as Circourt said, 'perhaps with Catholic forms and ceremonies, with Protestant morality and with dogmata about which no-one will trouble himself'.[19] De Circourt thought that there could be no question of imitating the Anglican system, 'but a Church tailored to the Russian pattern could be tried'.[20] But without any suggestion of schism a quiet reconciliation was developing between *gallicanisme ecclésiastique* and *gallicanisme parlementaire*. In the mid-sixties the Parisian churchmen were recommending to the ministère des Cultes as a policy for stemming the tide of ultramontanism exactly the methods which a dozen ministres des Cultes had urged their governments to adopt: limiting the power of the Nuncio to communicate with the bishops, curbing the growth of the religious orders, and starting a government-funded journal which could express the ideas of French theologians and religious philosophers. Maret found the ministry ready to agree that it might not be impossible even to win back the parish clergy, by offering them higher salaries and granting security of tenure, the long-hoped-for *inamovibilité*; it would have been a masterstroke of policy, but the problem was always to persuade public opinion to accept the necessary increase in the ministry's budget. In December 1864 Maret and Darboy were responsible for the government's invoking the Organic Articles to ban the publication in France of *Quanta cura* and the Syllabus of Errors, and at that time Maret made a suggestion which twenty years earlier would have been regarded as typical of *gallicanisme parlementaire*: to deal with future papal documents in the same theocratic vein as the Syllabus, he told Baroche, there should be a committee of senior bishops *chaired by the ministre des Cultes* which could decide on an official position and communicate with the papacy.[21] Towards the end of the Empire the gallicans were deterred from an even closer alliance by the possibility, visible in the politics of 1868 and 1869, that government in the future might fall into the hands of anticlericals and socialists; they were unprepared for the more subtle danger that a future government, like that of the Liberal Empire at the

[19] Senior, *Conversations with Distinguished Persons*, vol. i, 274–5.

[20] Circourt to Cavour, 10 Dec. 1860, *Carteggio Cavour-Circourt*, 282. Kergorlay also explored the question of a separate French Church in his manuscript notes for a projected book on Church and State.

[21] Maret's memorandum to Baroche, 27 Dec. 1864, AN F. 19. 1934.

time of the Vatican Council, might be benevolent but non-interventionist and might not think it worth while to deploy the influence of the State for the benefit of one party in an ecclesiastical dispute.

By 1870, as a result of co-operation between the leading gallicans and the ministry over episcopal appointments, there were forty-two men of gallican sympathies in the French episcopate, most of whom were ready to support a broadly gallican position at the Vatican Council, although with varying degrees of determination. The three sections of the Appendix emphasize the continuity of influence and tradition. Section (A) lists seven senior men who had been in the episcopate in 1853 and had been active in the controversies leading the encyclical *Inter multiplices*: Mathieu, Rivet, Marguerye, Dupont des Loges, Dupanloup, Bonnechose and Lyonnet. Section (B) includes thirty-one bishops appointed between 1853 and 1870, the first group from the Parisian circles of the *archevêché*, the Faculty of Theology and the École des Carmes, and the second group from provincial milieux. Section (C) adds the names of four elderly bishops in poor health who did not attend the Council but who had strongly gallican backgrounds and sympathized with the Minority.

Section (A) of the Appendix may stand without further comment. With regard to (B.i), the Parisian group, Maret's greatest coup had been the promotion of Georges Darboy first to the bishopric of Nancy in 1859, and then to succeed Morlot at the *archevêché* in 1863. Darboy was already unpopular at Rome long before his nomination but after his resistance to Rome over the temporal power question in 1860 and the Syllabus in 1864, and a series of battles he fought to prevent the Curia from interfering in the archdiocese of Paris, Pius IX lumped him with Napoleon III as two of the greatest 'enemies of the Holy Church' for whom the Pope prayed every day, he told a French visitor, that they would be humiliated as they deserved.[22] So many of the Parisian clergy were raised to the episcopate—Le Courtier, Ravinet, and Cuttoli from the *archevêché*; Lavigerie, Meignan, and Maret himself from the Faculty of Theology, although Maret had to be content with

---

[22] Houtin, *Le Père Hyacinthe dans l'Église romaine*, 203, 264. Pius IX made a very dismissive remark on hearing that Darboy had been shot as a hostage by the Communards in 1871.

the bishopric of Sura *in partibus infidelium* because the
Pope would not recognize him as bishop of any French diocese;
Cruice, Hugonin, and Foulon from the École des Carmes;
Baudry, the professor of dogma at Saint-Sulpice, and Bécel and
Christophe from amongst the *curés* of Paris[23]—that the ministry
received pointed reminders about equally good candidates
waiting their turn in the provinces. The provincial dioceses
provide very good evidence of gallican continuity. The list (B.ii)
continues with two bishops, Ginoulhiac and Ramadié, who had
belonged to the scholarly and radical circle of Montpellier; both
of these had links with Maret, and so did Dubrueil, appointed
archbishop of Avignon in 1863; two from the Sulpician background of Lyons, Callot and David, both active in the resistance
against the Roman liturgy; two friends of Dupanloup who shared
his ideas on the structure of the Church, Place and Sola; two
from Mgr Féron's strongly gallican circle at the *évêché* of
Clermont, Grimardias, who had been vicar-general, and Dours
who was Rector of the Academy of Clermont during the
ecclesiastical crisis of 1850 to 1853; three from the gallican milieu
of Autun, Devoucoux, who had been Marguerye's secretary,
Thomas, who had been his vicar-general, and Landriot, a
brilliant graduate of the Autun seminary who had later been
associated with the Faculty of Theology in Paris; Delcusy, who
had served under Marguerye at Saint-Flour; and eight who had
been pupils, secretaries, or vicars-general to other distinguished
gallicans of the older generation like Baudry, Robiou of
Coutances, Rivet of Dijon, and Mioland of Toulouse. The last
bishop listed in this group, Gueullette, had been influenced in the
opposite way: he had been vicar-general to the crabby and
insolent ultramontane bishop of Moulins, Mgr de Dreux-Brézé,
an experience which would have turned Louis Veuillot into a
gallican.

The Minority bishops of 1870 were thus in a direct line of
succession which ran back from Maret, Darboy, and Hugonin to
the earlier generation of Bouvier, Mazenod, and Affre, and
through them to Emery and Frayssinous at the beginning of the
concordatory period. In social composition they were very like

[23] Cruice, Baudry, and Christophe died before 1870. Another lecturer at the École
des Carmes, Isoard, was sent to Rome as the French government's Auditor of the
Rota.

the gallicans of 1850, coming mainly from the urban middle classes,[24] but they had more contact with the secular universities: the impression arises of a *clergé doctoral,* scholars rather than administrators. By the standards of their lay counterparts in the academic world they had a thin record of publication, but in terms of intellect and learning at least nine of them—Maret, Cruice, Ginoulhiac, Darboy, Meignan, Lyonnet, Hugonin, Guilbert, and Dours; perhaps it is invidious not to name others—were admitted to be genuinely distinguished. The senior clergy, on the whole, led busier lives than most civil servants, judges, or university lecturers, each of the priests in the Faculty of Theology, for example, having parish duties or posts at the *archevêché* on top of their university teaching, and few of them had time for reflection or publication once they became bishops; but their main handicap as authors was the Index. From 1853 to 1869 the gallican clergy published safe devotional works but, from fear of the Roman censorship, nothing at all substantial on ecclesiology or Church history. Lyonnet, who had written several volumes on gallican themes during the forties and had been lucky to escape being condemned with Lequeux, published nothing after 1852. Philosophical work like Hugonin's thesis on Aquinas attracted immediate attention from the Index. Meignan's *Les Évangiles et la critique* in 1864 shows his awareness of recent German progress in biblical studies but is almost unreadably cautious about reaching conclusions.

They were, nevertheless, unmistakeably gallican in that they had a common interest in strengthening the defences of the Church of France for some future struggle with Rome. Each of them, in 1870, had good reason to remember the condemnation of books and the encyclical of 1853, the older bishops as direct participants at that time and the younger generation as seminary directors or vicars-general and secretaries to bishops in the thick of the conflict, and they looked back at *Inter multiplices* not as a defeat but as a stimulus to the development of a more effective *gallicanisme ecclésiastique.*

[24] Without necessarily drawing any specific conclusions, it may be noted that the social origins of the ultramontane and gallican bishops of 1870 broadly repeat the pattern of 1850: of the 42 who were aligned with the Minority, 27 (64 per cent) had middle-class or upper-class backgrounds and good educational opportunities in their early lives; of the 40 Majority bishops, only 7 (17.5 per cent) had middle or upper-class backgrounds, and 33 came originally from farming or working-class families.

The gallican–liberal Minority at the Vatican Council

The gallican bishops had scarcely dared to hope that in the atmosphere created by the temporal power crisis and the Syllabus of Errors Rome would take the risk of calling a General Council, and they had greeted the announcement in 1865 with a certain degree of optimism. 'In the broad daylight of discussion' at a Council, as Maret said, there was surely no chance of an ecumenical gathering of bishops endorsing papal absolutism; the rights of the national episcopates would be defined and the power of the Roman Curia reduced.[25] 'If we know how to prepare for the Council', Maret told Lavigerie, 'new destinies will open for the Church and for the world'; but it soon became apparent that they were more likely to be buried under an ultramontane landslide. The bishops who were invited to Rome for a jubilee celebration in 1867 found themselves taking part in extraordinary ceremonies designed to glorify 'the Pope-King' and were urged to put their signatures to a draft address which virtually conceded papal infallibility or even, as some thought, papal omnipotence. Throughout 1868 and 1869 all the signs coming from the committees working in Rome on preparations for the Council, from the campaign being mounted by the *Civiltà Cattolica* and *L'Univers* 'to prepare Catholic minds', and from publications by leading ultramontanes like Manning and Dechamps, indicated that gallicans and liberals in the Church were facing a potential disaster. Although papal infallibility was not yet formally on the agenda Roman sources were predicting that it would be defined at the Council by acclamation, without debate, in 'an explosion of the power of the Holy Spirit'. As a theological proposition the doctrine itself was a serious enough challenge, but it was accompanied by the threatening corollaries and implications which ultramontane publicists were determined to read into the concept of an infallible Pope. Within the Church, it was being said, infallibility was to destroy all centrifugal forces, put an end to ideas of local or national independence, and allow the Roman Curia in future to legislate with irresistible authority; and Veuillot and the *Civiltà* were maintaining also with absolute conviction that infallibility would produce a fundamental and permanent change in Church–State relations because the Catholic

[25] On Maret and Lavigerie before the Council, Montclos, *Lavigerie*, chap. 9.

world would be compelled to recognize the authoritative force of a whole range of papal documents of the past: *L'Univers* cited *Unam Sanctam* in which Boniface VIII proclaimed the right of the Papacy to control civil governments, and from more recent times *Mirari vos* of 1832 which condemned liberal institutions and the freedom of the press, *Tuas libenter* of 1863 condemning the freedom of scientific and historical research, and, of course, *Quanta cura* and the Syllabus of Errors. The eighty propositions of the Syllabus had been expressed in a baffling series of double negatives, with footnotes which made their meanings even less clear, but one of the Roman committees was said to be translating the Syllabus into a list of unambiguous anti-liberal commandments to be approved by the Council, so that there could be no further discussion of 'liberal interpretations'. Veuillot announced cheerfully that after the Council Catholics would be a disruptive element in all liberal societies, and would work for the abandonment of the constitutional and parliamentary system and the founding of a new Holy Roman Empire.[26]

Only a handful of *exaltés* amongst the laity were ready for this programme; but Veuillot's real following was in the presbyteries. *L'Univers* had been allowed to reappear in 1867 as part of the general relaxation of the press laws in that year and had immediately regained its ascendancy over the parish clergy. The effects of the débâcle of 1853 in the seminaries, the purging of textbooks and the resignations of gallican professors, were clearly visible in the younger generation of clergy. Priests who graduated in the 1860s knew practically nothing about Bossuet or the tradition of the Sorbonne and had never heard of Bailly or Lequeux. Every subject in their curriculum had been permeated with the theme of Roman supremacy, and they were ready to follow Veuillot into the most extreme theocratic illusions. Throughout 1869 *L'Univers* distributed thousands of printed *fiches* on which priests could 'vote' for papal infallibility and express their impatience with the gallican hierarchy; the results, published in *L'Univers*, were a warning to the bishops of what they could

[26] *L'Univers* from 11 July 1868 onwards is a superb source for the preliminaries to the Council, and Veuillot's part in organizing the press campaign can be seen in V/BN 24228. A letter from Mgr Freppel to Dupanloup, 17 Feb. 1869, Dupanloup/AN AB XIX 526, is an example of the leaks from the commissions meeting at Rome; and see J. Kenens, three articles on the forthcoming Council in the *Revue contemporaine*, ciii, cvii, and cxi (1868–9).

expect in their dioceses if they sided with the opposition at the Council. The leading gallicans were thus in an uncomfortable and contradictory position, hated by the overwhelming majority of their clergy, but at the same time enjoying the cordial support of the *Revue des deux mondes*, the *Journal des débats*, the *Institut*, the Collège de France and the most influential members of the *Corps législatif* and the Senate. They knew from their contacts in these circles that there was a general feeling, shared by Catholics and non-Catholics alike, from Kergorlay and Arnaud de l'Ariège to Thiers and Jules Simon, that the hope of sensible Church–State relations in the future depended on a vigorous opposition at the Council being able to interrupt the ultramontane momentum: if the extremists won it was easy to foresee a troubled period of conflicts and reprisals in France, extending well beyond the 1870s. There was particularly strong encouragement from the *femmes savantes* who formed an important fraction of the educated laity, like Mme de Forbin who wrote in 1869 that 'the Church will always be Catholic, Apostolic, and Roman, but it must become more and more Catholic and Apostolic, and less and less Roman';[27] and an unexpected degree of support from the *école du Correspondant*, Montalembert, Falloux, Foisset, Broglie, and Cochin, the heirs of the liberal-ultramontane tradition going back to the time of Lamennais and *L'Avenir*, originally very hostile towards gallicanism. Montalembert and his circle had persisted for two decades with the sisyphean task of persuading the reading public that it was possible to be ultramontane and still believe in the principles of 1789, and that the papacy was the true patron of science and learning. Rome had treated them consistently with patronizing sarcasm, and subjected them to a series of rebuffs and humiliations—a devastating neo-Thomist analysis of their attempt to reconcile Catholicism and liberalism, pursued by the *Civiltà Cattolica* in a number of influential articles during the 1850s; a decree of the Index in 1862 condemning a book sponsored by *Le Correspondant*, the abbé Godard's *Les Principes de 1789 et la doctrine catholique*; the condemnations of the congress of German scholars at Munich and the Malines

---

[27] Quoted by Léon Séché, *Les Derniers Jansénistes*, vol. iii, 138. I am writing a separate study of the laity in this period, of which a part will be based on the correspondence of the women who were friends and *dirigées* of some of the leading clergy.

Congress in 1863; and the Syllabus in 1864. By the end of the
sixties they were disoriented and disillusioned. Montalembert,
suffering from a painful terminal illness, was more outspoken
about the papacy than his colleagues on *Le Correspondant* dared to
be and was using more truculent language than any of the
gallican bishops: France, he said, had sunk to being 'a mere
waiting-room to an ante-chamber of the Vatican'; the ultramontanes were 'sacrificing justice, truth, reason and history as a
holocaust to the idol they have erected in the Vatican'. Twenty
years earlier, in 1849, Montalembert and Falloux had been
responsible for the decision by the Assembly of the Second
Republic to send a French military force to restore the Pope to
Rome, and in 1860 Montalembert had thrown himself into the
defence of the papacy, risking what was left of his political career
and ruining his long-standing friendships with Italian liberals;
had he known then, he reflected in 1869, what was to become of
the Church under Pius IX, 'not a single French soldier would
have marched in defence of the temporal power'. In an open
letter to the *Gazette de France* he said that he was happy to stand
with the gallicans. He tried to stiffen the opposition by urging
Newman and Döllinger to go to the Council as theologians, and
he told Archbishop Dechamps of Malines that a declaration of
infallibility in anything like the terms being considered at Rome
would be the beginning of a long decline for the Church: it would
lose its adherents not by dramatic defections of whole nations, as
had happened in the Reformation, but subtly, imperceptibly,
Montalembert said, by classes and social groups, the educated
and politically active Catholics who cared for reform and
progress would drift away.[28]

Before setting off for Rome at the end of 1869 Dupanloup,
Darboy, Ginoulhiac, and a number of the other gallicans issued
pastoral letters expressing at least a guarded optimism about the
result of the Council. It would be 'a dawn and not a sunset', in
Dupanloup's phrase. The debates would be moderate, learned,
courteous and, above all, free; the decisions would reassure the

[28] On Montalembert and the *école du Correspondant* before the Council, *Le
Correspondant*, issue of Oct. 1869; J.-R. Palanque, *Catholiques libéraux et gallicans face au
Concile du Vatican 1867–1870* (Aix-en-Provence 1962); Montalembert's letter to
Döllinger, 7 Nov. 1869 and other correspondence, in S. Lösch, *Döllinger und Frankreich*
(Munich 1955), 159–64, 175–7; Montalembert's letter to Lallemand, Jan. 1870, in
Lecanuet, *Montalembert*, vol. iii, 466–7.

Catholic world. There would be no novelties, no sudden acclamations, no explosions. The most distinguished bishops of Europe and America, they said, were not likely to agree to abolish their own rights. *Le Correspondant* endorsed this last point in particular: who could imagine 'the States-General of the Church' voting to establish monarchical absolutism? The French were aware of the groundswell of anti-infallibilist opinion amongst the bishops of Germany and Eastern Europe and in the German theological faculties, and there were known to be 'gallican' parties in the English, Irish, and American episcopates; even in Italy some of the Piedmontese bishops had shown signs of opposition to Curial centralization and the concept of a separate and personal infallibility of the Pope, and there were striking individual dissenters like Mgr de Mérode, the Papal War Minister, Carlo Curci, the senior editor of the *Civiltà Cattolica*, the abbot of Monte Cassino, and Canon Audisio of the Lateran who was quoted as supporting 'a reaction of the periphery against the centre'; most extraordinary of all, the abbé Chaillot, the founder of the *Correspondance de Rome* and later secretary of the Congregation of Bishops and Regulars, had left Rome and had reappeared in Paris as editor of an ultra-gallican newspaper, *L'Avenir catholique*, filled with very well-informed satire on the papal court and the Curia.[29]

It had been obvious to Rome that the opposition would include the archbishops of most of the major cities of Europe and some of the most formidable intellectuals in the Church, and Curial officials had been dubious about the very idea of inviting people who failed to recognize the pressing need for a tighter and more centralized ecclesiastical structure, and who would want to waste time in historical and theological argument: one cardinal predicted that 'the French and Germans will come and turn our Congregations upside down'. The preparations for neutralizing this awkward element were well in train before the Council assembled, and when they arrived in Rome the Minority bishops could see that their problems were even more serious than they

[29] The untenable position taken by Pius IX over the Roman Question in 1859–62 had already caused a number of defections in the higher ranks of the Curia, including Curci and Passaglia who were both in favour of conciliation with the new Italian government and the abandonment of the temporal power, and Cardinal d'Andrea, Prefect of the Index, who left Rome and set up a schismatic *Chiesa Nazionale* in Naples, although he later submitted to the Pope.

had imagined. They had known in advance that there would be an infallibilist majority from Italy, Spain, and Latin America but they were astonished at the additional numbers of bishops without dioceses, bishops *in partibus,* Curial officials, vicars-apostolic, and missionaries directly subordinate to the Roman Congregations; and any hope they may have had of influencing the overwhelming majority faded when they discovered the rules of procedure. Draft statements of *schemata* had been prepared covering each of the main areas of discussion, the Catholic faith, the Catechism, the Church and the papacy, in the hope that the Fathers might be tempted to vote for these drafts without too much debate for the sake of avoiding a long Council. The commissions to draw up these *schemata* and supervise the discussions were stacked with determined infallibilists, elected in a swift manœuvre before the opposition had found its bearings. Amendments of substance and suggested matters for discussion had to be passed through a commission *de postulatis* appointed by the Pope, which was reluctant to accept any suggestions in a gallican direction. In January 1870 the French Minority submitted a *postulatum* relating to the draft *schema* on the Church, calling firstly for a clear definition of the rights and status of bishops and their freedom from censure by Curial Congregations, and secondly for a series of administrative reforms including provision for regular General Councils at ten- or twenty-year intervals, and the internationalization of the Curia to make it possible for national episcopates to nominate members to important Roman committees; this document was not even acknowledged.[30]

The debates themselves were often hard to follow because of the bizarre accoustics of the transept of Saint Peter's and the varieties of Latin pronunciation. The cardinals who acted as presidents of the sessions allowed the opposition bishops to make their speeches, but also allowed them to be shouted down by impatient members of the Majority, as happened to Strossmayer

---

[30] The following brief account of the Council is an attempt to convey the problems presented to the gallican bishops, and does not claim to do justice to the complex debates and negotiations; in particular it does less than justice to the German and East European Minority. From the literature on the Council, see especially Emile Ollivier, *L'Église et l'État au Concile du Vatican,* 2 vols. (1877); R. Aubert, *Vatican I* (1964), which draws on a wide range of sources; E. Dublanchy, 'Infaillibilité du Pape', *DTC*; J. Hoffman, 'Histoire et dogme: la définition de l'infaillibilité pontificale à Vatican I', *Revue des sciences philosophiques et théologiques,* lxii–lxiii (1978–9).

when he appealed for justice for Protestant theologians, and to
Haynald who pointed out that a Pope had initiated certain
changes in a breviary now condemned by the Congregation of
Rites. But the fundamental question relating to the freedom, and
ultimately the validity, of the Council proceedings concerned the
very concept of a Majority and Minority. The cogently argued
and sometimes passionate speeches by the opposition leaders,
especially by Strossmayer, Hefele, Kenrick, and Darboy—even
Maret, in spite of his deafness and his weak voice, was so effective
that the president of the session abruptly closed the debate as
soon as Maret had finished speaking—made it obvious that there
were profound divisions of opinion in the Church, and that the
Council did not have the 'moral unanimity' which had been
recognized in the past as the mark of valid conciliar decisions.
Demonstrating this lack of consensus, many of the opposition
felt, ought to be enough to win their case; but the problem of
moral unanimity was solved by a Roman ruling that decisions
were to be arrived at by simple majority vote. The Majority in
1870 was impervious to brilliant speeches. The point about
unanimity was crucial to the gallican position that there should
be one area of undoubted doctrine accepted by the mind of the
whole Church, and another area of permissible opinion. In an
article published in March 1870 Döllinger argued that moral
unanimity was fundamental if a Council claimed to be expressing
truths which had always been held in principle by the Church: a
decision taken by simple majority suggested that the majority
itself was uneasily conscious that it was not expressing the mind
of the Church. Lagrange, Dupanloup's vicar-general, published
a study *De l'unanimité morale nécessaire dans les Conciles* arguing that
if more than a hundred bishops were against a decision it could
not be theologically valid. The question was heard: would the
Holy Spirit be present in a decision taken by a majority of one,
and that one perhaps having been asleep throughout the debate?
Yes, certainly, the more extreme *ultras* replied, because those who
were willing to vote with the majority would be the only real
Catholics present. Dechamps suggested later in the Council that
bishops who wanted to limit papal supremacy should be
excommunicated, after which there would have been less trouble
in achieving unanimity; at the same time thoughtful and
conciliatory Majority leaders like Pie of Poitiers, who distanced

themselves from this kind of fundamentalist zeal, treated the question of unanimity and the other procedural grievances seriously and tried to put forward reasoned arguments defending the organization of the Council, although without convincing the supporters of the Minority. 'This immense scandal will be regarded with contempt by civilized people and nations', Adolphe Perraud of the Oratory wrote to Dupanloup; 'it will bring us all into complete disrepute ... You must fight on against the ineptitude and prejudice of the proceedings; it is the fight of Simon Maccabeus, and God will aid you!'[31]

The opposition bishops felt compelled to vote for the first of the principal drafts presented to the Council, the constitution *Dei Filius* on the basic truths of the Christian faith, in spite of their reservations about its pedantic and quarrelsome tone, because it was essential in the early stages of the Council for the Minority to avoid being branded as blind opponents of the Holy See: if they could be seen voting for this objectionable document, they thought, they would be on stronger ground in resisting the worse things still to come. The draft *schema* on the Church, *De Ecclesia Christi*, was so much worse that several bishops had to be dissuaded from leaving Rome after reading it. All its emphasis was on the Pope, and even some ultramontane speakers felt that the *schema* reduced the Church to an appendage of the papacy. The Pope's jurisdiction over every diocese was defined as *ordinaria atque immediata*; there were only a few lines on the hierarchy, and nothing specifically about bishops. General Councils were mentioned mainly to anathematize anyone who said that there was a right of appeal to a Council from a papal decision. The temporal power was declared to be a gift of Providence to the Pope himself. The chapters on Church–State relations (XIII–XV) went some way towards putting the Syllabus of Errors into a positive form, virtually claiming the right of the Church to disallow civil legislation and condemning the whole complex of constitutional systems arising from the idea of the sovereignty of the people. This last section of the *schema* found its way into the press and caused such an unfavourable

---

[31] Perraud to Dupanloup, 22 Feb. 1870, Dupanloup/AN AB XIX 526. In the second century BC the Maccabean family had fought to preserve the rights of an independent Judaism against the efforts of the Seleucid king Antiochus IV to impose pagan rituals in Judaea.

reaction in the foreign ministries of the Catholic states that the organizers of the Council were put momentarily on the defensive, and after a month of energetic debate the opposition succeeded in having the whole of *De Ecclesia* withdrawn for redrafting. When it was brought back again in May 1870, however, it contained a new chapter *De Romani Pontificis Infallibilitate*—of which, as it happened, the preliminary draft had been written by the same Mgr Giuseppe Cardoni who nearly twenty years earlier had given his professional opinion in the case of the abbé Lequeux and the Index that the papacy should turn a blind eye to the gallican doctrines held in various parts of Europe—and in response to intense lobbying by the Majority leaders, who were furious with the way *De Ecclesia* had been treated, it was announced that the debate on papal infallibility would begin without further delay, overruling protests that it was illogical to debate the infallibility of the Pope before having defined the infallibility of the Church.

The case against infallibility which the French Minority brought to the Council can be assessed in a number of important publications in 1869: the pastoral letters on the forthcoming Council by Dupanloup, Darboy, and Ginoulhiac, the *Lettres sur l'Infaillibilité* by Alphonse Gratry, and above all in Maret's two-volume treatise *Du Concile général et de la paix religieuse*. Maret's book is of capital importance. The draft chapters were seen and approved by an *ad hoc* panel representing a broad spectrum of gallican churchmen from both the older and the younger generations: Mathieu, Dupanloup, Ginoulhiac, Darboy, Meignan, David, Hugonin, Ramadié, and Lavigerie in the hierarchy, and two priests, Icard of Saint-Sulpice and Valroger of the Oratory.[32] It became the main theoretical text of the French Minority, echoed constantly in their speeches during the Council. Maret was in close touch with Döllinger and other German theologians in 1869 and took into account a number of points which the French and Germans had in common, but *Du Concile général* was fundamentally grounded in Bossuet and the gallican classics, and

---

[32] H. L. C. Maret, *Du Concile général et de la paix religieuse: la Constitution de l'Église et la périodicité des Conciles généraux: Mémoire soumis au prochain Concile œcumenique du Vatican*, 2 vols. (September 1869); and see Montclos, *Lavigerie*, 410–13, and Lösch, *Döllinger und Frankreich*, 468–9. All of the group listed above approved the text, with minor reservations, but Dupanloup, Lavigerie, and some others were against publishing the book before the Council met.

in the Sulpician doctrine of Emery and Frayssinous. In this tradition, although papal infallibility was a proposition which individual theologians might hold, there were insuperable obstacles in logic and in history to defining it as a dogma. In defining a 'new' dogma the Church is doing no more than finding fresh language to explain more fully something always held by Catholics. The French implicitly rejected the Spanish and Jesuit traditions according to which revelation could be expressed in a progressive series of logical deductions from secure premises, issuing in new and infallible dogmata. Surely, it was argued, not every possible logical deduction could be an infallible truth, even if the premises were divinely guaranteed? The 'new' truth had to be an organic and inevitable growth, absolutely consonant with everything already believed, clearly implicit in the corpus of scripture, the Fathers and tradition: it had to be, so to speak, an apple growing on an apple tree—but the apple tree had sprouted a flagrantly exotic fruit, a positive mango, which the infallibilists were hailing as the ultimate triumph of apple cultivation. Maret and Gratry followed Bossuet in their emphasis on the early Councils, carrying the argument beyond the status of the Gallican Church and into broader issues of the historical relations between Popes, Councils, and episcopates, and the nature of spiritual authority in the early centuries of Christianity. Gallicanism, Maret wrote in this final and definitive manifesto, was not in any way an aberration or a heresy. With allowance made for the necessities of changing times over almost two millenia it remained true that the Church had grown up as an elective and constitutional monarchy, in which authority resided jointly in the Pope and in the bishops. In the matter of jurisdiction, the authority of the Pope and the liberty of the bishops existed side by side; neither diminished the other. No previous Pope had ever claimed a separate and personal infallibility; infallibility was an attribute of the Church, expressed by the Pope after consultation with the episcopate. No papal statement could be irreformable in itself because Councils, expressing the mind of the Church, retained the right to correct or censure Popes. The arguments were still basically those of the Sulpician *Mémoire* of 1852, with the structure now underpinned by a long and closely documented study of how authority had been exercised at twenty-two General Councils, from which

Maret drew his points in a series of lucidly written expositions.[33]

Between May and July 1870 the Minority managed to give an adequate presentation of this case, in spite of the time-limit on speeches and the need to approach matters like the theological judgements of past Popes obliquely and tactfully to avoid provoking noisy demonstrations. But they had imagined that historical arguments would be persuasive and perhaps decisive, and they were thrown off balance by the Majority's treatment of history. Texts and documents were mishandled to prove a deeply unhistorical case that a separate papal infallibility had been acknowledged throughout the Church even in the earliest centuries; but when pressed on some particular point, most Majority speakers took the line that history was irrelevant: arguments drawn from the Councils of Ephesus and Chalcedon were agreed to be interesting, but, it was said, they failed to recognize the way in which the Holy Spirit could renew and develop doctrine by acting directly through the papacy, transcending history;[34] and the extremists simply condemned any appeal to the past, or to the so-called Vincentian rule that a doctrine had to have 'universality, antiquity and consent', as an insult to the papacy. It had been expected that the infallibilist side would find it embarrassing to deal with the case of Pope Honorius, who had endorsed the Monothelite position on the divine will in a judgement of 634 only to have his decision overturned by the Council of Constantinople in 680, and to be condemned as a heretic by Pope Leo II; but Honorius was brushed aside: if he was wrong about Monothelitism—which some infallibilists disputed—then he cannot have been speaking *ex cathedra.*

As the Council went on there was an erosion of confidence amongst the opposition. Defections and compromises began as early as January 1870. Ginoulhiac had told Dupanloup before

[33] R. Thysman criticizes Maret and by implication the whole gallican school for relying too much on examples from antiquity and neglecting the main developments of ecclesiology in the medieval period—as Bossuet also had neglected them—and for accepting too readily that some of the assemblies of the first six centuries of Christianity deserved to be called 'general councils': 'Le gallicanisme de Mgr Maret et l'influence de Bossuet', *Revue d'histoire ecclésiastique*, lvii (1957), 402–65.

[34] The anti-historical case was argued by several Majority speakers, and permeates the work published by Mgr Cardoni during the Council, *Elucubratio de dogmatica Rom. Pontificis infallibilitate* (Tipografico della Propaganda, 1870).

leaving for Rome that he hoped to see the episcopate 'rejecting the passive role assigned to it . . . going beyond our usual reticences and timidities',[35] but in the highly charged atmosphere of Rome it was easy to be reticent and timid. Although the cardinals who controlled the commissions often went out of their way to be courteous, the seventy-eight-year-old Pope treated the Minority bishops with malicious frivolity, sending congratulatory letters to ultramontane authors in which he described the publications on the Council by Maret, Dupanloup, and Gratry as 'vain hostile sophisms' and 'stupid, irrational and anti-Catholic', and commiserating with priests from Paris, Lyons, and Orleans for having to put up with bishops who were the Pope's personal enemies. The papal presence increasingly loomed over the Council proceedings, intervening to have Minority amendments struck out and showing obvious disapproval after major speeches by anti-infallibilists. *L'Univers*, which now had an effective readership of three-quarters of the parish clergy, reported each humiliation of a French bishop, and Veuillot's newsletters from Rome emphasized the low standing of the Minority leaders with the Holy See. The rest of the French press was sympathetic, although some Catholic laymen thought that the Minority was behaving altogether too mildly and tactfully at the Council. A group of politicians and diplomats offered to produce a set of pamphlets supporting Dupanloup's position;[36] but he declined because he hoped to persuade the government itself to intervene at Rome to have the Council prorogued. The cabinet had followed the proceedings closely and was particularly interested in the fortunes of Maret and Darboy; Napoleon III had offered Maret a private subsidy for the expenses of publishing *Du Concile général*. A booklet produced by Maret's circle in Rome, *Ce qui se passe au Concile*, had conveyed a strong impression that Catholic governments had very good reasons to be concerned about the path the Council was taking. After considerable lobbying, however, by Dupanloup in favour of intervention and by Bonnechose and Lavigerie who raised theoretical and practical reasons against it, the government decided not to act. An intervention by one Catholic state acting alone would have been a diplomatic diaster, and the Foreign

[35] Ginoulhiac to Dupanloup, 14 Oct. 1869, Dupanloup/AN AB XIX 526.
[36] M. Johanet to Dupanloup, 5 Mar. 1870, Dupanloup/AN AB XIX 526.

Ministry was not convinced that a concerted action could be arranged even with Bavaria and Austria, in spite of the amount of correspondence that was known to be passing between Rome, Munich, and Vienna. After the change of government in April Émile Ollivier's view prevailed, that it would be a mistake with very long-lasting consequences for the State to interfere in a doctrinal conflict within the Church.

Left to face the increasingly rebarbative debates, with support in France uncertain at best and with depressing news arriving every day from their mutinous dioceses, a number of the opposition bishops drifted away from the Minority and attached themselves to the *Tiers parti* which had coalesced around Cardinal de Bonnechose, in the belief that since a definition of infallibility could not be avoided it would be better to co-operate with the Majority in the hope of attenuating the wording of whatever final formula was arrived at. Behind the decision of each man who gave up outright opposition there was a complex of motives, some theological and some personal. Lavigerie, for example, a protégé and close friend of Maret, had been made archbishop of Algiers in 1867 and was dazzled by the prospect of the conversion of Africa, which he felt could never be accomplished if the Catholic Church itself was divided on fundamental questions of authority. Two hundred million souls, he wrote to Maret in 1869: 'if you only knew how everything else disappears before that'; in any case, he said, he had 'an invincible horror of the quarrels which break out between Catholics'; Maret suspected that he had an invincible horror of being on the losing side.[37]

The famous retreat of the Minority, when the anti-infallibilist bishops left Rome in a body to avoid having to vote in the final session on 18 July, a historic blunder which was judged very harshly by contemporaries who had hoped for more resolute behaviour, has to be seen against the background of the final weeks of the Council. Until the last days of debate in July the Minority still hoped to avoid a definition that the Pope possessed a separate and personal infallibility, above and apart from the Church. In the end, although they could not see that there was any need to disturb Catholic consciences by imposing it as an article of faith, they would have accepted a formula declaring the

---

[37] Montclos, *Lavigerie*, 426–9.

Pope infallible when he expressed the mind of the Church, ascertained by consulting the episcopate; but from the tone of the Majority speeches and amendments it was clear that the tide was running strongly in the opposite direction. Although some of the Majority made thoughtful speeches indicating that they accepted limits to the extent of infallibility and the exercise of the papal *magisterium*, others who obviously represented an overwhelming number of the infallibilist rank and file insisted that there could be no compromise on the basic point of infallibility being a separate and personal attribute of the Pope. One speaker after another declared that rather than founding a Church, Christ had founded an apostolic succession of divinely guided Popes, around whom a Church had grown up; that the Church in a General Council had only a minor and secondary degree of infallibility through its association with the Pope; that absolutely nothing more was needed for the Church to meet the challenges of modern science, history, philosophy, and political theory than for Catholics to surrender their minds to the judgement of the Pope, who could act rapidly and decisively on the Church's behalf; that the Pope had no need to consult the episcopate because he was himself the mind of the Church. The opposition listened with incredulity to intelligent and experienced bishops saying, in effect, that they could not possibly give their allegiance to an authority which was so feeble and irresolute as to want to consult their opinions. Cardinal Rauscher's proposed formula *utens consilio et requirens adjutorium universalis Ecclesiae* was refused, and all other amendments requiring papal statements to have the consent of the episcopate or the subsequent assent of the Church were struck out. On 11 July Mgr Gasser, bishop of Brixen, was authorized to explain the doctrine as it was understood by the commission responsible for the draft, a gesture meant to reassure the Minority bishops who were still pressing for amendments. It was manifestly absurd, Gasser said, to bind the Pope, who was himself the supreme interpreter of Scripture and tradition, always to consult the episcopate when defining doctrine; but he might indeed find it desirable to consult them on some occasions, as he had done with regard to the dogma of the Immaculate Conception. This reassured nobody. Bishops, Gasser explained, did retain an authority derived not from Rome but from the earliest days of Christianity; but he hoped everyone could see the impossibility of including such a concept in the text of a formal definition. He went on, even less reassuringly, to envisage developments of papal infallibility, which eventually—the Minority imagined a future *Dictatus papae*—might extend beyond revealed truth to embrace 'dogmatic facts' and the condemnation of errors.[38] Gasser did not dispel a suspicion in the minds of the Minority, based on hard experience, that infallibility would cover a final centralization and petrifaction of Church government because it would mean in practice the infallibility of the Roman Curia. What became of the idea of separate and personal infallibility when the Popes, in general, did not write their own encyclicals? *Inter multiplices* was known to have been written by Cardinal Recanati, and the dogmatic definition of the Immaculate Conception in 1854 had been put together by a committee which had used some phrases contributed by Veuillot and Guéranger. The encyclicals of the sixties dealing with important points of doctrine and discipline, *Jamdudum cernimus, Maxima quidem, Tuas libenter, Quanta cura,* all of them initiated and written in the Curia—were they in any degree infallible statements?

Arguments in this vein were kept alive by theologians until the second half of the twentieth century. The definition itself, put to a vote on 13 July in a form more moderate than the extreme ultramontanes would have liked, said nothing about infallibility being a quality that could be delegated to subordinates: the Pope was declared infallible when as supreme pastor and doctor he defined a doctrine on faith or morality to be accepted and believed by the whole Church. The full text of *Pastor aeternus,* however, laid down an interpretation in the sense most favourable to the papacy of the scriptural texts relating to the foundation of the Church, and put an end, for the time being, to all theories of pluralism, collegiality, and episcopal autonomy. One clause, suggested by Manning and inserted by the Pope's express instruction, declared anathema anyone who denied the plenitude of power and jurisdiction of the papacy in all aspects of Church government and discipline; it was generally taken to be aimed at Maret and Darboy. In the ballot 451 bishops voted *placet*; 88 *non placet*; 62 *placet juxta modum,* of whom about 40 belonged to the opposition and the rest were ultramontanes who wanted the

---

[38] Cuthbert Butler, *The Vatican Council* (London 1962), 386 ff., gives a good account of Gasser's speech.

definition strengthened; and more than 70 bishops actually in Rome preferred to be absent. Of the French Minority, 23 voted *non placet*, and 11 either voted *placet juxta modum* or did not attend the voting. One of the latter group, Le Courtier, threw all his conciliar documents into the Tiber.[39] The dogma was to be proclaimed on 18 July. On 15 July a delegation led by Darboy, Ketteler, and Ginoulhiac pleaded with the Pope to allow an amendment formally recognizing the need for 'the testimony of the Church' in infallible dogmatic statements. But it was precisely this hope on the Minority side of rescuing something, however small, from the general débâcle that made the Majority leaders all the more determined to push their victory as far as possible. For Dechamps, Senestrey, Manning, and their theologians at the Council, the historical and ecclesiological arguments had been secondary. They saw personal infallibility as the Church's main weapon in a definitive struggle against that persistent and threatening entity 'the Revolution'. The rapid developments in science, history, philosophy, and biblical criticism in the latter half of the nineteenth century, a second and more dangerous phase of the European Enlightenment, could be dealt with, they thought, only by an unprecedented tightening of the structure of the Church, closing ranks round an inspired and infallible leader. Every potential source of disruptive 'independence' had to disappear; the Church's powers of resistance and survival would be undermined if gallicans found any excuse to claim, after the Council, that they still retained even a vestige of autonomous jurisdiction, or a right to be consulted.[40] The only result of the Minority delegation, therefore, was to provoke a last-minute addition to the text declaring that 'definitions by the Roman Pontiff are irreformable in themselves, and not by virtue of the consent of the Church'. At this point Darboy and Haynald urged that the Minority, whose numbers they estimated altogether at over a hundred, should attend the public session and boldly vote against the final form of the dogma to demonstrate that there was no consensus or moral unanimity at the Council; but Dupanloup managed to persuade nearly all of the Minority

[39] The French bishops who did not vote for infallibility on 13 July 1870 are indicated with asterisks in the list of the French Minority in the Appendix.
[40] See Y. Congar, 'Bulletin d'ecclésiologie', *Revue des sciences philosophiques et théologiques*, lxii (1978), 65–95.

leaders to leave Rome, arguing that a demonstration in the face
of the Pope would be a scandal and would be misunderstood by
the Catholic world; and so there was a general exodus.

Amongst the laity there were many who felt deprived of
leadership and example at a crucial moment. The circle of
liberals who had relied on Dupanloup as their champion,
Cochin, Lavedan, Johanet, Mme Craven, Mme de Menthon,
were thunderstruck. Circourt, an unforgiving observer, wrote
that 'this party of cowards fled back to their dioceses instead of
staying to vote "no", and afterwards submitted for the sake of
unity, as if truth did not matter'.[41] Leaving Rome does seem, in
retrospect, to have been a disastrous tactical mistake; but the
submissions are perhaps easier to understand. The Franco–
Prussian War broke out on the day after the Council ended,
dividing the French from their colleagues in Germany and
Eastern Europe so that there was no possibility of a concerted
protest or even a conference. Throughout the last months of 1870
the senior gallican clergy had to go through their personal
dramas of submission to Rome while trying to deal every day
with the pastoral problems of a defeated country, and to adjust
their minds to a radical change of government. Many of them
were convinced by the argument that prevailed in the dioceses
and universities of Germany, that dissent over the Council
decrees could lead to a schism which might have more ruinous
effects than the Reformation; Strossmayer, Hefele, and Hohenlohe,
all of whom thought the Council invalid, found practical and
pastoral reasons for submitting. The signs from Rome were that
although the dogma would be explained and re-explained there
would be no time spent in persuading individuals. Intense
administrative pressure was applied by the Curia to the Minority
leaders, making their dioceses more or less ungovernable until
they submitted. The Pope had said immediately after the
Council that infallibility was the most fundamental principle of
Catholic doctrine, and had spoken of the Minority bishops with
scorn and dislike. The French submitted with painful reluctance,
and in the end abjectly and without preserving much dignity—
even Darboy had to pretend that he had always believed in the
dogma itself and that he had simply been against the opportune-

---

[41] Manuscript, 'L'Église gallicane', Circourt/BN 20501.

ness of a definition—but the laity should not have been too ready to criticize men who remembered the treatment of Lequeux, Bouvier, and Sibour, and faced the real possibility of condemnations by the Index, the loss of their dioceses, and eventually, for persistent *réfractaires,* excommunication and humble lives as schoolmasters or as pastors of tiny dissenting congregations. The later careers of several French bishops who had been at the Council suggest that they remained unreconciled. One, Las Cases, left instructions in his will that his funeral panegyric should describe him accurately as an opponent of papal infallibility and not merely an inopportunist. To follow them into the 1870s, a period of frustration and regret for all the old gallicans, would outrun the limits of this book. We may end with Dupanloup, writing in about 1872 in the hope that his manuscript would be given to a new Pope to be elected after the death of Pius IX, and imagining the calling of another Council

to finish the work of the Council [of 1870] by reconciling society with the Church, restoring to an honoured place the broad traditions of the old ecclesiastical government . . . giving back to the bishops their legitimate initiative and autonomy, and thus the authority which they have a right to exercise in the government of the Church . . . to restore the sharing of power throughout the hierarchy, and the counterpoise of a salutary control in place of dictatorial proceedings.

It was a task, Dupanloup added, to challenge a Pope of the stature of the greatest churchmen in history.[42]

---

[42] 'Rapport au Pape', Dupanloup/AN AB XIX 524: chap. 13.

APPENDIX

The French Minority bishops at the Vatican Council, with notes on their backgrounds before being raised to the episcopate.

The asterisks indicate those who did not vote for papal infallibility on 13 July 1870.

(A) THOSE WHO HAD BEEN BISHOPS BEFORE 1853

*Mathieu (Besançon)	Saint-Sulpice, after beginning career as a barrister; vicar-general of Paris under Mgr de Quélen, and *curé* of the Madeleine.
*Rivet (Dijon)	Saint-Sulpice; *curé* at Versailles under Mgr Blanquart de Bailleul
*Marguerye (Autun)	Bayeux seminary (Sulpicians); secretary to Cardinal de Rohan, then vicar-general to Mgr Simony at Soissons.
*Dupont des Loges (Metz)	Saint-Sulpice; vicar-general to Mgr Morlot at Orleans
*Dupanloup (Orleans)	Saint-Sulpice; headmaster of Saint-Nicholas-du-Chardonnet; prolific writer on political and educational questions.
*Lyonnet (Albi)	Saint-Irénée, Lyons; vicar-general at Lyons; biographer of Cardinal Fesch and other gallican prelates, author of three treatises on ecclesiastical law.
Bonnechose (Rouen)	*Avocat général* of Besançon; trained for priesthood under Louis Bautain; superior of Saint-Louis-des-Français at Rome.

(B) BISHOPS APPOINTED 1853–1870

(i) from the Parisian milieu

*Darboy (Paris)	Nancy seminary; editor of *Moniteur catholique* under Sibour; vicar-general of Paris under Morlot.
*Maret (Sura)	Saint-Sulpice; academic posts; co-editor of *Ère nouvelle* in 1848; dean of Faculty of Theology at Sorbonne; nomination as bishop of Vannes refused by Pope.
*Le Courtier (Montpellier)	Saint-Sulpice; vicar of *Missions Etrangères*, then vicar-general of Paris and archpriest of Notre-Dame.
*Foulon (Nancy)	Saint-Sulpice and École des Carmes. degree in letters; published editions of some works of Plato and Ovid.
*Meignan (Châlons)	Le Mans seminary, pupil of Bouvier; studied at four German universities, wrote on biblical criticism; *curé* of Saint-Louis-d'Antin, Paris.
*Bécel (Vannes)	Vannes seminary; called to Paris by Morlot as *curé* of La Trinité; author of *L'Age de raison* (1856).
*Hugonin (Bayeux)	Protégé of Dupanloup as student; Saint-Sulpice and École des Carmes, doctorate of Sorbonne; thesis on matter and form in Aquinas; director of the Carmes.
*Cuttoli (Ajaccio)	Saint-Sulpice; principal secretary of the *archevêché* under Morlot and Darboy.
Lavigerie (Algiers)	Saint-Sulpice and École des Carmes, doctorate of Sorbonne; protégé of Baudry and Maret; lecturer in Faculty of theology, then Auditor of the Rota in Rome.
Ravinet (Troyes)	Saint-Sulpice; secretary to Affre, later one of Sibour's vicars-general.

264 Appendix

(ii) from provincial milieux

*Ginoulhiac (Grenoble)	Montpellier seminary (Lazarists); seminary instructor with wide influence throughout Gallican Church; author of *Histoire du dogme catholique* (1852).
*Ramadié (Perpignan)	Montpellier seminary; protégé of Thibault, and friend of Maret and Ginoulhiac.
*Callot (Oran)	Saint-Irénée, Lyons; member of the Sulpician Order, professor of theology at the *École des hautes études*, Lyons; vicar-general, and led the opposition to the Roman liturgy in the diocese.
*David (Saint-Brieuc)	Saint-Irénée, Lyons; member of Order of the *Chartreux de Lyon*; musician and amateur archaeologist.
*Place (Marseilles)	Barrister, entered priesthood at 33; close friend of Dupanloup; studied at Rome, was adviser to French Embassy under Second Republic; later superior of *petit-séminaire* of Orleans.
*Sola (Nice)	Educated at Turin, and became bishop of Nice when it was an Italian city. Strongly influenced by Dupanloup in 1860s.
*Grimardias (Cahors)	Clermont seminary (Sulpicians); secretary to Féron and archpriest of Clermont cathedral.
*Dours (Soissons)	Dax seminary; joined *Université*, headmaster of *lycée* of Laval, later Rector of Academy of Clermont, belonged to Féron's circle at the *évêché*.
*Devoucoux (Evreux)	Autun seminary (Sulpicians); secretary to Marguerye at Autun.
*Thomas (La Rochelle)	Autun seminary and Saint-Sulpice; vicar-general to Marguerye, friend of Darboy and of R. P. Hyacinthe.
*Colet (Luçon)	Versailles seminary, pupil of Rivet who later called him to Dijon as secretary; then vicar-general of Morlot at Tours.

*Guilbert (Gap)	Coutances seminary (Sulpicians); superior of *petit séminaire* of Mortain; diocesan administrator under Robiou. Author of *La Divine synthèse* (1864).
*Bravard (Coutances)	Sens seminary; vicar-general to Jolly at Sens.
*Las Cases (Constantine)	Liberal Bonapartist background; married, with family, entered Saint-Sulpice at 49 after wife's death; pupil of Baudry who called him to be vicar-general at Perpignan. Friend of Maret, Lavigerie, and Angebault.
*Hacquard (Verdun)	Versailles seminary; vicar-general to Gros at Versailles.
*Belaval (Pamiers)	Toulouse seminary (Sulpicians); vicar-general to Mioland at Toulouse.
*Gueullette (Valence)	Moulins seminary; vicar-general to Dreux-Brézé at Moulins, who placed him under an interdict for disobedience in 1857.

Four bishops aligned with this group when the Council began voted *placet juxta modum* on 13 July 1870:

Dubreuil (Avignon)	Toulouse seminary; vicar-general of Thibault at Montpellier.
Bernardou (Sens)	Saint-Sulpice; vicar-general to Dupuch at Algiers.
Landriot (Reims)	Autun seminary, later at Faculty of Theology in Paris.
Delcusy (Viviers)	Saint-Flour seminary; recommended for episcopate by Marguerye and Lyonnet.

(C) GALLICAN BISHOPS WHO DID NOT ATTEND THE COUNCIL

Delamarre (Auch)	Coutances seminary (Sulpicians); headmaster of State college, and took law degree; vicar-general to Robiou at Coutances.

Féron (Clermont)	Saint-Sulpice; old friend of Mathieu of Besançon; administrative post at Evreux under Salmon du Chatellier.
Guérrin (Langres)	Besançon seminary; vicar-general to Mathieu at Besançon.
Pompignac (Saint-Flour)	Saint-Sulpice; member of Sulpician Order; protégé and close friend of Lyonnet.

Index

Each French bishop's name is followed by the name of the most important diocese or dioceses he occupied during the period discussed in the book.